The MARKET MECHANISM and ECONOMIC REFORMS in CHINA

Studies on Contemporary China

THE POLITICAL ECONOMY OF CHINA'S
SPECIAL ECONOMIC ZONES
George T. Crane

WORLDS APART
RECENT CHINESE WRITING AND ITS AUDIENCES
Howard Goldblatt, editor

CHINESE URBAN REFORM
WHAT MODEL NOW?
*R. Yin-Wang Kwok, William L. Parish, and Anthony Gar-On Yeh
with Xu Xueqiang, editors*

REBELLION AND FACTIONALISM IN A CHINESE PROVINCE
ZHEJIANG, 1966–1976
Keith Forster

POLITICS AT MAO'S COURT
GAO GANG AND PARTY FACTIONALISM
IN THE EARLY 1950s
Frederick C. Teiwes

MOLDING THE MEDIUM
THE CHINESE COMMUNIST PARTY
AND THE *LIBERATION DAILY*
Patricia Stranahan

THE MAKING OF A SINO-MARXIST WORLD VIEW
PERCEPTIONS AND INTERPRETATIONS
OF WORLD HISTORY
IN THE PEOPLE'S REPUBLIC OF CHINA
Dorothea A. L. Martin

POLITICS OF DISILLUSIONMENT
THE CHINESE COMMUNIST PARTY
UNDER DENG XIAOPING, 1978–1989
Hsi-sheng Ch'i

THE MARKET MECHANISM AND
ECONOMIC REFORMS IN CHINA
William A. Byrd

Studies on Contemporary China

The MARKET MECHANISM and ECONOMIC REFORMS in CHINA

WILLIAM A. BYRD

An East Gate Book

M. E. Sharpe, Inc.
Armonk, New York
London, England

An East Gate Book

Available in the United Kingdom and Europe from M. E. Sharpe,
Publishers, 3 Henrietta Street, London WC2E 8LU.

Library of Congress Cataloging-in-Publication Data

Byrd, William A.
    The market mechanism and economic reforms in China / by
William A. Byrd.
            p.   cm. — (Studies on contemporary China)
    "An East gate book."
    ISBN 0-87332-719-5
        1. China—Economic policy—1976–   . 2. Industrial management—
China. 3. Industry and state—China. 4. Supply and demand—China.
I. Title. II. Series.
HC427.92.B97   1991
338.951—dc20   90-8105
                                                                              CIP

Printed in the United States of America

TS   10   9   8   7   6   5   4   3   2   1

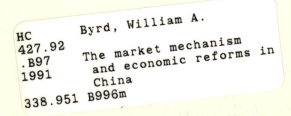

Contents

Tables   vii
Preface   ix

1. Introduction   3

2. Prerequisites for Effectively Functioning Markets   19

3. Markets in Chinese Industry   44

4. The Impact of Markets on Chinese Industrial Enterprises   69

5. The Redistributional Role of Chinese Economic Planning   103

6. Plan and Market in the Chinese Economy:
   A Simple General Equilibrium Model   132

7. Assumptions, Limitations, and Extensions of the Model   153

8. Market Price Trends and Market Integration   171

9. The Atrophy of Central Planning in Chinese Industry   195

10. Conclusions   218

Notes   226
References   237
Index   245

Tables

2.1 Elements for Effective Competition, Enterprise Efficiency, and Rational Market Adjustment   41

3.1 State Plan Shares for Key Industrial Producer Goods, 1980–88   51

3.2 Direct Marketing of Rolled Steel, Cement, and Trucks, 1980–84   52

3.3 Share of Enterprise Direct Marketing of Various Industrial Products, 1987   53

3.4 Procurement of Industrial Producer Goods by the Material Supply System Outside of Mandatory Plans, 1983–86   54

3.5 Composition of Procurement of Industrial Goods by the State Commercial System, 1980–82   56

3.6 Share of Industrial Enterprises in Total Retail Sales, 1952–87   57

3.7 Transactions at Urban and Rural Free Markets, 1965–87   58

3.8 Plan and Market Shares for Qingdao Sample Enterprises, 1984   59

3.9 Shares of Market Input and Output Transactions for a Sample of Industrial Enterprises, 1984–85   61

4.1 Names and Abbreviations of Sample Enterprises   70

4.2 Market Conditions, Product Characteristics, Technology, and Enterprise Response, 1982–83   73

4.3 Input and Output Inventories of Sample Enterprises, 1982   75

4.4 Direct Marketing and Exports, 1980–82   79

4.5 Financial Indicators, 1980–82   83

4.6 Investment Rates, 1980–82   84

5.1 Plan Fulfillment by Chinese State-Owned Industrial Enterprises, 1965–84   111

5.2 Fulfillment of Production Targets by Chinese State-Owned Industrial Enterprises, 1965–84   112

5.3 Constraints on Chinese Industrial Enterprise Decision Making, 1985   113

5.4 Plan Shares for Different Types of Enterprises, 1984   114

5.5 Illustrative Calculations of Embodied Rents, 1985   122

5.6 Profitability and Retained Profits in Twenty State-Owned Industrial Enterprises   124

8.1 State Plan and Shanghai Market Prices for Steel Products, 1979–89   172

8.2 State Plan and Shanghai Market Prices for Other Industrial Producer Goods, 1979–89   173

8.3 Market Price Trends, Average, 1987–89   175
8.4 Correlations between Levels of Market Prices in Shanghai
      and Various Other Cities, 1984–87   178
8.5 Correlations Between Monthly Changes in Market Prices in Shanghai
      and Other Cities, 1984–87   179
8.6 Tests of Market Integration   188
8.7 Productwise Configurations of Test Results   189
8.8 Citywise Configurations of Test Results, One-Period Lag Structure   191
9.1 Share of Coal Output by Different Types of Mines, 1978–85   209
9.2 Direct Marketing by the No. 2 Auto Plant, 1980–87   211
9.3 Fulfillment of State Plan Contracts, 1987–88   215

Preface

THIS BOOK is based on my Ph.D. dissertation for the Department of Economics of Harvard University, submitted in final form in May 1987 and extensively revised for publication in 1988 and 1989. Research and writing for the dissertation occurred over a lengthy period of time during which Chinese industrial reforms were themselves unfolding, roughly from 1981 to 1987. It focused on the first phase of reforms in Chinese state-owned industry, which lasted from the late 1970s until the mid-1980s. During the process of subsequent revisions, newly available data were incorporated and developments in 1987–88 were covered in the analysis, to the extent possible.

The political events culminating in the massacre at Tiananmen Square on June 4, 1989, and major changes in China's top leadership that occurred at the time had a substantial impact on the progress of market-oriented reforms in Chinese industry, as well as more broadly on the reform program as a whole. But by mid-1990 it was clear that a wholesale reversal of reforms already implemented had not occurred, and there were some signs of a cautious renewal of interest in reform. In any case, this book can shed light on the underlying economic dynamics and tendencies, even though the influence of political developments, which are hard to predict at this point, must be acknowledged.

A word about the technical level of economic analysis used in this study. Chapters 1–5 and 9–10 are nontechnical in nature and hence should be accessible to nonspecialist readers and noneconomists. Chapter 6, on the other hand, presents a formal theoretical model and analysis, which may be largely incomprehensible to noneconomists. Chapter 7 is a continuation and extension of chapter 6 and thus would not be very informative in the absence of an understanding of the latter. Chapter 8 has a mixture of fairly simple descriptive analysis in the first part and formal econometric testing in the second part. Thus, noneconomists may wish to skip from chapter 5 to chapter 9, between which there is some continuity of thought, looking at the first half of chapter 8 on the way. In terms of knowledge about China and the Chinese economy assumed, the goal has been to develop a fairly self-contained narrative that does not require detailed prior knowledge of the Chinese economy, but which also will prove to be of interest to China specialists.

This book could never have been completed without the active support and encouragement of a number of people. Dwight Perkins provided an invaluable combination of encouragement, patience, and substantive advice. He painstakingly read every draft of every chapter, including a number that turned out to be false starts. Janos Kornai, who became actively involved at a somewhat later stage, carefully read a complete draft from cover to cover and provided important suggestions on structure as well as detailed substantive comments. Martin Weitzman also provided useful comments.

Among colleagues at the World Bank, Gene Tidrick encouraged me not only to complete the study but to make it a high-quality effort; he provided numerous ideas, comments, and suggestions that are reflected in various parts of the work. Adrian Wood also read and commented on early drafts of a number of chapters. Other people who provided useful comments and suggestions on various chapters include Richard Ericson, Barry Naughton, Christine Wong, and participants at several academic conferences where earlier versions of some chapters were presented. The book also has benefited from my intensive involvement in a program of collaborative research between the World Bank and the Institute of Economics of the Chinese Academy of Social Sciences, including in particular the use of research materials from the project on Chinese state-owned industrial enterprise management (RPO 673–14). More generally, numerous Chinese reform-oriented researchers have knowingly and unknowingly provided valuable inputs into this book as well as inspiration for the task of writing it.

Responsibility for the presentation of information, observations, conclusions, and any errors in the book rests solely with the author. In particular, the views, findings, interpretations, and conclusions herein should not be attributed to the World Bank or to its affiliated institutions.

Financial support from Harvard University, NDEA Foreign Language Area Studies (FLAS) Fellowships, a National Resource Fellowship, and a Schumpeter Prize Fellowship facilitated the earlier stages of my dissertation research and is gratefully acknowledged.

Chapter 6 and parts of chapter 7 are based largely on my article "Plan and Market in the Chinese Economy: A Simple General Equilibrium Model," which appeared in the *Journal of Comparative Economics* 13, 2 (June 1989). In addition, an earlier version of chapter 9 was published in the *Journal of Comparative Economics* 11, 3 (September 1987). Permission from Academic Press to use material from these articles is gratefully acknowledged.

Neither the thesis nor the book could ever have been completed without the great understanding, encouragement, patience, and forbearance exhibited by my wife Rabia, who bore much of the burden from my involvement in research and writing at the same time that I was holding a full-time job. This book is dedicated to her.

The
MARKET
MECHANISM
and
ECONOMIC
REFORMS
in CHINA

1. Introduction

THIS IS a study of China's attempt since the late 1970s to reintroduce markets into its urban industrial sector. Development of markets for industrial goods is only part of China's wide-ranging economic reforms designed to improve economic efficiency and promote rapid growth, development, and modernization. Yet it is a crucial part, without which the reform package as a whole cannot get off the ground. Market-oriented reforms have been moving China away from the pattern of administrative control over short-term resource allocation, which is found in traditional centrally planned economies along Soviet lines. This makes theoretical and empirical research on the development of the market mechanism all the more important. But neoclassical and other Western modes of economic analysis cannot be applied to the evolving Chinese situation in a simpleminded manner, since economic institutions in China sharply depart from those in a capitalist market economy.

Scope of the Study

This study is organized around the general theme of the expansion of the role of the market mechanism in the distribution of Chinese industrial goods. This choice of focus is related to the stage and accomplishments of reforms so far, which have made considerable progress in this area. It would not necessarily be as appropriate in looking at other sectors of the economy, where the constellation of reforms may be somewhat different, or at a later time, when goods markets may no longer be a major issue in reform. But in terms of the situation in Chinese urban industry (primarily state-owned industry) through the mid-1980s and into the late 1980s, the emergence, expansion, functioning, and impact of goods markets has perhaps been the most crucial development.[1]

The selection of markets for industrial goods as the central topic means that other aspects of reform are approached from the perspective of their effect on and relation to this aspect. The market mechanism is examined in depth from a number of different perspectives, while other reforms are looked at in a more subsidiary light, primarily trying to ascertain whether and to what degree they are prerequisites for the success of market-oriented reforms. Since the latter do require at least a certain degree of progress in reform implementation in other spheres, the study will necessarily touch on such areas as greater autonomy for enterprise decision makers, profit retention for state enterprises, bonuses for workers and managers, price reform, tax reform, changes in internal enterprise organization, and so on.

The study will not, however, give significant attention to some key areas of reform and certain critical parts of the reform process. In the first place, it is a study of economic reform and hence will not cover political, social, and cultural developments, even though these are important and in certain respects critical for the success of economic reforms. Within the sphere of economic reforms, certain specific topics are almost completely excluded: agricultural reforms; development of nonagricultural activities in rural areas, particularly township and village industries; reforms in the ownership system and internal structure and management arrangements for both state and nonstate industrial enterprises; reform and change in the factor allocation system (land, labor, and capital); reforms in the banking system; and reforms in public finance and taxation.

Historical Background

The historical context has had an important influence on Chinese industrial reforms.[2] Chinese industry was dominated in the prereform period by state-owned enterprises of various types. The state sector accounted for about 78 percent of gross industrial output value in 1978 (State Statistical Bureau 1983, 215; 1985a, 239). There was a substantial nonstate sector of collective enterprises, which grew rapidly in the 1970s with the expansion of rural commune- and brigade-run enterprises. Nonstate enterprises in the prereform period were under the jurisdiction of government supervisory agencies or rural communes and brigades and probably were not controlled and managed in a way greatly different from small state-owned enterprises. They had to rely much more on obtaining inputs and selling outputs outside the state plan, however.

Chinese industry was characterized by a wide range of firm sizes and technological levels in most industries. The former resulted partly from promotion of small-scale industry under local government or rural collective supervision in the 1970s. The latter was partly related to differing plant sizes but also reflected the continued existence of older plants using obsolete technology.[3] As in other centrally planned economies, but to a considerably lesser extent due to its lower level of development, China's industrial structure was "top-heavy," dominated by some very large plants set up in the 1950s and thereafter, which accounted for a disproportionate share of total industrial output.

Most Chinese industrial enterprises had only a single main plant; multiplant firms were a rarity, and outside the rural collective sector firms with several different main product lines were virtually unheard of. Many ancillary activities were integrated within enterprises, however, and there were strong tendencies toward backward integration, a common pattern in centrally planned economies characterized by chronic shortage. Activities integrated within larger state enterprises typically included machinery repair and manufacturing, production of components, heat treatment, production or mining of raw materials, and a host of services for employees, ranging from workers' housing and meals to day-care facilities, medical care, commuter transport, pensions (which came to be paid by each firm to its retirees out of current revenues on a completely unfunded basis), and even in some cases public security. Enterprises in the late 1970s also had substantial responsibilities to provide employment for workers' dependents: a worker's child had the right to ''replace'' his or her retiring parent, and in practice many firms had to find some kind of work for all workers' children. Chinese state-owned industrial enterprises thus had become key social institutions for their employees and dependents.

Both state and nonstate enterprises were under the hierarchical supervision of at least one government supervisory agency—industrial bureaus at provincial, municipal, and county levels; industrial ministries at the central level. Many firms were under ''multiheaded leadership'' of more than one level of government, while other government agencies often intervened in enterprise affairs and day-to-day management.[4] In the early 1970s a massive decentralization of the administrative supervision system for state enterprises was instituted. Most enterprises directly under ministries were put under provincial or local control. Combined with the rapid growth of small-scale rural industry (at the county, commune, and brigade levels), this meant that administrative supervision of industrial enterprises became somewhat decentralized and fragmented along territorial lines.

Enterprise autonomy vis-à-vis government supervisory agencies was extremely limited in the 1970s. Administrative decentralization of government supervision did not translate into greater scope for independent enterprise decision making. There was (and continues to be) a symbiotic patron-client relationship between firms and their immediate supervisory agencies. The latter could help the former in dealing with a complex administrative environment but at the same time were to a large extent evaluated bureaucratically on the basis of the performance of the firms under their jurisdiction. This may have enhanced the ability of enterprises to get favorable deals from the bureaucracy.

Though Chinese state-owned industry was governed by administrative fiat, this does not mean that it was thoroughly or comprehensively ''planned'' in any real sense. Centralized planning was crude and relatively weak, and large parts of industry were not really included in central planning in the 1970s. Local and provincial government agencies played an important role in economic decision making and resource allocation, but they did not do detailed, comprehensive planning within their own domains.

Given administrative control over resource allocation, markets for industrial goods were underdeveloped. The decentralization and fragmentation of control as well as the crude nature of production planning did, however, leave some major gaps that encouraged certain informal resource allocation mechanisms to emerge, some of which were similar to markets. These mechanisms, discussed in chapter 3, were themselves distorted by the existing administrative system and indeed tended to be managed by local authorities rather than enterprises. Nevertheless, they helped create the potential for development of more genuine market mechanisms in the reform period.

Product prices were administratively controlled and remained fixed over long periods of time. The prices of most important industrial producer goods remained constant between 1967, when a price freeze was imposed during the Cultural Revolution, and the late 1970s or early 1980s. In any case, prices did not serve as the primary guide for resource allocation. Prices for the same good in different jurisdictions could vary, primarily due to supply factors (for example, smaller, backward plants needed higher prices to cover their higher costs) and to a lesser extent as a result of cross-subsidization by localities, which sometimes charged higher prices for outside sales and lower prices for local users. The decentralization of planning and industrial administration was accompanied by a lesser degree of administrative decentralization of authority over price setting, but there is no evidence that local and provincial governments were any more flexible in this regard than the central government. Market price determination was not relevant for most industrial products.

Another interesting feature of the immediate prereform situation was the virtually complete absence of financial incentives at the enterprise and individual levels. Enterprises did not retain any of their profits, and workers had no performance- or profit-related bonuses.[5] Some financial incentive systems were instituted for provincial and local governments and in some cases for agencies supervising enterprises,[6] but these did not affect firms directly. The bonus system for workers was not restored until 1978. Thus, in the realm of financial incentives, the Chinese system in the immediate prereform period lagged behind the Soviet system, where bonuses for workers and profit retention by enterprises had long been acceptable practice.

Chinese industry was characterized by extreme rigidity of factor allocation and severe problems of factor immobility, aggravated by the "cellularization" of the economy in the 1970s (Donnithorne 1972). Land, labor, and capital in the state sector were subject to allocation by administrative decrees, and given the difficulty of reallocating factors once they were assigned to firms, enterprise factor endowments tended to be highly uneven. The factor allocation system was a major, if not the predominant, source of inefficiency and waste in the system.

Poor product quality was a severe problem, to the point that large amounts of national industrial output had to be discarded as useless. There were periodic massive campaigns to write off substandard, damaged, or nonfunctional inventories of goods and equipment in the hands of industrial and commercial firms. Similarly, lack of technological progress was manifestly evident, both in continued production of obsolete products, without even marginal improvements, and in backward process technologies.

Chinese state-owned industry in the immediate prereform period suffered from tremendous inefficiency and slack. There was great waste of factors of production (including labor as well as land and capital), and inefficiency in the utilization of material inputs and energy as well. Total factor productivity in state industry grew slowly or stagnated between the late 1950s and the late 1970s, a poor record considering the rapid industrial growth that occurred in this period (see Tidrick 1986, 1–5). New estimates of total factor productivity growth by Chen et al. (1988), based on careful adjustments of the data, show an average increase of only about 1 percent per year. Moreover, these estimates are based on exclusion of the three years 1958–60, on the grounds that data for those years are unreliable, and discounting of data for five other years between the late 1950s and late 1970s. Inclusion of these years in calculating average annual productivity growth would almost certainly lower estimates to near-stagnant levels.[7] Hence China's impressive industrial growth in the prereform period (9.7 percent per year in real terms from 1957 to 1978) was achieved primarily through increases in factor inputs rather than efficiency improvements.

Various explanations have been advanced for the poor performance of Chinese industry. Naughton (1988) has noted the huge, to a large extent wasted investments that went into the "Third Front" defense industrialization program in China's interior provinces. He claims that this alone is sufficient to explain poor utilization of capital in China in the prereform period. Others cite the politicization of economic decision making, weaknesses in the planning apparatus, and other related aspects. Decentralization of administrative control over enterprises also had a problematic impact on industrial performance (see Wong 1986). But there is no doubt that systemic features of the Maoist economy as outlined above had a major adverse impact on efficiency. Certainly this was the perception of reformers and policy makers at the outset of the reform process in the late 1970s.

Chinese Industrial Reforms

Pervasive inefficiency and the need to shift from a Soviet-style extensive growth pattern to intensive growth based on improved efficiency of resource allocation were the underlying economic factors giving impetus to economic reforms starting at the end of 1978. Political changes of course played a crucial role particularly in determining the timing of economic reforms. The death of Mao Zedong and downfall of the Gang of Four in 1976 and subsequent political developments had an important impact but will not be discussed here.

Reforms have been haphazard, often seemingly chaotic, and highly ad hoc in their implementation. There has been no overall reform blueprint or plan, and specific reforms in particular spheres of the economic system often do not appear to have been planned or thought out in any detail. Implementation in some areas has sometimes far outrun the expectations of central authorities, whereas in other areas little progress has been made despite strong reform directives from the center. There has been a great deal of local experimentation, which has resulted in significant differences in the pattern and timing of reforms across localities and provinces.

Under these circumstances, economic reform in China has been to some extent a "natural" process, with a kind of "natural selection" at work. Numerous different methods and solutions have been tried out in different places; those that fit in well with the existing, evolving system and did not generate strong opposition have survived, prospered, and become part of the system. On the other hand, reform proposals and experiments that did not fit in as well or led to opposition did not get off the ground, progressed slowly (if they were sponsored by central authorities), or simply disappeared (which may have happened to many local experiments).

In this process the greatest progress has been made where resistance to reforms was weakest; for example, enterprise profit retention and bonuses—firms and their employees clearly benefit from increased flows of financial resources—and the expansion of the role of the market mechanism, which helped fill the vacuum left by weak and fragmented planning. By the same token, however, many reforms have become adapted to the existing system, which may distort their content and impact. For instance, workers' bonuses to a large extent became more or less fixed-income supplements, with minimal incentive effects. Moreover, by the late 1980s the progress of the reform program as a whole was increasingly being held back by bottlenecks in spheres of the system where change was resisted. Hence, reforms in Chinese urban, primarily state-owned industry have involved a process of evolution and change based on conflicts between old and new elements in the system and a considerable degree of fluidity in institutional arrangements as well as changing formal and informal rules governing behavior of different agents.

Main Elements of Industrial Reforms

Despite the lack of overall guidelines and often haphazard implementation, there is an underlying "package" of industrial reforms, which fits together in terms of both logical interrelationships and actual implementation. The underlying structural coherence of Chinese industrial reforms is only implicit and appears to have emerged from experience rather than from conscious thought at the beginning of the reform process. Nevertheless, the main features of reforms in Chinese state industry can be understood as components of this package.

The set of reforms initially promulgated in the late 1970s included: (1) a degree of enterprise decision-making autonomy in production, and to a lesser extent in investment; (2) reinstitution of financial incentives at the enterprise and individual levels; and (3) expansion of the role of the market mechanism in the allocation of industrial goods and corresponding reductions in the role of planning and administrative allocation (see Byrd 1983b). The components of this initial reform package are closely interrelated and mutually reinforcing. Considerable progress was made in achieving both (2) and (3), initially much less with (1). Since 1984, however, there has been a renewed focus on implementing (1), which is a cornerstone required for other reforms to be meaningful.

Expansion of the role of the market mechanism in resource allocation is the central focus of this study and hence is not incorporated in this introductory discussion. Financial incentive schemes for state enterprises, starting with the reinstatement of the "enterprise fund" scheme and institution of profit retention pilot programs in late 1978, are discussed later in this chapter. Bonuses for employees were reinstated relatively early, but their incentive effect is in question, given that they were subject to ceilings (later a highly progressive bonus tax), treated as income supplements by many if not most workers, and distributed in an egalitarian fashion by most enterprises, at least until the mid-1980s. Enterprise autonomy in business decision making, a key building block of urban economic reforms, was pushed forward gradually and intermittently.

Other reforms can be understood in the light of this initial package. Price reform is needed so that market price signals accurately reflect scarcity values in the economy. Financial incentives for enterprises do not work well unless there is a certain degree of enterprise financial discipline, or if performance criteria for enterprises are distorted. Reforms in the system of investment financing and decision making help realize (1) by giving greater scope for independent enterprise investment decision making. Even changes in the ownership system, not discussed here, are part of this effort to institute genuine enterprise decision-making autonomy, subject to market-based "natural" (as opposed to administrative) financial and economic constraints. Recent moves to "socialize" the pension system for state enterprises also are in part designed to strengthen managerial autonomy in enterprise decision making, and to begin to alleviate the burden of the social responsibilities of enterprises toward their employees.

By the mid-1980s, industrial reforms clearly had begun to move beyond the initial package, though like the measures mentioned above they also can be viewed as efforts to "complete" it. Reforms in the factor allocation system included attempts to restructure the banking system and give it greater independence in loan decisions; inculcation of greater flexibility in labor allocation; and limited moves toward development of capital markets and capital market instruments. There was also relaxation of administrative controls over factor allocation, better factor pricing, and, in a more limited, hesitant, uneven manner, the development of factor markets. Reforms in factor allocation systems have made less progress than has occurred in the development of product markets. This has major implications for the basic reform package, in particular reducing the ability of otherwise autonomous firms to respond to changing market conditions.

There was much focus on reforming the ownership system in the late 1980s. This did not, except in smaller enterprises, involve wholesale privatization but rather strove to achieve stronger and more responsible exercise of ownership functions by government agencies vested with ownership rights over state enterprises. Widespread experimentation with stock and bond capital issues tied ownership reforms in with capital market development.

Another major current of second-stage enterprise reforms has been the focus on strengthening the position of the factory director in relation to the party committee and its secretary, the workers' union, and other actors. This led to contractual responsibility systems between government supervisory agencies and enterprise directors, which attempted to clarify the latter's position and incentives and minimize intervention by the former.

The restructuring of the banking system and establishment of a separate central bank in 1984 were part of the effort to enhance and improve macroeconomic control through use of indirect policy instruments. The success of industrial reforms is intimately linked to the ability to maintain adequate macroeconomic control as direct micro controls over enterprise decisions and activities are weakened.

Overall progress in reform implementation has been in many respects considerably greater than might have been expected. Financial incentive schemes for enterprises are universal. As is documented in chapter 3, a substantial and increasing share of the output of most industrial products is being allocated through markets rather than by administrative directives. Progress has also been made toward enterprise autonomy, though this has been more uneven. There have been substantial changes in prices and in the mode of price determination. Whether reform implementation has reached the point where there are now well-functioning markets in Chinese industry is a key question addressed by this study.

Chinese industrial reforms have made little or no progress in some areas, however. Enterprise autonomy and the factor allocation system have already been mentioned. Firms have gained some de facto independence and a higher status in relation to their supervisors, but the strong, formally quasi-hierarchical links between particular firms and government agencies remain. Within this context, reforms may have increased enterprise bargaining power without necessarily enhancing enterprise autonomy. This could mean a switch from a fairly strong hierarchical relationship not toward free market interactions but rather toward a bilateral bargaining situation between enterprise and supervisory agency. Some decentralization and loosening of control have occurred in the factor allocation system, but China's urban state sector is still far from having functioning markets for land, capital, and especially labor. The combination of weak and fragmented administrative allocation and the lack of well-functioning factor markets has meant continued inefficiency and waste, uneven factor endowments, and inability to reallocate factors across users (see Byrd and Tidrick 1987).

Reforms are also "missing" in certain other spheres. For example, changes in the ownership system for state enterprises were minimal up to the mid-1980s; subsequent reforms were highly visible but did not appear to result in fundamental changes. Ownership reform of some kind may be necessary, however, to achieve enterprise autonomy within a framework of public ownership. Development of legal codes, institutions, and protections has been slow and has contributed to the continuation and even aggravation of pervasive bargaining in the economic system. In certain respects the social responsibilities of enterprises toward their employees have increased rather than decreased since the late 1970s.

Some reforms that have been widely implemented are still incomplete. Enterprise financial autonomy is subject to negotiations with government authorities and hence remains unstable. Particularly in investment decision making, enterprise autonomy is hampered by political and administrative interventions and by continuing government control over external sources of investment funds, including bank loans. Market functioning is a major question, given the administrative environment and strong influence of government supervisory agencies.

Despite all these problems and caveats, Chinese industrial reforms clearly have been successful in narrow terms: implementation of some of the main provisions has been widespread, and the bulk of state-owned industrial enterprises have been "reformed" at least to some extent. But in terms of achieving the goal of improved efficiency in the economy, they have been less successful. Rapid growth has occurred, but it has been far slower than in the dynamic nonstate industrial sector. Moreover, it has been accompanied by rapid growth of factor and nonfactor inputs. There is some evidence of improving efficiency at the aggregate level in Chinese state industry since the late 1970s, as indicated by total factor productivity growth (see Chen et al. 1988), but this has not been spectacular, is hard to measure, and can be affected by a host of different factors not directly related to industrial reforms.[8] In any case, only part of the backlog of inefficiency, waste, and backward technology inherited from the prereform period has been regained.

State Enterprise Reforms

Enterprise reforms got off to a modest start in a few factories in Sichuan Province as early as October 1978. The Third Plenum of the Eleventh Chinese Communist Party Central Committee in December 1978 formally inaugurated the era of reforms, and a number of local pilot programs of enterprise reform sprang up, culminating in the national "experiment in expanding enterprise autonomy" promulgated in July 1979. The heart of these early reforms was restoration of enterprise profit retention (10–30 percent of above-quota profits in the case of the national system). There were also experimental profit tax systems, "dividend" systems, and other variants. Most enterprises were allowed to retain a higher proportion of their depreciation funds as well. The bonus system for workers, restoration of which had begun in 1977–78, was virtually universal by 1979.

Not surprisingly, given the attractiveness of profit retention to firms, these schemes spread rapidly; by the end of 1980, 6,600 state-owned industrial enterprises, accounting for 16 percent of their total number but 60 percent of total state-sector industrial output value and 70 percent of profits, had instituted some form of profit retention scheme. Though profit retention marked a great step forward compared with the prereform system of virtually 100 percent profit remittance to the state, enterprise incentives were still not very strong. Moreover, many firms complained about "ratchet effects," whereby good performance in one year was punished by higher targets in subsequent years.

In 1981–82, various forms of the "economic responsibility system" came to the fore. These involved fixing targets for profits to be turned over by enterprises to the government, with very high enterprise retention rates from above-quota profits (often 60–80 percent, sometimes 100 percent). Since targets were based on negotiations between firms and their supervisory agencies and could be adjusted from year to year or even within the year, the new system provided considerable flexibility in the face of market or other shocks. But its ad hoc nature weakened the incentive effects of the economic responsibility system. Moreover, it apparently led to a hemorrhage of government revenue, since enterprises and supervisory agencies could effectively conspire to reduce flows of profits to the public finance system.

The third stage, and in a certain sense the culmination of first-phase state enterprise reforms in China, was the gradual move to a profit tax system in 1983–85, which was in part a reaction against the excesses of the economic responsibility system. Various experimental profit tax systems had been instituted in ten (later expanded to over four hundred) enterprises, starting in 1980. In 1983 a nationwide profit tax system was promulgated; profit tax carried a uniform rate of 55 percent, but due to price distortions and other "objective factors" that made profitability vary greatly across enterprises and industries, an enterprise-specific "adjustment tax" also was imposed on most large or medium-sized enterprises. Enterprises in industries with very low profitability paid tax at rates effectively well below 55 percent, or in some cases none at all. Despite these problems, the profit tax system represented a major step toward the creation of a genuine tax system, and adjustment tax rates for most firms were subsequently gradually reduced. By 1985 the bulk of state enterprises were at least nominally operating under the new profit tax system.

Another current of state enterprise reforms, which had been present all along but received greater emphasis after 1984, was the effort to delineate clearly and strengthen the position of the director as the primary operational decision maker of the enterprise. While early reforms had attempted in at least some spheres successfully to give enterprises greater decision-making powers, the question of what person or organizational structure within the firm would exercise this authority remained unresolved. The party committee, headed by its party secretary, had been the supreme decision-making entity in the prereform period. The first step in moving away from this system was the introduction of a system of factory director responsibility under the overall leadership of the party committee. Various experiments involving the Workers' Representative Assembly as the highest decision-making body and election of factory directors by the workers were tried out in some firms. But the general trend throughout the period of reforms, and especially after 1984, was for the factory director to assume the role of ultimate decision maker and representative of the enterprise in dealings with outside agencies. This trend culminated with the promulgation of the ''Regulations on the Work of Factory Directors in State-Owned Industrial Enterprises'' in September 1986, along with companion regulations on the respective roles of the enterprise party committee and Workers' Representative Assembly. These at least in principle gave final authority to the factory director, though he was supposed to consult with other actors on major decisions. Perhaps most important, the director was granted substantial authority over personnel decisions within the enterprise.

The factory director responsibility system and the factory director fixed-term goal responsibility system were manifestations of this new emphasis. The former began on an experimental basis in 1984, and by 1986 it had been tried out in 27,000 state-owned industrial firms. It actually meant little more than the concrete implementation of the regulations for factory directors, though it must be remembered that the factory director responsibility system predated the regulations by as much as two years. It was specified that managerial rewards could exceed the pay of an average worker by 100–300 percent, but the mechanism for determining managerial pay was left unclear. The fixed-term goal responsibility system involved setting specific tasks and targets for the factory director, against which performance was evaluated at the end of his term in office. The system was designed to combat the tendency of directors in fixed-term jobs (introduced in September 1984) to pursue short-term goals at the expense of the long-term development of their enterprises. As in the case of the director responsibility system, reward mechanisms and linkages were not very well specified.

Starting in 1986 and widely implemented in 1987–88, ''contractual'' responsibility systems became for a time the major focus of state enterprise reform efforts. These included leasing, the contract management responsibility system (later made into the dominant ''umbrella'' scheme), the enterprise management responsibility system, and the asset management responsibility system. Despite their variation and complexity, these different schemes had some main elements in common. In the first place, they all involved a contract-based relationship between the enterprise or its manager and the supervisory agency with jurisdiction over the firm. In theory, the contracts were between equals and supposedly were entered into voluntarily, which superficially marked a sharp departure from earlier schemes. With some exceptions, the director entered into the contractual relationship as a representative of his enterprise. Thus there was in principle a strong element of personal responsibility. To work at all, these schemes required the factory director to be in a position of authority commensurate with his responsibilities. In many firms the implementation of contractual responsibility systems hence led to a substantial increase in the powers of the director. Another common feature was the assumption of substantial risk by the director, with greater, performance-linked variability in his rewards. In the asset management responsibility system, for example, it was specified that the director's rewards could exceed the average worker's pay by as much as 1,000 percent. Finally, most of the contractual responsibility systems involved multiyear targets and incentives, to ameliorate any ratchet effect.

Though contractual responsibility systems represented a major effort to deal with the problems of earlier, incomplete reforms, by 1988–89 issues related to the restructuring of state ownership had come to the fore. Various kinds of shareholding systems for state enterprises had been experimented with in a limited way earlier, and state enterprises have increasingly resorted to issuance of capital market instruments. But subsequently the stock system also came to be viewed as a means of changing ownership and the exercise of ownership functions with respect to state enterprises. The issue of ownership rights for workers or for other public agencies also has come up in the context of shareholding or joint stock systems, which would be a convenient vehicle for diversifying the ownership structure of state enterprises.

Overall, by the late 1980s Chinese state enterprise reforms were in a ferment, in some ways similar to the initial phase of local experimentation in the late 1970s, but at a more advanced stage and a more sophisticated level. There was a groping toward solutions to problems that had hindered reforms earlier, in the face of continuing obstacles. The evolution of reformist thinking has involved an increasing recognition of the fundamental nature and complexity of barriers to dynamism and efficiency improvements in Chinese state industry, with a consequent search for deeper, more fundamental solutions. But as of the late 1980s, it was too early to tell how far these efforts would proceed and the extent to which they would succeed. Moreover, political developments in the middle of 1989 and related changes in China's top leadership may well have put at least a temporary stop to efforts to ''deepen'' state enterprise reforms.

Key Questions Addressed by This Study

This study attacks a number of issues related to the development of the market mechanism in Chinese industry. The most fundamental question concerns the prospects for the emergence and durability of effectively functioning markets that are conducive to dynamic industrial growth and development (hereafter referred to as dynamic markets) in China. Most of the study grapples with this question, which is difficult not only in itself but because the answer to the general question of the conditions required for dynamic markets in any country is necessarily somewhat vague and ambiguous.

A number of different approaches, each posing and answering questions of its own, are used to address this issue. The abstract approach seeks necessary and sufficient conditions for dynamic markets based on theoretical considerations and models. Using certain assumptions, mathematical models of planning and markets can be constructed. Conditions required for dynamic markets also can be ascertained by studying international experience and case studies. But applications of the results of this theoretical and empirical analysis to Chinese industry must be based on a thorough understanding of the situation in China and recent patterns and trends.

Once there is some understanding of the conditions required for dynamic markets, the next question is whether these prerequisites are or will be attained in Chinese state-owned industry. This is a crucial issue that cannot be ignored, though it is difficult to identify such conditions in the first place, and even more so to apply them to China. The question can be broken down into specific subquestions based on different prerequisites, and also depending on whether the question relates to the present (and immediate past) or the foreseeable future.

The questions addressed by this study can also be classified in another way. Some relate to what has happened in China so far and have a primarily empirical bent. The underlying concern is the extent to which functioning markets have already emerged in China. The quantitative share of markets in industrial activity is obviously an important indicator in this respect, for which a considerable amount of data is available. Even more important is the qualitative functioning of markets and their impact on transactors and particularly on industrial producers, which can be evaluated through case studies. A closely related question is whether and to what extent the development of markets in Chinese industry is hindered by obstacles embedded in the system. Identification of these obstacles and their precise roles is an important policy-related task.

Another set of questions relates to the logical and theoretical implications of what is going on in China, which may provide some clues as to the likely course of events in the future. The goal is to try to ascertain the inherent tendencies in the evolving Chinese industrial system and their strength relative to other forces that may support or hinder reforms. What are the static and dynamic implications of China's evolving plan/market system? How do these affect the future prospects for markets in Chinese industry? How do the different economic and administrative or political forces at work interact and influence trends? To address these questions requires some theoretical analysis and modeling.

This study will not be able to answer all of these questions definitively, because of its limited scope and the problematic nature of the questions themselves. Nevertheless, the more fundamental underlying issues should be kept in mind during the detailed analysis of particular topics.

Outline of the Study

Chapter 2 looks at the prerequisites for dynamic markets, based on theoretical considerations and with some attention to international experience. It starts by trying to come up with a working definition of the market mechanism, in the light of contrasting views of its role. It then searches for necessary or sufficient conditions for dynamic markets, rejecting some candidates and looking in more detail at others. Effective competition receives considerable attention as one of the most crucial prerequisites. The chapter ends with a classification of different types of market situations based on the presence or absence of various preconditions.

Chapter 3 presents available evidence on the quantitative significance of markets for Chinese industrial goods and makes a preliminary attempt to evaluate how they function. There is first a brief look at the limited role of markets in the prereform period. Then the quantitative share of markets for industrial products is assessed at the aggregate level, for producer goods, for consumer goods, and at the micro level for several samples of firms. There is strong evidence that the role of markets in Chinese industry is significant and that their share of total transactions has been rising. Finally, the chapter looks at obstacles to well-functioning markets, such as various kinds of government interference, the impact of unreformed parts of the economic system, and market segmentation and regional or local protectionism.

Chapter 4 analyzes the response of Chinese state-owned industrial enterprises to market forces during the reform period. It starts by classifying different enterprise response patterns. Then it looks at how response differs as between a sellers' market (excess demand) and a buyers' market (excess supply). Technical, financial, and other aspects that may influence enterprise response are also discussed, but it is argued that market conditions are the crucial determinant. The chapter then analyzes the response of government authorities to market forces, which can either dampen or intensify market conditions but typically does not reverse them. Patterns of market competition and price adjustments are also reviewed. It is suggested that competition in Chinese industry may resemble competition in international trade more closely than competition within well-integrated national markets. Finally, the chapter looks at the crucial issue of dynamic trends and overall performance, focusing primarily on buyers' markets and the period 1978–82.[9]

Chapter 5 looks at the changing role of planning in Chinese state-owned industry, concentrating on short-term production planning and administrative allocation of enterprise outputs and material inputs. The chapter first briefly describes the different roles of planning and the main features of the prereform situation. Then it argues that planning in Chinese industry has lost its direct role in short-term resource allocation, as well as any role in mobilizing enterprise effort and resources through its impact on incentives. By the same token, planning no longer facilitates government control over the economy in the short run.

With the dissipation of its other roles, planning now plays a primarily redistributional role, which is analyzed in the chapter. Chapter 5 also discusses the generation and flow of rents in the Chinese planning system and "rent-seeking behavior" engendered.

Chapter 6 moves on to a formal theoretical analysis of plan and market in the Chinese economy. It presents a static general equilibrium model, in which part of the total output or supply of each good is allocated by plan at fixed prices, part by the market at flexible prices that equilibrate nonplan supply and demand. Plan input allocations and output targets are modeled as minimum constraints on the flows of goods to and from different agents. Other important features of the model include rigidity of enterprise factor endowments, enterprise profit maximization subject to constraints imposed by plan targets, fixed nominal wage rates, and a highly simplistic modeling of final demand. Under certain conditions, an equilibrium solution to the model does exist. Moreover, if all firms engage in market transactions for all of their inputs and outputs at the margin, the resulting equilibrium solution is no different from a market equilibrium in the absence of planning and therefore is Pareto-optimal. In this situation, planning may have no effect on resource allocation, as was argued in chapter 5. When plan targets "constrain" the choices of economic agents, certain results still apply.

Chapter 7 looks critically at the assumptions embedded in the model, particularly those required to generate its main results. It also examines the weaknesses and limitations of the model. For the most part these do not invalidate the results, though caution is necessary in interpreting them. The chapter also looks at some possible extensions of the model. In most cases these do not drastically change its results. The major exception is allowing product variation within plan categories, which permits the model to display many of the features of chronic shortage found in centrally planned economies. Finally, the chapter formalizes the concept of rents developed in chapter 5 and incorporates it into the model.

Chapter 8 analyzes the performance of Chinese markets for industrial producer goods based on market price data, using a methodology developed in the 1980s for the study of markets for agricultural goods in developing countries. This method can be used to assess the degree to which different local markets are "integrated"—linked to each other through rapid, equilibrating price adjustments—or "segmented," with unrelated price movements. Market price trends in the 1980s also are reviewed and analyzed, particularly the near-stability of market prices for many goods between late 1985 and early 1988.

Chapter 9 looks at dynamic patterns and trends that have been at work in Chinese industry, as the "two-tier" system of resource allocation and pricing emerged for goods whose plan prices were kept artificially low and faced a chronic sellers' market. It is suggested that the inherent economic incentives of the two-tier system and the difficulty of monitoring and punishing diversion of goods from plan to market channels have led to a secular tendency for the share of the market in total supply to rise and for its importance relative to planning to increase. There are pressures to hold down the absolute volume of plan-allocated supply, to reduce it through legal or illegal means, to decontrol prices, and to sharply raise plan prices to reduce the incentives for diversion. These trends are documented with case studies of some key industrial products.

Chapter 10 recapitulates the main conclusions of the study and pulls together the arguments of different chapters. It does not attempt to summarize the contents of the book as a whole, however.

2. Prerequisites for Effectively Functioning Markets

THE ULTIMATE objectives of Chinese reformers were simple: rapid, sustained economic growth and improvements in living standards, which over a period of several decades would permit China to achieve a satisfactory level of living for its populace and later to "catch up" with the developed nations.[1] Substantial improvements in the efficiency of the Chinese economy are required to meet these objectives, not just the massive resource mobilization and capital investments that generated growth in the past.[2] Therefore, improving economic efficiency has assumed the status of a goal on nearly the same level as rapid growth and higher living standards.

The twin requirements of maintaining a socialist political economic system and maintaining some degree of control at the macro level have constrained measures to achieve faster economic growth. The latter was often expressed in the article of faith that "China is a planned economy" and in the implicit presumption that it would remain so.[3] It was also a highly practical concern: there is a deep-seated fear of macro instability and inflation in China; poor performance in this area would threaten the government and the reformers at its helm even more than perceived ideological deviations.

These two constraints set ideological and political limits to the kinds of reforms that could be proposed and implemented; they also acted as ex post obstacles by causing reforms that were seen to have "gone too far" to be pulled back. Nevertheless, these limits receded considerably over time, and practices that would have been impossible in the late 1970s were accepted at least provisionally in the mid- to late 1980s. The political developments of April–June 1989, however, and the ouster of Party Secretary Zhao Ziyang and his radical reformist followers undoubtedly have resulted in tighter ideological and political constraints on reform, particularly in sensitive areas like ownership changes, private enterprise development, and labor market reforms.

Other goals of reformers have had a decidedly "intermediate" character: they were valued only because they could further ultimate objectives, and if they were found not to promote them they could be discarded relatively easily. The goal of expanding the role of the market mechanism fell in this category, as did price reform, financial incentives, and devolution of decision-making authority to economic agents (which was not valued in itself or for political reasons). Given this orientation on the part of reformers, Chinese reforms have had a pragmatic, experimental character.

A key intellectual underpinning of China's reform effort is that greater use of markets as a resource allocation mechanism and less reliance on planning and administrative controls will improve economic efficiency, which in turn will further the ultimate objectives of rapid long-term growth and rising living standards.[4] Hence, it is useful to think of reforms as an attempt to institute a functioning market system, partly supplementing, partly supplanting the existing system of administrative allocation. Even if markets are only meant to cover part of the economy, they have to work well in the spheres where they are permitted. Thus, it is important to ascertain how markets function in economic systems where they are the dominant mode of resource allocation, before asking whether and how they can work in mixed systems. This leads to the critical question of what minimum prerequisites must be satisfied for an effective market system.

Contrasting Views of the Market Mechanism

Western economic theory does not present a unified viewpoint on this question. Several different strands of thought can be distinguished; they are outlined only briefly here.

The Neoclassical Perspective

In the standard neoclassical model of perfectly competitive markets, a number of assumptions are necessary to generate mathematically demonstrable existence and efficiency properties. Decision-making authority in the hands of market participants, their self-interested motivation, and decentralization of information are required. Goods traded in each market are assumed to be homogeneous, so prices are the only information needed to make production, purchase, and sales decisions. There is only one price for each good, and prices adjust appropriately in response to changes in supply and demand conditions. There are numerous buyers and sellers, with each transactor too small to affect the market price or overall market conditions. Moreover, each agent acts as if he could buy or sell whatever quantity he wanted to at the going market price. Agents are motivated solely by the desire to maximize profits from their activities. Markets must be complete, that is, there must be functioning markets for all goods and services in the economy.

With these assumptions and some others relating to technology and preferences, the neoclassical model has strong efficiency properties and achieves Pareto optimality: there is no more efficient way of allocating a given endowment of resources, in the short run or, with stronger assumptions, in a dynamic setting. The demonstrable efficiency and Pareto optimality properties of the neoclassical model to a large extent explain its popularity.

Unrealistic Assumptions and Conditions

Few real-life markets closely resemble the neoclassical ideal, even though they function reasonably well in the short run and are consistent with rapid growth and economic development in the long run. The number of transactors in many markets is small enough that some of them have a major impact on market conditions. Monopoly and oligopoly theories try to come to grips with this by abandoning perfect competition. In the neoclassical framework the adverse impact of departures from perfect competition on efficiency is easy to demonstrate. But markets with imperfect competition can be characterized by dynamism, growth, and technological progress.

Even when the number of transactors is large, market participants have strong incentives to be price-takers only when the market is in equilibrium, the only time they are actually free to buy or sell as much as they want at the going market price (Arrow 1959). If there is excess demand, buyers are quantity-constrained, whereas in a situation of excess supply, sellers are quantity-constrained. Most markets are continually adjusting toward an equilibrium that itself changes over time and may never be achieved exactly. Enterprises facing excess supply may be able to sell more by lowering their output prices, even in the short run, which implies that each enterprise faces falling demand curves for its output. Monopolistic competition models could be an appropriate tool of analysis in this situation (see Chamberlin 1956).

Another problem area is the price adjustment mechanism. Very few markets are characterized by the equivalent of an auctioneer and a tatonnement process whereby prices adjust quickly to market equilibrium. A variety of different modes of price formation have arisen naturally over time, depending on product characteristics, industrial structure, the pattern of consumption or use, institutional arrangements, and other factors. In a few markets, with virtually homogeneous products or a reliable standardized grading system that creates homogeneous products and with a very large number of transactors and transactions, a centralized exchange mechanism may emerge. Prices adjust rapidly, and the market may closely mimic the neoclassical perfectly competitive market model. Examples include staple agricultural goods, pure metals, and financial securities. In these types of markets, secondary and speculative trading tends to be common.

For differentiated manufactured goods, price setting by producers is the norm. Wiles (1977, 243–44) argues that if goods are storable, producers price to cover full cost plus a profit margin and will change price lists infrequently due to the costs involved (new price lists, new price labels for goods, changes in accounts, etc.). Moreover, the information carried by prices cannot be conveyed to buyers unless prices remain fixed for at least short periods of time. Purchase decisions take time, and would-be purchasers could not go about this task without some confidence that sellers' offers will remain valid for a while. Producers may engage in occasional or frequent discounting. With short-run fixed prices, sales are determined by demand; inventories and excess capacity serve as buffers to meet unexpected surges.

If goods are not storable (as in the case of services, transport, and electricity), then various forms of marginal cost pricing may emerge. This does not generate financial insolvency as long as there are periods when marginal cost is above average cost as well as below it. Where marginal cost is below average cost due to economies of scale, marginal cost pricing does lead to chronic financial losses, severe competition, bankruptcies, and mergers. After decades of difficult experience, U.S. companies have "learned" more stable pricing behavior, sticking to full-cost pricing and engaging in nonprice competition, along with discounts and sales (Clark 1961).

Even when there are large numbers of transactors on both sides of a market, adjustment toward equilibrium may be quite different depending on the mode of price determination.[5] Transactions outside of equilibrium can have an effect on the equilibrium outcome. In some functioning markets, prices are subject to external controls by government authorities, an even greater departure from the neoclassical model.

The assumption of product homogeneity across firms does not hold for most goods. This leads in the neoclassical framework to the theory of monopolistic competition with differentiated products, if there are numerous transactors. The lack of product homogeneity may make it easier for producers to maintain constant prices, even if market conditions are changing in the short run. The costs of changing prices are the same, whereas the costs of not changing them are less, because differentiation means that individual firm demand curves are less elastic.

Given the lack of product homogeneity and the relative slowness of price adjustments, prices cannot convey all relevant information to buyers and sellers. Unless there is a centralized market exchange institution, information about actual transaction prices also may be difficult to obtain. As a result, real-world markets have a variety of mechanisms for generating and disseminating price and nonprice market information. Sometimes this is done privately through services that market participants are willing to pay for, but the externalities involved often make it necessary for the government to become involved in collection and dissemination of market information. Similarly, government standards, grading specifications, and inspections are examples of government intervention to help markets function more smoothly.

The assumption of complete markets is unrealistic in the case of multiperiod dynamic analysis, but also even from a static perspective. When markets are incomplete the efficiency properties of the neoclassical model are to a large extent lost. Yet, in the real world, economies with incomplete markets can be conducive to efficiency, growth, and economic development.

Toward a More Realistic Working Definition

What, then, is an appropriate definition of the market mechanism? Markets entail voluntary exchange of goods by self-interested individuals or entities for each other or for money. The autonomy of transactors is a crucial element. They are free to enter and exit the market and to accept or refuse transaction offers. Another important element is decentralization of information and its flow through horizontal rather than vertical channels. A third is the existence of market prices. Finally, the motivation of self-interest on the part of transactors is an integral element.

This bare-bones definition is sufficient for our purposes and encompasses markets in precapitalist and centrally planned economic systems as well as in capitalist market economies. Not all markets that fit this description, however, promote or even are consistent with long-term rapid economic growth and development and technological progress. Many markets have existed in an economic situation of near-stability or very slow long-term growth, even though they may have had a corrosive impact on traditional institutions and practices over time. Thus the question of prerequisites for markets to play a dynamic role in stimulating efficient economic development, rather than merely to function and survive, looms very important.

The Market Mechanism as Process Rather than State

The most cogent critique of the neoclassical view of the market mechanism is that of the Austrian School, which broadly includes Joseph Schumpeter (1934; 1950) as well as the line of economists stretching from von Mises to Hayek (1945; 1948; 1984), Kirzner (1973; 1979), and others. Common to their perspectives is a focus on the market mechanism as a dynamic process rather than on market equilibrium states. Innovations and informational improvements are constantly affecting the perceived possible courses of action of economic agents, so it is meaningless to assume that they are maximizing benefits in a framework of fixed, known constraints. Economic agents are not even fully aware of their utility functions.[6]

In the Schumpeterian view, dynamic markets are often in fundamental disequilibrium. The economy is occasionally buffeted by major innovations that dominate any tendencies toward equilibrium that may have been at work as previous innovations were being absorbed. These innovations result in premature (in terms of physical lifetime) obsolescence of existing capital in the economy. Firms must struggle to keep up with new innovations and if possible be at the forefront in order to survive over long periods of time. From this perspective, temporary monopolies are not harmful and instead may even be helpful in promoting innovations. The process of economic development in market economies is one of "creative destruction."

Hayek also views the market mechanism primarily as a process rather than as an equilibrium state. But unlike Schumpeter, he stresses its equilibrating role, which permits the knowledge, plans, and actions of different agents to converge toward consistency over time. The end result of the market process is something like neoclassical market equilibrium, though because of disturbances, changes in plans and perceptions, and new developments, a stable, stationary equilibrium is never reached. Though he recognizes the usefulness of the analysis of equilibrium states, Hayek considers the "discovery process" and knowledge enhancement that occur during market adjustment as the main role and benefit of the market mechanism.

Hayek's approach is not fundamentally contradictory to that of Schumpeter, though their assessments of the prospects for capitalism disagree sharply. Hayek focused on the "normal" workings of the market mechanism and the tendencies for agents to correct their mistakes and misperceptions over time, which implies a tendency toward equilibrium. Schumpeter, on the other hand, concentrated his attention on long-term economic development, where disequilibrating innovations and "creative destruction" play the key role.

Other economists also have viewed the market mechanism as a process rather than as a neoclassical equilibrium state. J. M. Clark (1961) saw competition as a "dynamic process" that was the driving force behind the market mechanism as a means of promoting economic progress. I. M. Kirzner (1973) emphasizes the role of competition and entrepreneurship in the market process, which he views in much the same light as Hayek. These perspectives all differ fundamentally from the neoclassical approach in their focus on the adjustment process that occurs under the market mechanism.

Neoclassical economics has absorbed some of these criticisms. Stability of equilibrium has all along been an important topic in general equilibrium analysis. The economics of information has shed light on many of the questions that Hayek and others of the Austrian School raised. In the 1970s, various "disequilibrium" approaches emerged, which look at the behavior of markets outside of equilibrium and the "spill-over" effects of disequilibrium in one market on other markets. Extensions of neoclassical theory have tended not to push beyond the limits of constrained maximization by agents, even though the constraints and outcomes may be stochastic rather than determinate. Thus, a more fundamental aspect of the Austrian critique of neoclassical economics, that the insulation and "privatization" of information in market participants renders even the standard microeconomic tool of constrained maximization invalid, does retain its force.

The view of the market mechanism as a dynamic process has much to recommend it. Markets involve misperceptions and mistakes by the various market participants; improvements and convergence over time as mistakes are rectified and information is communicated through the market; and continual disturbances and new developments, which either dominate the tendencies toward equilibrium (Schumpeter) or prevent a stationary equilibrium state from being reached (Hayek). In a reforming centrally planned economy like China, this perspective takes on even greater importance. Market institutions and arrangements are not well established in Chinese industry. A large part of the task of reforms is to create and nurture well-functioning markets. For this, an understanding of the dynamics of the market mechanism is essential.

The lack of established market institutions, arrangements, and traditions in Chinese state-owned industry means that the basic framework of the market mechanism is still in flux. This is another reason for focusing primary attention on the market process rather than on equilibrium states. Institutional and structural changes in the Chinese industrial system have been so great that tendencies toward equilibrium have to a large extent been submerged.

Prerequisites for Effectively Functioning Markets

What is required for markets to work effectively and in a way that promotes efficiency, growth, economic development, and technological progress? The minimum set of elements in any functioning market or market system is clearly insufficient. There are many examples in precapitalist economies of markets that may have functioned well in balancing supply and demand at flexible prices, in a general economic situation of stagnation or very slow long-term growth. Similarly, functioning markets in centrally planned economies, like free markets in the USSR at which peasants can sell the produce of their private plots, may improve resource allocation, but they have not been dynamic stimulants of long-term growth and technological progress. This section looks at some prerequisites for dynamic markets, including autonomy of transactors, price flexibility, financial discipline, middlemen and arbitrage (secondary trading), entrepreneurs and entrepreneurship, and the allocation of factors of production.

Prerequisites for Autonomy

Autonomy of transactors has already been mentioned as a basic element of functioning markets. But what degree of autonomy is necessary for dynamic markets, and what elements in the economic system are consistent with this degree of autonomy? How can autonomy of transactors be preserved when those responsible for transactions are not formal owners of the goods being transacted or of the organizations doing the transactions? These questions cannot be answered in any but the most general way but should be kept in mind.

One obvious candidate for prerequisite status is *private ownership of the means of production.* Some, like von Mises (1936), argued that an economy without private ownership cannot be dynamic and efficient, whereas advocates of "market socialism" have come to the opposite conclusion. Broadly speaking, ownership need not be vested directly in the economic agents transacting in the market or their chief decision makers, since in widely held corporations ownership is largely separated from control yet markets play a dynamic role. What is important is that agents producing for and transacting in markets have a considerable degree of autonomy, whether or not they own their enterprises. This requirement is consistent with a variety of different ownership forms, possibly including public ownership.

With vigorous competition from the private sector and minimal government intervention, publicly owned enterprises at least sometimes can perform as efficiently as private firms. One study compared two major Canadian railroad corporations, one government-owned and the other private, that competed directly against each other in a competitive, deregulated environment (see Caves and Christensen 1980). Total factor productivity grew rapidly in both companies, but slightly faster in the government-owned company than in the private company (3.1 percent versus 2.5 percent per year). At the end of the period under study, total factor productivity in the two railroads was almost the same. There is nothing in this carefully researched study to indicate that the public enterprise is less efficient than its private competitor.

This study is an exception not only in its methodological care but also in its results: other comparisons of public and private enterprises in market economies have found the former to be less profitable and efficient than the latter. But this does not necessarily mean there are inherent problems with state ownership. The usual pattern of state ownership combined with heavy regulation and a noncompetitive or only weakly competitive environment does lead to problems, but ownership may not be the primary cause.

The key issue for Chinese industry is whether it is possible to have competitive markets in a system dominated by publicly owned firms. Efficient, dynamic public enterprises in mixed economies operate in an environment dominated by private ownership, where there are credible private competitors. As long as the government does not provide undue protection or help to its own firms, a competitive market environment is possible. Achieving this may be much more difficult, however, when all large firms are state-owned. When two or more enterprises in the same market are under the supervision of a single government agency, the latter may try to dampen competition between them in order to protect its interests in both. The danger of detailed government regulation may also be greater if the main market participants are government-owned. But the most serious adverse impact of pervasive government ownership may simply be the absence of strong competition from a healthy private sector.

The tendency toward government control and stifling of competition may be ameliorated if government ownership is dispersed across different agencies, levels of government, and territorial jurisdictions (World Bank 1985, 166; also see Hua et al. 1989). But the nature of dispersal is crucial. In China, supervisory authority is scattered across numerous different government organizations, but each enterprise is closely tied to one or two agencies that exert control and take a strong interest in the welfare of "their" firms. Enterprises under different administrative hierarchies may compete fairly vigorously, and government-sponsored market-sharing schemes may be hard to impose and maintain. Such competition remains distorted, however, since government organizations will intervene to protect their firms from "excessive" competition even if they do not interfere extensively in enterprise operations. As a result, barriers to internal trade and fragmented domestic markets may become widespread.[7]

This is quite different from a situation in which government agencies for the most part have only a small stake in any individual enterprise and in any case have much the same interests as ordinary stockholders. In West Germany, for example, public ownership of industrial and financial concerns is widespread but is dispersed across different levels of government, with few government entities having large ownership stakes in particular firms (World Bank 1985, 167). Governments and other social entities largely act like ordinary shareholders, and in any case there is strong competition from the private sector. Dispersed public ownership may generate requirements for tradable ownership shares and secondary markets, which could be hard to meet in a country like China.

This all suggests that the key prerequisite for autonomy of firms is not ownership per se but rather the absence of heavy-handed, detailed government regulation of enterprise activities. Private ownership is no guarantee that government will not impose extensive regulation, but dominant public ownership may make it difficult for the government to avoid such involvement, though in principle a variety of different ownership systems may be consistent with the degree of enterprise autonomy required for dynamic markets. Particularly when concentrated and involving close relationships between firms and particular agencies, public ownership carries a great threat to enterprise autonomy.

Long-Term Price Flexibility

Completely flexible prices could be viewed as a prerequisite for well-functioning markets. But there are examples of markets that work efficiently even in the face of external (to the market participants) price controls. Moreover, in many cases price flexibility is limited by market participants in their own interests. Certainly this is true in oligopolistic situations with price leadership. But some price rigidity may be desired by producers in any case, because time is required for price signals to have an impact on would-be purchasers. There are also costs to changing prices, which would tend to inhibit very frequent small changes. Thus there may be a considerable degree of continuity between self-imposed price rigidity in markets and weaker forms of externally imposed price controls.

The "administered-price thesis" developed by Gardiner Means (1935; 1972) asserted that many industrial prices are rigid over considerable periods of time. Stigler and Kindahl (1970) attempted to refute this hypothesis with new data on actual transaction prices. Carlton (1986), using the same data but focusing on individual transactions rather than on averages, showed that in American industry during times of low general inflation, prices have tended to be rigid, often for periods of over one year. For some products, correlations between price changes across transactors also are low. Thus, price rigidities can be present even in a competitive situation and in the absence of price controls.

Whereas short-term price flexibility and continuous price adjustments do not seem to be necessary for dynamic markets, this is not true over longer periods of time. Price rigidities generated by market participants do not persist very long in the face of major changes in market conditions. Thus, long-term inflexibility is generally the result of externally imposed price controls, which to be effective must be accompanied by restrictions against entry and overexpansion (if the controlled price is artificially high), or by rationing of demand or inflows of funds in one form or another (if the controlled price is artificially low). Long-term price rigidity distorts incentives and financial flows and is highly inimical to market dynamism.

Financial Discipline and Profit Orientation

Profit orientation of some kind is a prerequisite for markets to function in the first place; it is a logical concomitant of one of the basic characteristics of markets—self-interested behavior. The real question is what degree of orientation toward profits is necessary. In a competitive situation, a strong aversion on the part of enterprises to incurring losses combined with a desire to achieve rapid growth is probably sufficient. A distinction should also be made between the short run and the long run, since aggressive, strategic behavior designed to increase market share may be costly in the short run yet maximize profits over the long run if successful.

To have strong incentives to cut costs, improve products, meet customer needs, and innovate, producers should be under pressure based on limits to and a high perceived value of financial resources. Enterprises in centrally planned economies typically lack this pressure, and numerous problems arise from the "soft budget constraint" (see Kornai 1980; Kornai and Matits 1984). Changing enterprise behavior in this respect is likely to be a key prerequisite for dynamic markets over the long run, but it is by no means easy to achieve. As will be discussed later in this chapter, the issue of enterprise financial discipline is closely related to market conditions, in particular chronic shortage, and hence to the degree of effective competition.

Middlemen and Arbitrage

Middlemen—commercial intermediaries—buy from producers, or from other middlemen in a chain of transactions that eventually leads to producers, and sell to the consumer or final user, either directly or through a chain of middleman transactions. Middlemen provide numerous commercial services, ranging from location changes to some final processing of the product or even its assembly. Arbitrageurs also buy and sell commodities as their main activity, but they generally do not provide any commercial service. They can, however, contribute to smooth, continuous adjustment of market prices and (in futures markets) hedging of risks by other agents. Both middleman transactions and arbitrage are oriented toward making commercial profits.

Issues raised by commercial intermediation and arbitrage are important for several reasons. First, ideological concerns come into play. Second, commercial organizations were generally suppressed and weakened during the Cultural Revolution period, and "speculation" has been looked upon with disfavor throughout the history of the PRC. Third, both activities, arbitrage especially, undermine control by the planning system; similarly, they undermine price controls. Finally, in an environment like China's, with many highly distorted prices and underdeveloped markets, profits from arbitrage are exorbitantly high and often undeserved, which tempts authorities to forbid it on "equity" grounds.

The need for middlemen and arbitrage varies greatly for different types of commodities. At one extreme, real-world markets characterized by something close to perfect competition have a great deal of secondary trading and arbitrage, which may be essential to "thicken" the market enough to allow smooth, continuous adjustments. But in many markets for differentiated products, where producer-posted prices and buyer-determined quantities are the norm, arbitrage and secondary trading are not evident. This does not mean, however, that they would not arise if profit opportunities existed. Hence, the potential for arbitrage may be important in preventing exploitation by existing market participants.

Reliance on commercial intermediation is obviously the most efficient alternative for many goods. But for others, particularly differentiated capital goods, direct transactions between producer and end-user may be the best solution. The need for commercial intermediation and the optimal number of links in the chain of transactions depend on product characteristics, the final use to which goods are being put, and industrial structure.

A related question concerns the extent to which commercial units and arbitrageurs should be permitted freely to engage in profit-seeking activity. This is somewhat analogous to the issue of industrial enterprises moving into new lines of products, but it is generally much easier to shift into trading new goods than to change the production process so as to make new products. The role of commercial intermediaries is hence closely linked with the degree of price flexibility in the system. If prices are rigid (and hence distorted), then controls over commercial activity as well as arbitrage are likely to be necessary.

Given the desirability and necessity of commercial intermediation and arbitrage in at least some markets, blanket prohibitions would undoubtedly be harmful. Any attempt to dispense with commercial intermediation entirely or keep it under tight government control would obviously be counterproductive. Extensive arbitrage may not become politically acceptable, however, until price reforms and further market development have narrowed the profits that can be earned through this activity.

Entrepreneurship

Entrepreneurship has many definitions and an extensive literature.[8] There is disagreement about its meaning and role, but authorities on the subject are unanimous in asserting that entrepreneurship is a crucial element left out of the standard neoclassical market model. At the broadest level, entrepreneurship consists of human alertness to profit opportunities that arise in the process of market adjustment and willingness to take actions to appropriate such "entrepreneurial profits." The exercise of entrepreneurship at one extreme can have a profound effect on the structure of the economy and its subsequent development (Schumpeter 1934; 1950), while at the opposite extreme it involves a host of minor activities that improve the efficiency of a market economy and allow it to function more smoothly (Kirzner 1973).

Based on this broad definition, anyone who plays an active role in taking advantage of market opportunities is an entrepreneur, while entrepreneurship is a critical part of the market process. Without countless minor adjustments and appropriation of profit opportunities by agents, market adjustment would not occur. Entrepreneurial alertness and action generate the tendency in markets toward improved knowledge on the part of participants and greater consistency in their plans and actions over time, or in other words the tendency toward market equilibrium. At the same time, major innovations, effectively brought into the marketplace by entrepreneurs, can have a profoundly disequilibrating impact. While entrepreneurship "in the small" can smooth the process of market adjustment, "in the large" it may be destabilizing (while stimulating economic progress).

Entrepreneurship may be restricted or discouraged, impeding market functioning. Discrimination against "outside" entrepreneurs, a chronic problem in many developing countries, is one example. Limits on entrepreneurial rewards also can harm incentives. Tight controls over managerial rewards in state enterprises inhibit exercise of entrepreneurship by their managers. These could be reinforced by ideological or administrative discrimination against entrepreneurs.

An environment where entrepreneurship is at least tacitly permitted and a significant portion of entrepreneurial profits can accrue to those who generate them would appear to be a prerequisite for well-functioning markets. This kind of environment is difficult to create in a partially reformed, centrally planned economy, particularly one in which entrepreneurial profits are not supposed to be appropriated by individuals. Restrictions on autonomy of enterprise managers also dampen entrepreneurship. Middleman transactions and arbitrage, already discussed, are examples of entrepreneurship broadly defined. The problems the Chinese system has had in accepting these activities provide some indication of the difficulties in fostering entrepreneurship more generally in Chinese industry.

Factor Allocation

Are functioning markets for factors of production (labor, capital, and land) a prerequisite for dynamic industrial goods markets? Factor markets may not be needed for effectively functioning goods markets in the short run, but rational factor allocation may well be essential for dynamic markets over the long run. Adjustment of factor endowments is a key instrument of enterprise response to market forces. If this instrument is difficult to use because of rigidity in the factor allocation system, both enterprise-level and industrywide adjustment may be severely hindered. China's factor allocation system is fragmented, rigid, and a major source of inefficiency, despite some reforms and evolution of the system in the 1980s (Byrd and Tidrick 1987).

The minimum required degree of rationality and flexibility in the factor allocation system may fall considerably short of fully functional factor markets, however. Labor markets in all countries are subject to distortions and rigidities. Land transactions also are restricted in various ways. Financial markets do not function efficiently in many countries, some of which have experienced rapid growth and development. Thus, what seems to be critical is reasonably effective mechanisms for adjustment of enterprise factor endowments over time in response to the forces and incentives emanating from goods markets. This condition can be met with less than perfect factor markets, though markets covering at least part of total factor allocation may be essential.

Competition

Corresponding to the views of the market mechanism discussed earlier, there are different conceptions of market competition and its role. In neoclassical perfect competition there are so many competitors that none of them individually can affect the market price or the actions of other competitors. The layman's idea of competition is much more that of a conscious struggle to keep up with the market (if there are many competitors) or with particular competitors (if there are few). The latter concept fits much better with the view of the market mechanism as a process rather than an equilibrium state. Competition in this view is simply the independent effort by different businesses and individuals to make sales and profits in a situation in which a number of other agents are striving to do the same thing. Autonomy of agents and voluntary transactions together imply choice, at least as to whether or not to undertake a certain transaction at all.[9] Whenever there is more than one potential opposite number, agents also have a choice regarding with whom to conclude a market transaction. This leads in a natural way to activities on the part of market participants to influence choices made by those on the other side of the market, which is the essence of competition.

Competition is a dynamic process (Clark 1961). Depending on its nature and strength and the kinds of activities it stimulates, competition may play a crucial role in promoting efficiency, growth, and technological progress. Two main questions arise in this context: (1) the optimal type, degree, and arena of competition; and (2) the prerequisites for unfettered competition.

Types of Competition

Competition can be classified by several different criteria: (1) the number of transactors on each side of the market and the impact each has on the market; (2) actual versus potential competition; (3) the arena in which competition occurs (price versus nonprice competition, business competition versus competition for rents); and (4) general market conditions (buyers' market versus sellers' market). The last of these is discussed in the following section.

At one extreme, monopoly in theory results in restriction of output and higher prices. At the opposite extreme, perfect competition has strong static efficiency implications. The combination of the two is monopolistic competition (Chamberlin 1956), where each producer has a unique product for which he is a monopolist facing a downward-sloping demand curve, but there are many sellers of similar goods, each too small to affect market conditions for the "product group" as a whole. In between the two extremes are various forms of imperfect competition, with relatively few transactors, at least some of them of a size large enough that they individually can have an impact on prices, market conditions, and each others' activities.

Even if the number of market participants is small, as long as entry is relatively easy and unrestricted they may compete as if their number were larger. To have meaningful potential competition, the threat of new entrants must be credible to market participants. Various kinds of barriers to entry then become important. Some may be technical or "natural"; others are erected by market participants to deter entry and allow them higher profits or an easier life; still others are created by the government, either in its own interest or at the behest of market participants. Potential competition from prospective entrants is important because it may support dynamic markets even if the number of actual transactors is very small.

Nonprice competition is more important than price competition in many markets. This encompasses product characteristics, design, and usefulness; product quality; advertising; location, convenience, and availability; and postsale service and warranties. Product differentiation can be beneficial for consumers, because it is valued in itself or because consumers with different tastes have different preferences. Similarly, product variation for intermediate and capital goods may have similar benefits for users.

From this perspective, nonprice competition is extremely important and does not necessarily have the negative efficiency implications sometimes ascribed to it. If there are economies of scale, there is a trade-off between cost considerations, which would dictate production of very large amounts of only a few different kinds of products, and consumers' and users' desires, which would be served by greater variety. Lancaster (1979) developed a model in which determinate results are obtained by a combination of product differentiation/monopolistic competition and economies of scale.

Product variation and monopolistic competition have implications for the impact of price controls. If price controls or rigidities inhibit price competition, the focus of activity can easily shift to nonprice competition. This is often beneficial, as long as the controlled price is high enough to allow attractive profits. In a situation where producers or sellers face a downward-sloping demand curve that they can influence by incurring additional costs, a firm facing an artificially low price for its output would engage in less than the optimal level of costly activities to make products more attractive to the demand side, since it cannot make additional profits by raising the price and demand exceeds supply at the controlled price anyway. Correspondingly, a demand-constrained enterprise facing a controlled price above the market equilibrium level would tend to engage in more than the optimal level of costly activities to make products more attractive to the demand side, since this would increase demand.[10] This can be interpreted as a decrease in variety caused by price controls and greater emphasis on product differentiation in the presence of artificially high prices.

Similar issues arise with product quality and advertising. If improved quality is accompanied by continued availability of the lower-quality goods and there is appropriate price differentiation, then quality improvements are likely to be beneficial, in the same way that increasing the number of product varieties is. On the other hand, with a single product whose quality can be varied, it is possible to have excessively high as well as excessively poor quality. Moreover, bogus quality "improvement" can serve as a means of getting around price controls in a shortage situation. As provision of relevant information to would-be purchasers, advertising is unambiguously beneficial. But if it manipulates preferences or choices in a way that does not improve welfare, it is harmful or at least wasteful. In China, where there has been a dearth of good market information, the positive impact of advertising probably has been more important than any possible negative effects, at least so far.

Among the different arenas of competition, rent-seeking behavior can have harmful consequences. If the government generates lucrative rents for certain activities through policies, regulations, or other interventions, firms may compete vigorously to appropriate these rents, which will use up resources and distort incentives. Competitive rent-seeking behavior may be similar in motivation and outward form to vigorous, dynamic competition in markets. But whereas competition in the market arena is a positive force, this is not true of competition to gain access to benefits conferred by the bureaucracy or political system. Even when conditions are otherwise suitable for vigorous, dynamic market competition, enterprises can be distracted from this and directed toward wasteful and harmful rent-seeking competition by government policies and regulations. Rent-seeking behavior in the Chinese context is discussed in detail in chapter 5 and incorporated into a formal model in chapter 7.

Schumpeterian, Hayekian, and "Effective" Competition

Three strands of thought focus on the role of competition in a market economy: the dynamics of "creative destruction" (Schumpeter 1934; 1950); competition as a "discovery procedure" that moves the economy closer to equilibrium (Hayek 1984); and "workable" or "effective" competition (Clark 1961). All of these theories disagree sharply with the neoclassical view.

Schumpeter's theory of economic development emphasized competition among entrepreneurial capitalist firms. Large enough to influence the markets in which they compete, they feverishly strive for temporary monopoly profits, which could be generated by a new innovation or by other factors, like heavy advertising or a better distribution network. The process of development in a dynamic capitalist or corporate economy is precisely this search, sometimes successful, often not, for temporary monopoly profits that are constantly eroded by "catching up" or "leapfrogging" on the part of competitors. In Schumpeter's model, competition, like the innovations on which it is based, is not an equilibrating force but rather a stimulus to economic development that is profoundly threatening to the status quo.

From this perspective, static efficiency losses due to monopoly or collusive oligopoly are unimportant compared with the dynamism induced by the search for profits. Permanent, unassailable monopoly indeed would be a problem, but Schumpeter argues that this is extremely rare. Even persistent monopolies may not be harmful, if they constantly pursue innovation to keep ahead of potential competitors.

Schumpeter's theory, intended to explain dynamic capitalist development, focuses on new and important innovations, which are the key to improved efficiency and longer-term economic growth and development. It can also be applied, however, to less important competitive measures. Indeed, the Hayekian view of competition as a process through which the facts (or "givens") of the situation in the market are gradually discovered by the participants and their inevitable initial misperceptions and mistakes are corrected is basically consistent with Schumpeter's approach.

For Hayek, competition is essentially a "discovery procedure," which by its very nature improves the functioning of markets and moves them toward (but not actually to) equilibrium. An essential ingredient and consequence of competition is its communication of new and improved information through the market. Though competition involves a struggle to keep up with and move ahead of rivals, its result is adjustments by market participants that improve the functioning and efficiency of the economy.

Clark's concept of "effective competition" arose from a critique of what he saw as the overly negative implications of theories of imperfect competition developed in the 1930s. He saw competition as a "dynamic process":

> Competition between business units . . . is the effort of such units, acting independently of each other . . . each trying to make a profitable volume of sales in the face of the offers of other sellers of identical or closely similar products. . . . The process normally involved rivalry, though this may or may not be direct and conscious. . . . It is the form of discipline that business units exercise over one another, under pressure of the discipline customers can exercise over business units by virtue of their power of choosing between the offerings of rival suppliers. Competition presupposes that businesses pursue their own self-interest, and it harnesses this force by their need of securing the customer's favor. (Clark 1961, 9, 13–14, 16)

Competition, according to Clark, occurs in three main arenas: product selection and design, selling effort, and price. To compete in these three areas, firms must devote resources to them, which in turn requires efficient and low-cost production so that this can be done while still earning profits.

Clark goes further and asks what conditions are required to have healthy competition in an industry, which promotes economic progress over the long run. One prerequisite is that businesses must be motivated by self-interest, though they need not be pure profit maximizers. Another, more implicit, is the ability of customers to exercise the "exit" option and switch suppliers. Also implicit in Clark's approach is the idea that there must be at least the possibility of earning profits (with efficient, low-cost production). Price-setting by firms must be constrained, however, by willingness of competitors to undercut them if excessive profits are being earned. Conditions *not* required for effective competition according to Clark include price-taking behavior by firms; a competitive struggle to excess with only one winner; profit maximization; strong competition at all times—sometimes competition can be dormant without damaging effectiveness; and a large number of active participants in the market.

All three views of competition see it as a dynamic process, an essential component of the market mechanism. Competition is also closely linked with entrepreneurship. Kirzner (1973) asserts that competition is an essential ingredient of the market process and of what he defines as entrepreneurship. While effective competition is a prerequisite for well-functioning markets, entrepreneurship may itself be a prerequisite for effective competition. Competition as described by Schumpeter, Hayek, and to a lesser extent Clark inherently involves entrepreneurship broadly defined.

Prerequisites for Effective Competition

In the area of price and nonprice competition, one negative conclusion outweighs the complexities in other aspects: vigorous price competition is generally not essential for dynamic markets. This does not mean that flexibility of prices over the medium and long term is not necessary. But in the short run, competition can and for many kinds of goods indeed should focus on nonprice aspects. Development of new products and varieties is a major form of innovation, which can be stimulated by nonprice competition. However, the "optimal" kind and degree of nonprice competition vary greatly across products and industries. Another negative conclusion is that vigorous competition should be restricted to the arena of reasonably well-functioning markets. If it is diverted into competition for rents generated by government actions, it can become harmful and wasteful.

Potential competition is crucial in many markets with relatively few active participants. It is particularly necessary in the face of outright monopoly or near-monopoly. If natural barriers to entry are high, potential competition is weakened and vigorous active competition is required. With a large number of market actors, potential competition is less important.

The number of active market participants required to stimulate effective competition and promote dynamism is rather small, provided that collusion is absent. Even a very small number of participants may be prevented from colluding to gain monopoly profits by the threat of potential competition. Only collusive, short-sighted oligopoly and true monopoly, neither facing viable potential competition, are necessarily inimical to dynamic markets.

The history of the metal can industry in the United States, Great Britain, and West Germany provides a striking example of how even very small numbers of competitors in a market can compete vigorously and effectively, provided there is no collusion (see Wagner 1980; Hessian 1971). Industrial structure in the United States was something close to a duopoly for many decades. But the metal can industry faces strong competition from alternatives like cardboard cartons, and some of the largest users of cans (brewing companies) produce some of their own and hence provide a credible threat of entry if independent can manufacturers take advantage of their market position. Even with only two main competitors, the U.S. metal can industry did well in terms of innovations, productivity and efficiency improvements, and cost reductions. Price competition through discounting of list prices for large customers was common. Nonprice competition also was severe, resulting in good service and high quality.

In Great Britain, on the other hand, a single firm had a virtually complete monopoly for over two decades. The metal can industry there was very slow to introduce the two-piece aluminum can, the main innovation of the past several decades. Labor productivity in British can-manufacturing plants in the early 1970s was only a fraction of that in the U.S. industry, despite larger plant sizes. The West German can industry also has been dominated by a single firm. Though West Germany introduced the two-piece aluminum can before Great Britain, labor productivity in the early 1970s was close to that in Great Britain and only one-third the U.S. level.

This example indicates that there can be effective competition even with only two competitors, as long as outright collusion is prevented, whereas a single dominant firm can result in inefficiency and slower technological progress, particularly if potential entrants are legally or otherwise prohibited from becoming active competitors. Too many participants in a market, on the other hand, might scatter resources, make research and innovation more difficult (the pooling of risky activities in large corporations could not take place), and might not provide lucrative opportunities for entrepreneurs or innovators.

Freedom of entry is required for meaningful potential competition and hence is a crucial prerequisite for effective competition. *Freedom of exit* also is needed to achieve smooth, efficiency-improving market adjustments. If firms that cannot keep up with the competition are not permitted to exit from the scene, market dynamism, flexibility, efficiency, and functioning may be impaired. Indeed, inability to exit may force the system to generate obstacles against new entry, or against rapid growth by successful competitors.

Market Conditions, Competition, and Efficiency

In addition to the prerequisites for effective competition discussed above, market conditions can be a crucial determinant of its presence or absence and strength and can greatly affect the impact of competition on efficiency. This section explores some key concepts and distinctions relating to market conditions and then looks at different possible combinations of these factors and their likely effect on competition and efficiency.

Some Basic Definitions

Careful distinctions should be made among different terms used to describe market conditions: equilibrium versus disequilibrium; buyers' market versus sellers' market; and excess demand versus excess supply. Static equilibrium is a clear concept—total demand and supply for a commodity are equal at the market price. Excess supply is then a situation where prices are too high, whereas if there is excess demand prices are too low. The distinction between equilibrium and disequilibrium also is clear in this context: the latter involves a price different from the equilibrium market-clearing one, while in the former the price is "right" and clears the market.

The concepts of buyers' and sellers' markets (see Kornai 1980) superficially can be equated with excess supply and excess demand, but this is an oversimplification. Kornai links the term sellers' market to chronic shortage in centrally planned economies, where it is not meaningful to consider that the only problem is "wrong" prices and that a suitable price increase would clear the market. He argues that in a chronic shortage situation no feasible price increase would clear the market, since there would be excess demand at almost any price authorities or economic agents determine. Economic behavior and institutions become adapted to chronic shortage, which then becomes self-reinforcing, unlike a temporary period of excess demand in a market that is at or near equilibrium most of the time.

As Kornai notes, a key indicator of chronic shortage is the level of inventories held by users relative to those held by producers. In a sellers' market, output stocks will be run down to the point where "stock-outs" (sellers running out of inventories and being unable to meet demand) are common. Producers have no incentive to build inventories because goods can be sold as soon as they are made. To protect themselves from future stock-outs, users hoard goods, which exacerbates shortage. Hence, there can be severe chronic shortage even though production and actual use of commodities are roughly equal, and inventories are concentrated in the hands of users.

Just as the chronic sellers' market cannot be equated with excess demand during temporary market disequilibrium, the concept of the buyers' market is not identical to that of temporary excess supply. There are really two types of buyers' markets: One involves a problem of severe excess supply or capacity, either in the economy as a whole or for a particular industry. The former could be the result of a recession or restrictive macroeconomic policy, the latter of a radical change in conditions not foreseen by most market participants and investors. This kind of buyers' market in principle could be eliminated by suitable changes in prices or in macroeconomic policy. Excess supply also can be engendered by fixed prices above the equilibrium level, which are prevented from falling to equilibrate demand and supply.

This first type of buyers' market emerged at least briefly for many Chinese industrial products (see chapter 4). Sometimes there has been overinvestment, in response to high administratively set prices, priority allocation of investment resources to the industry concerned, or both. In other industries such as machinery, drastic cutbacks in government-sponsored investment have led to buyers' markets. But these types of buyers' markets still have only a short history in China, and, more important, they involve excess supply that in principle is attributable to price distortions.

The second type of buyers' market cannot be equated in a simplistic way with excess supply, and feasible price adjustments (this time in the downward direction) might not eliminate it. The "chronic" or "normal" buyers' market is one in which supplies are freely available from adequate stocks in the hands of producers and sellers, but in which these agents have no incentive to lower their prices and clear out their stocks over the long run. There may also be some excess capacity in the industry concerned or nationwide, but again there is no incentive for the holders of this capacity to cut prices drastically in order to utilize it fully.

Some not unrealistic assumptions are required to justify this kind of behavior. Demand is uncertain, and there is a real cost to producers and sellers from stock-outs. In static terms, this cost is just the profits forgone from missing out on transactions. But in industries where much business involves "repeat" sales to customers who tend to return to the same vendor, the cost of a stock-out can be much greater: new customers may turn away permanently, and loyalty of regular customers also may be weakened. So the costs of carrying inventories (interest charges, deterioration, warehouse space, etc.) can be set against the hard to forecast but nevertheless substantial costs of stock-outs. Maintaining a certain level of excess capacity, if production can be adjusted faster than new capacity can be added, also allows smoother adjustment to short- or medium-term demand fluctuations.

This suggests that in a well-developed market system, producers and sellers will hold considerable inventories and may also maintain some excess capacity, purely in the interest of maximizing profits. Thus, the "normal buyers' market" in mature market economies should be traced not to macroeconomic policies or rigidities imposed on market participants, but rather to their self-interested behavior. The term used for this kind of buyers' market, to distinguish it from excess supply induced by high prices, inappropriate investment decisions, or restrictive macro policy, is "buffered equilibrium," where markets are basically in equilibrium with ample stocks and excess capacity to take care of temporary fluctuations in demand.

If there is chronic shortage, buyers will queue and compete to obtain available supplies, whereas competition among producers or sellers will be nonexistent. The latter have no trouble selling all they can produce; there is no cost to stocking out; output inventories are bought up immediately; and there is no benefit from building up excess capacity. Sellers also have no incentive to be concerned about quality, product variety, or innovation, especially if this is costly in terms of forgone current production.

On the other hand, in either type of buyers' market, competition among producers will be intense and that among buyers relaxed. This will be true even if in their own self-interest producers do not cut product prices to the point where they run down their stocks. The buyers in the system have a great deal of choice and do not need to maintain large stocks as a buffer against fluctuations in their own demand.[11] The bulk of inventories are held by sellers rather than buyers.

Key Distinctions for Analysis of Market Functioning

One critical distinction is between a buyers' market and a sellers' market. But such markets must be further subdivided into excess demand; chronic shortage or chronic sellers' market; excess supply or buyers' market; and "normal" buyers' market or "buffered equilibrium." Another distinction relates to the presence or absence of effective competition, which is only partly determined by market conditions. A lasting sellers' market precludes effective competition among sellers, but a buyers' market by no means guarantees effective competition. Still another key distinction relates to the presence or absence of enterprise financial discipline, or the "soft budget constraint" (Kornai 1980, chap. 13). On the supply side, the soft budget constraint can imply lack of concern about holding down costs in a buyers' market situation, whereas on the demand side it can mean irresponsible, for practical purposes unlimited, demand for goods in short supply. Thus financial discipline is in principle distinct from market conditions, though the two may be closely related in practice. A final distinction involves price flexibility, over the medium term if not in the short run. A sufficient degree of price flexibility allows market adjustments to take place, even if at a slow pace. Completely rigid prices, on the other hand, freeze market conditions once adjustment to the given price has been completed.

These six distinctions generate a matrix of possible market situations with different implications for competition and efficiency. A schematic framework is presented in table 2.1 of the elements that go into different kinds of markets and competitive situations. Each column indicates presence or absence of a certain element, each row a different market outcome, divided into two groups according to whether or not there is effective competition.

The absence of effective competition can be due either to market conditions (sellers' market) or to the lack of certain other prerequisites discussed earlier (for example, a situation of monopoly or collusive oligopoly). These possibilities are shown in the first two rows of table 2.1. In either case there may be a considerable degree of enterprise financial discipline and medium-term price flexibility. But without effective competition these are not sufficient to ensure efficiency and appropriate market adjustment. Enterprise financial discipline, however, would reduce the X-inefficiency associated with monopoly, while price flexibility would reduce and eventually eliminate excess demand, generating conditions for effective competition. In practice, a situation of chronic excess demand is not likely to be associated with enterprise financial discipline and price flexibility.

The remainder of table 2.1 shows that it is possible to have a situation of effective competition associated with enterprise-level inefficiency, poor market adjustment, or both. If enterprise financial discipline is weak, then the buyers' market is probably one of disequilibrium excess supply rather than a "normal buyers' market" or "buffered equilibrium." Weak financial discipline implies that adjustment to a buyers' market by means of exit will be minimal, which in turn suggests that the situation is unstable and hence will not settle into a normal pattern, particularly if prices are not flexible. Inflexible prices in any case are not likely to be associated with buffered equilibrium over the long run. Flexible prices, on the other hand, mean that long-term excess supply is not possible and hence that either the situation is only temporary or that it does involve buffered equilibrium.

The third row of table 2.1 represents a situation where there is effective competition but X-inefficiency at the enterprise level and poor adjustment for the market as a whole. Effective competition does not, in this framework,

Table 2.1

Elements for Effective Competition, Enterprise Efficiency, and Rational Market Adjustment

Market situation	Excess supply[1]	Buyers' market[2]	Other prerequisites for effective competition[3]	Enterprise financial discipline	Price flexibility
No effective competition					
Sellers' market	N	N	Y or N	Y or N	Y or N
Other reasons	Y		N	Y or N	Y or N
Effective competition					
Inefficiency at firm level and poor market adjustment	Y	N	Y	N	N
Micro efficiency but poor market adjustment	Y	N	Y	Y	N
Micro inefficiency and effective market adjustment	Y		Y	N	Y
Micro efficiency and effective market adjustment	N	Y	Y	Y	Y

1. Excess supply refers to the disequilibrium situation where supply exceeds demand and the price is above the equilibrium level.
2. Buyers' market refers to what has been called the "normal buyers' market" or "buffered equilibrium" in the text.
3. The other prerequisites for effective competition were discussed earlier in this chapter.

necessarily imply strong enterprise efforts to reduce costs and improve the efficiency of their operations in other ways.[12] Nor does it imply anything about market adjustment. The fourth and fifth rows involve absence of enterprise financial discipline and X-efficiency or efficient market adjustment, but not both. The fifth row may be particularly relevant for China, showing a situation where flexible prices should eliminate excess supply over the medium term but where enterprise financial discipline is missing. This combination has conflicting implications for the kind of buyers' market or excess supply that is present. One factor (price flexibility) generates a tendency toward "normal" buyers' markets or buffered equilibrium, while the other (financial indiscipline) at least to some extent militates against it. In the final row, all of the identified prerequisites are met, and the situation is something close to that of well-functioning markets in industrialized capitalist economies.

Summary

This chapter has identified a number of prerequisites for well-functioning markets. But a set of sufficient conditions has not been established, except, trivially, all the elements actually found in markets that manifestly function well and promote efficiency, growth, and innovation over the long run.

Among the critical elements, effective competition comes close to being the essence of well-functioning markets. Two related questions have been addressed: what constitutes effective competition, and what conditions must be satisfied to have effective competition. Some possible candidates for prerequisite status, such as an atomistic industrial structure or quickly adjusting prices, are not essential. Others, like noncollusion, unrestricted entry, long-term price flexibility, entrepreneurship, and suitable market conditions, would seem to be necessary for effective competition.

Another element that appears to be necessary for well-functioning, dynamic markets is decision-making autonomy for market transactors and particularly for producers. This autonomy must include freedom to respond to the market in a dynamic manner, not just freedom to decide whether or not or with whom to engage in particular market transactions. Thus it encompasses investment decision making, innovative effort, and related long-run decisions, as well as production and marketing. Freedom of entry as an exercise of autonomy by economic agents is crucial.

An appropriate ownership system may be very important as a prerequisite for dynamic markets. The question of whether public ownership is inherently inimical to such markets remains open; some counterexamples do exist. What clearly is dangerous is aspects of public ownership that interfere with the autonomy of market transactors, free entry, and competition.

As already mentioned, long-term price flexibility also is a prerequisite for well-functioning markets. This could be compatible, however, with a variety of short-run rigidities and possibly even external controls.

Another crucial prerequisite is a certain degree of financial discipline in producers and transactors. Otherwise demand will always be pressing against supply. Probably even more important, weak financial discipline reduces the incentives for improved efficiency and cost reductions that are an essential ingredient of well-functioning markets. The need for a strong profit orientation on the part of enterprises by no means implies that profit maximization is necessary; avoidance of losses and a desire to grow by responding to market needs are probably sufficient in a situation of rapid development and effective competition.

Related to financial discipline is the need for mechanisms to ensure that weaker competitors make the necessary adjustments and that unviable ones exit from the scene. Inability to allow exit may be one of the most damaging aspects of public ownership systems.

A final prerequisite for well-functioning markets is good information flows that agents can respond to in their decision making. This does not require perfect information—in fact, imperfect information creates opportunities that enterprises can take advantage of. But a minimum network of information flows is needed to assure that flagrant opportunities for rent seeking due to market imperfections are eliminated, and that the market is as broad and "thick" as possible.

3. Markets in Chinese Industry

IN CHINA since 1978, the role of the market mechanism in the distribution of industrial products has expanded greatly, while that of administrative directives and controls has correspondingly diminished. This development, a crucial part of economic reforms, is documented in this chapter. A survey of market price trends in the 1980s and an econometric analysis of local market price movements to evaluate the degree to which markets are "integrated" are presented in chapter 8.

The Prereform Situation

Did prereform markets or market-like allocation mechanisms facilitate the rapid development of markets in Chinese industry since the late 1970s? Certain precursors to the market mechanism and even some genuine markets for industrial goods did exist in the prereform period, which undoubtedly eased the subsequent transition. But prereform developments were severely limited in important respects.

The Weakness of Central Planning and Resulting Vacuum

The prereform planning system is discussed in more detail in chapter 5. Here it suffices to note that the weakness and fragmentation of central planning in the prereform period left a vacuum in the economy's resource allocation mechanism that had to be filled in some way to keep the economy operating. Ad hoc administrative directives by government authorities at the provincial and local levels undoubtedly played the major role. Another obvious response was promotion of self-sufficient industrialization and autarky at the provincial and local levels (see Lyons 1986). The vacuum left by weak planning also stimulated some more market-like mechanisms to arise, however, both as part of the disaggregation of the relatively coarse targets and allocations handed down by the planning system and as a supplement to planned allocation. These extra-plan mechanisms, discussed below, were fairly tightly controlled by lower-level government supervisory authorities.

Administrative fragmentation and the unreliability of central planning, particularly with respect to flows of commodities across territorial jurisdictions, led in the 1970s to the emergence of interregional exchange of industrial commodities under the auspices of provincial and to a lesser extent local governments. Thus, a "market" in interregional trade arose, with provincial and local government authorities as the main actors.

Extra-Plan Mechanisms

Some of the extra-plan methods for allocating or reallocating industrial goods in prereform China were similar to those in other centrally planned economies. Enterprises with excess stocks of various inputs were encouraged to make them available to other firms in need of these goods, and local meetings were sometimes organized for this purpose. Exchange or outright barter of inputs among users was only one step further and appears to have been common in prereform China as it was in the Soviet Union. These were typical "second economy" practices in that they involved reallocation of inputs already supplied to users through the plan rather than primary distribution of output directly from producers.

A Chinese innovation to handle disaggregating and concretely specifying plan targets and linking particular suppliers to users was so-called materials ordering conferences. These were held by planning and material supply authorities and the ministry in charge of production of the goods concerned (for example, the Ministry of Metallurgy in the case of steel), usually twice a year. At these meetings, input allocations and output targets of firms were specified in terms of precise varieties, grades, and product specifications, and particular users were linked with appropriate suppliers. Materials allocation conferences could be massive affairs, often involving as many as ten thousand representatives of different ministries, provinces, and major enterprises. They must have been ponderous and unwieldy and involved pervasive bargaining. Nevertheless, they did bring buyers and sellers together face-to-face, and, more important, they did to some extent facilitate the subsequent development of periodic markets for industrial producer goods.[1]

It should also be noted that industrial enterprises or their supervisory bureaus were responsible for significant amounts of retail sales even in the prereform period. As can be seen from table 3.6, their share in retail sales of consumer goods and industrial inputs into agriculture was never below about 6 percent and rose steadily during the 1970s. It is unclear, however, whether these represented direct sales by enterprises or instead involved industrial supervisory bureaus. In any case, price flexibility was most probably nonexistent.

Another area where more voluntary, market-like mechanisms may have been at work at the enterprise level was sales by locally controlled firms to customers from outside the locality. Goods sold in this manner outside the plan often may have carried fairly high though still administratively determined prices, which could offset the impact on profits of sales at low prices to favored local users.

Interregional Markets for Local Governments

Provinces, and perhaps to a lesser extent local governments, appear to have begun to exchange important goods and materials with each other in the early 1970s. These exchanges were not pure barter but rather involved parallel, linked purchase and sales transactions, usually at the official state prices for the goods concerned. Unlike barter, these transactions could result in net financial flows in one direction or the other, if physical exchange ratios differed from the price ratios used.

It is difficult to gauge the magnitude of interregional exchange (often referred to as "materials cooperation") in the prereform period, but it was already fairly substantial by 1980, which indicates that it must have developed to a considerable degree by the late 1970s. Some provinces depended on materials obtained in this way to support their industrial development, the most notable example being coal for Jiangsu Province in the 1970s, which was probably a critical determinant of the province's rapid industrial growth during this period.[2]

Interregional exchange in the prereform period was limited in terms of both the products and the provinces involved. In some respects it resembled the use of foreign trade in a traditional centrally planned economy as a vent for short-term surpluses and source of goods to alleviate shortages. Nevertheless, its development helped set the stage for subsequent expansion under a more flexible regime during the reform period.

Limitations and Potential of Prereform Mechanisms

Prereform markets and market-like resource allocation mechanisms in Chinese industry were quite limited, particularly in their impact at the enterprise level. Prices were inflexible and administratively controlled, at the provincial and local level if not by the central government. Goods flows remained subject to provincial and local government direction, with little scope for enterprise autonomy. Even the transactors were often government agencies rather than firms. Finally, the share of these resource allocation mechanisms in total economic activity remained small, though it was growing. Thus, prereform practices only served to some extent to prepare the way for subsequent expansion of the role of the market mechanism in Chinese industry; they did not achieve major advances in that direction. The crudeness and fragmentation of planning and administrative control also was very important, since it left a vacuum that could naturally be filled by the market.

Industrial Market Development in China: A Brief Review

Before assessing the quantitative significance and qualitative aspects of markets for industrial products in China, a brief chronological review of the emergence and development of these markets is in order. Three major stages are apparent in the development of markets for industrial producer goods. (Trends were generally steadier in the case of industrial consumer goods.)

Initial Emergence, 1979–80

Development of markets for industrial goods in the early years of reform, though explicitly considered one of the main components of the reform package, was uneven and largely dependent on changing demand-supply conditions. The causation leading from emerging excess supply for certain industrial goods to expansion of market allocation for those goods is traced out, with examples, in chapter 4. Market allocation of goods in excess supply developed rapidly and its share in total production rose sharply, whereas for goods in chronic excess demand, market development was very limited. A good example of the former is machinery—for machinery producers under the jurisdiction of the First Ministry of Machine Building the share of total output value allocated through the market mechanism as opposed to directive planning rose from 13 percent in 1979 to 46 percent in 1980 (Byrd 1984, 92).

Some explicit institutional and policy measures helped promote the expansion of market allocation of industrial products. So-called markets for the means of production were established in some large cities starting in 1979, most notably Shanghai (see Byrd 1985a). Numerous industrial producer goods were traded at Shanghai and other markets, with apparently at least somewhat flexible prices, in 1979–80. Initially, however, quarterly trade fairs accounted for the bulk of the total value of transactions, which meant that the market functioned irregularly and may also explain the high degree of price variability for some goods.

Another important change was that companies in the material supply system increasingly engaged in outside-of-plan transactions, on behalf of local producers or to obtain needed supplies for local users. These ranged from holding trade fairs to purchasing and selling goods on consignment and various related activities. The share of material supply system transactions occurring outside the plan was fairly small in the initial stages, but the way was prepared for subsequent dramatic expansion.

Turning to industrial consumer goods, the most important early development was a major change in the methods by which the commercial system procured goods from industrial firms, starting in 1979. Four categories of commercial procurement were designated, two of which were supposedly completely voluntary on the part of both the producer and the commercial unit involved. In the early 1980s about 40 percent of commercial procurement occurred through these latter channels (see table 3.5 and accompanying discussion).

Overall, markets for industrial goods made a promising start during this period. But their quantitative significance should not be exaggerated; moreover, the market mechanism was vulnerable to administrative controls and perhaps even more to changes in market conditions.

Evolution under Price and Other Restrictions, 1981–83

There was some pullback from market-oriented industrial reforms with the macro-economic retrenchment and investment cutbacks of 1981, along with an unevenly enforced freeze on the prices of industrial producer goods imposed at the end of 1980. The effect on markets for the means of production was immediate—trans-actions at the Shanghai market plunged sharply starting from the second half of 1980, and numerous goods could no longer be traded due to price controls or other restrictions. It is likely that many market transactions for industrial producer goods moved "underground," and that "exchange" of goods for one another or for other scarce resources became widespread, though such a trend is hard to document. Numerous government directives and circulars prohibiting disguised price increases and related illegal activities suggest that they were common. Over-all, this was a period during which markets for industrial producer goods and market pricing made much less progress than earlier.

In the case of consumer goods, the impact of retrenchment was more limited. Moreover, market conditions for many industrial consumer goods shifted sharply toward excess supply in 1982, prominent examples being textiles and consumer durables such as watches. This encouraged expansion in the share of market allocation. Reforms in the commercial system proceeded at a steadier pace, gradually delinking the system from directive planning and permitting more widespread "entry" by different commercial units into different activities and localities. Price controls, especially at the retail level, were effective, however, throughout this period.

Post-1984 Flourishing

Starting in 1984, a major conscious push to expand market allocation for industrial products is evident. Moreover, this occurred in an overall demand-supply situation (excess demand) that had previously proved inimical to the market mechanism. The quantitative aspects of this flourishing of industrial markets are taken up in the following section. Here some of the policy highlights are noted.

In the first place, the share of output of a number of important industrial producer goods subject to distribution through the central plan declined sharply (see table 3.1 and accompanying discussion), a development that could only have occurred with the concurrence of central government authorities at the highest level. This trend opened the way for greatly expanded market allocation of industrial producer goods.

Existing and new marketplaces for industrial producer goods, the latter now termed Materials Trade Centers, proliferated. Specialized markets for trucks, steel, and other products spread widely under government encouragement. Wholesale markets for industrial consumer goods also were established in numerous localities.

Perhaps most important, price controls over industrial producer goods produced and traded outside the state plan were eliminated at the beginning of 1985. Similarly, price controls were relaxed for many consumer goods in phases, somewhat later. Despite remaining problems and continuing rigidities, this was a crucial policy development that allowed functioning markets even for industrial goods chronically in severe short supply at their state plan prices.

Accompanying these more visible and specific changes was an observable if not easily quantifiable trend toward marketization of the activities and outlooks of market participants. (This is brought out later in this chapter and to some extent in chapter 4.) It was encouraged by the explicit policy changes noted above, by the general proreform atmosphere especially in 1984–85, and, to some extent, by the dynamics of the evolving situation itself (see especially chapter 9).

It would be misleading to leave the impression that market development was relentless and unencumbered in the post-1984 period, however. There were problems with the qualitative functioning of markets, to be looked at later in this chapter, as well as some tendency toward putting market allocation under local or informal administrative controls. The general trend, however, was one of steady expansion in market allocation of industrial goods.

It is clear that from the institutional and policy perspective, important changes occurred that permitted and encouraged market allocation of industrial goods. These changes were reinforced—indeed, even initiated—by changes in the demand-supply situation in the late 1970s and early 1980s, but much less so subsequently.

Quantitative Significance of Industrial Product Markets

It is difficult to come up with reliable aggregate figures on market transactions in Chinese industrial goods, because of inadequate data, confusing definitions, and the inherent problem of distinguishing between market and nonmarket mechanisms at the margin. Different sources reported the share of market allocation in China's gross industrial output value as 10 percent in 1979 and an estimated 15 percent in 1980.[3] By the mid-1980s, a dramatic increase in the share of the market mechanism had occurred. In 1984 the share of industrial output value allocated by the central plan was reportedly 40 percent, and it was expected to decline to 20 percent in 1985 (*China Economic Yearbook* Editorial Committee 1985, II–3). The central plan portion apparently did decline by such a large margin in 1985, since the 20 percent figure for 1985 has been repeated in several sources.

The share of total industrial output value sold outside of the central state plan included some goods allocated by local and provincial governments as well as those traded through the market mechanism. But a large portion of non–centrally planned output did actually go through the market. The decline in the share of central plan allocations almost certainly has not been fully offset by increases in the share of local and provincial administrative allocation, though this may have occurred to some extent. Hence there has been a substantial increase in the share of market allocation.

The following discussion divides naturally into three parts. In China the administrative management system and apparatus for industrial producer goods and for consumer goods have been largely insulated from each other, the former under the supervision of the State Material Supply Bureau, the latter under the Ministry of Commerce and related organizations. Available firm-level data provide evidence on the quantitative significance of industrial product markets at the micro level.

Market Allocation of Producer Goods

As can be seen from table 3.1, shares of total output of important producer goods transacted through the central plan are significantly less than 100 percent. Moreover, there were substantial drops in the share of the central plan between 1980 and 1985, continuing through 1988. The most spectacular reduction was for timber, which fell from 81 percent in 1980 to 31 percent in 1985 and then further to about 25 percent in 1988. For rolled steel, the share fell from 74 percent in 1980 to 57 percent in 1985 and then to 42 percent by 1988. In the case of cement the decline was from 35 percent in 1980 to 14 percent in 1988.

A relatively low share of central plan allocations does not necessarily imply a high share for the market mechanism. But available information indicates that the share of market allocation as opposed to lower-level administrative control is relatively large and growing. Table 3.2 presents information on the direct marketing of rolled steel, cement, and trucks by producers in 1980–84, at three different levels: aggregate (for rolled steel and trucks), for large enterprises as a group (rolled steel and cement), and for an important enterprise in each of the three industries. These data are broadly consistent and show a substantial share of enterprise direct marketing. The figures for rolled steel and cement directly marketed by large producers are particularly striking because for smaller plants these shares were probably even higher. For cement and trucks, an upward trend in direct marketing is evident, whereas rolled steel shows considerable fluctuations. The sharp drop in enterprise direct marketing for the steel industry as a whole in 1983 was almost certainly spurious, however, since information on Anshan and other major steel plants indicates only a slight decline.

By 1987, direct marketing by enterprises had sharply increased, as is shown in table 3.3. Perhaps most strikingly, 71 percent of the metal-cutting machine tools made in China were directly marketed by their producers. The same was true of more than half of cement and trucks (considerably higher shares than in earlier

Table 3.1

State Plan Shares for Key Industrial Producer Goods, 1980–88
(percent of total domestic production)

	1980	1985	1986	1987	1988 (est.)
Coal	57.9	50.6	42.3	—	—
Timber	80.9	30.7	30.0	27.6	25.0[a]
Rolled steel	74.3	56.9	53.1	47.1	42.0[b]
Cement	35.0	19.4	16.2	15.6	14.0[a]
Nonferrous metals[c]	86.4	—	61.4	—	—

Sources: Ling (1986, 2); State Statistical Bureau (1988a, VI; 1989a, III); *China Economic Yearbook* Editorial Committee (1987, VI-170; 1988, IV-26); *Zhongguo wuzi bao*, March 7, 1989, 2.

a. Based on share of state plan contracts in total output. Contracts were substantially underfulfilled in 1988, so shares of actual deliveries of goods for state plan distribution were even lower.

b. Based on reported percentage decline in state plan contracts and increase in production.

c. Copper, lead, zinc, and aluminum (presumably total weight of these four metals).

years), nearly a quarter of rolled steel, and one-fifth of coal output. Only in the case of oil and petroleum products were relatively low shares of enterprise direct marketing recorded.

Another indication of the substantial and growing share of the market is the volume of industrial producer goods procured outside of mandatory plans by the material supply system. Table 3.4 shows that the state material supply system, which is responsible for planned distribution of industrial producer goods, also does a substantial amount of business outside the plan. Moreover, the share of such transactions in total procurement of the goods concerned rose sharply between 1983 and 1986. The total value of industrial goods arranged outside of mandatory plans by all levels of the material supply system in 1985 was 42.1 billion yuan, 41 percent of the total value of procurement by the system (Wu 1986, 10). This figure rose further to 45 percent in 1986 and 62 percent in 1987 (*China Economic Yearbook* Editorial Committee 1988, IV–27). By the late 1980s, the material supply system must have become oriented largely toward profitable activities outside the state plan, possibly to the neglect of plan transactions.

Interregional "cooperation" has become another major form of market allocation for industrial producer goods. The total value of interregional cooperation in industrial producer goods rose from 3 billion yuan in 1980 to nearly 5 billion yuan in 1983, before jumping to 9 billion yuan in 1984, 16 billion yuan in 1985, 26 billion yuan in 1986, and 35 billion yuan in 1987.[4] Shares of total output of

Table 3.2

Direct Marketing of Rolled Steel, Cement, and Trucks, 1980–84

	Ratio of self-sales to total output (percent)					
Item	1979	1980	1981	1982	1983	1984
Rolled steel[a]	3.6	10.6	19.9	14.4	3.5	—
Rolled steel by key steel plants[b]	—	15.7	22.2	18.4	5.9	9.6
Anshan Iron and Steel Company	6.0	11.0	14.0	11.0	10.0	12.0
Cement by large and medium-sized plants	—	5.8	7.0	8.1	7.8	8.8
Xiangxiang Cement Plant	—	—	8.0	11.7	13.2	11.9
Trucks	—	—	—	—	15.0	40.0
No. 2 Auto Plant[c]	0	0	53.3	58.6	16.6	21.4

Sources: Zhu Rongji (1985, 295); Zhou (1984, 357); interview information (October 1984 and August 1985).

a. The 1983 figure appears to be suspect, in view of the information provided by the Anshan Iron and Steel Company and the fact that the Capital Iron and Steel Company was allowed to market directly 15 percent of its total output during this period.

b. China's key iron and steel enterprises accounted for 66.2 percent of China's total production of rolled steel in 1984 (Ministry of Metallurgy 1986, 1).

c. The 1985 share of direct marketing in total production was 34.2 percent.

major industrial producer goods traded through interregional cooperation were significant and growing over time, even though not very large in most cases, falling in a range of 1–6 percent in 1983 and 2–7 percent in 1984.[5]

Interregional cooperation as a method of doing business has become regularized; there are meetings held by planning authorities each year, and suggested guidelines are published on the physical exchange ratios to be used in this trade. Though in the past central authorities attempted to manage and guide interregional cooperation, this was not very successful and appears not to have detracted from its essentially voluntary nature. The guidelines on exchange ratios only specify ranges, for example, with the gap between upper and lower recommended limits often exceeding 100 percent. Over 50 percent of the volume of

Table 3.3

Share of Enterprise Direct Marketing of Various Industrial Products, 1987
(percent)

Product	Share of enterprise self-sales in total sales	Product	Share of enterprise self-sales in total sales
Pig iron	12.8	Sulphuric acid	23.3
for steelmaking	5.4	Sodium bicarbonate	27.5
for casting	41.0	Soda ash	49.3
Rolled steel	22.5	Tire inner-tubes	47.2
Metal-cutting machine tools	70.7	Tire outer parts	42.1
Cement	52.4	Plate glass	62.3
Motor vehicles	53.3	Raw timber	37.8
Trucks	57.9	Coal	20.0
Large and medium tractors	37.1	Crude oil	1.3
Small tractors	55.2	Heavy oil	9.5
AC generators	79.9	Gasoline	12.6
		Diesel oil	12.2

Source: State Statistical Bureau (1988b, 460–72).

interregional cooperation is reportedly now conducted by counties, 30 percent by prefectures and cities, and only 20 percent by provinces. In the prereform period, by contrast, provinces most likely played the primary role. Interregional cooperation has become relatively fragmented, with numerous actors, to the point where something like a genuine market mechanism is probably at work.

A most striking manifestation of the expanded role of markets in the allocation of industrial producer goods is the development of so-called markets for the means of production starting in 1979 and materials trade centers starting in 1984, as well as specialized marketplaces for goods like trucks and steel. The growth and success of these markets hinged greatly on the presence or absence of administrative price controls. In 1979–80 market prices were at least somewhat flexible, and in any case, due to excess supply, some of them were below state prices. A price freeze at the beginning of 1981 greatly affected markets for the means of production, since they were highly visible and restrictions were easy to implement. Market transactions most likely continued but had to take the form of exchange[6] or were driven underground. It was not until 1984 and especially 1985 that price decontrol led to renewed rapid growth of business.

Total transactions at markets for the means of production were reportedly 3 billion yuan in 1979 (Liu Dingfu 1982, 36–37). By 1982, the volume of transactions apparently had doubled to 6.1 billion yuan.[7] Materials trade centers were

Table 3.4

Procurement of Industrial Producer Goods by the Material Supply System Outside of Mandatory Plans, 1983–86

	Share of total procurement			
Item	1983	1984	1985	1986
Coal	17.0	24.0	21.7	24.9
Rolled steel	24.0	22.8	31.9	33.5
Cement	22.0	28.0	31.6	35.7
Timber	11.0	20.0	32.5	38.8
Machinery and electrical equipment	Bulk of procurement is outside of plan			

Source: China Economic Yearbook Editorial Committee (1985, IV-32; 1987, V-25).
Note: Figures for 1985–86 may not be precisely comparable with those for 1983–84.

promoted only starting in 1984 (Wu 1986, 10). By the end of 1985 there were 644 such centers, and their total 1985 transactions were 10.5 billion yuan. This was equivalent to 9 percent of total material supply system sales. In 1986 there was a further rise to 17.4 billion yuan, or 15 percent of total sales by material supply units (*China Economic Yearbook* Editorial Committee 1987, V–25). In 1987, total transactions reached 24.3 billion yuan; in that year, 6.4 million tons of rolled steel, 11.3 million tons of coal, and 114,000 motor vehicles were among the products traded at these centers (ibid. 1988, IV–26). These markets are particularly important because of their visibility and the price signals they generate, which may well be used as reference for other market transactions which occur outside their bounds (see chapter 8). Transactions have increased to the point where significant proportions of total national output are bought and sold at materials trade centers.

Market Allocation of Consumer Goods

Consumer goods and industrial inputs into agriculture are handled by China's commercial system. Rationing of industrial consumer goods at the retail level was largely elmininated in the early 1980s, with the exception of certain famous brands and high-quality products. Hence, the retail consumer goods market has become largely free of direct quantity allocation, though still subject in varying degrees to price controls. These have been progressively relaxed, first in the case of "minor" commodities, then in 1986 for many consumer durables.[8] Shortage and surplus could coexist for different brands of the same type of good, like bicycles or electric fans, due to major quality differences and, until recently, price controls that did not reflect quality and brand-name differences adequately.

In wholesale commerce, a major reform instituted in 1979–80 divided goods into four categories: (1) unified distribution; (2) planned procurement; (3) procurement according to orders; and (4) selective procurement.[9] Type 1 goods were entirely subject to mandatory procurement by the state commercial system, except for new products made on a trial basis. For type 2 goods, the bulk of output including all production within the plan was subject to mandatory procurement, but firms were allowed to market part of above-plan output directly. Type 3 goods were procured through negotiations between producers and the commercial system on a voluntary basis, using enforceable economic contracts. Type 4 goods were purchased by the commercial system after inspection of finished products, also on a voluntary basis. The number of industrial goods subject to unified allocation under the Ministry of Commerce was reduced from 131 to 37 as a result of this new policy. By 1982 the number was further reduced to 11 (Zhou 1984, 489).

Table 3.5 indicates that the share of more market-like transactions (those in categories 3 and 4) in total procurement of industrial consumer goods and agricultural inputs was relatively high in the early 1980s (in the neighborhood of 40 percent). Moreover, the placement of goods in the different categories often lagged behind developments in the market. For example, cotton and cotton-synthetic blend cloth were listed as type 1 products, while watches and other consumer durables were considered type 2 goods (Ministry of Commerce 1984, 403). But there is evidence of large trade in watches outside the plan, which must have increased sharply as market conditions for ordinary varieties of watches shifted from excess demand to excess supply (Byrd and Tidrick 1984). Allocation of cloth also was loosened considerably in the early 1980s.

As in the case of industrial producer goods, one indicator of the importance of the market mechanism is the share of direct marketing by enterprises. Table 3.6 shows a downward long-term trend in the estimated share of industrial enterprises in total retail sales of industrial goods from the 1950s through the early 1970s. There was then a gradual increase during the 1970s, which picked up dramatically starting in 1979. By the mid-1980s the share was well over double that of the immediate prereform period. The plateau reached after 1985, at close to 20 percent, suggests that direct marketing had reached something like its "natural" level. (There are many valid economic reasons why industrial producers, particularly single-plant firms like those in China, would limit their involvement in retail commerce, even though this is increasingly unrestricted by the commercial system.) The qualitative changes in enterprise direct marketing (see chapter 4) have probably been even more important than its rising share in total retail sales.

The mirror image of enterprise direct marketing is the share of commercial agencies in the total value of industrial goods sold by producers. This share (including rural supply and marketing cooperatives in the commercial system)

Table 3.5

Composition of Procurement of Industrial Goods by the State Commercial System, 1980–82 (percent of total)

	Year		
Procurement category[a]	1980[b]	1981	1982
(1) Unified distribution	39.0	32.0	24.9
(2) Planned procurement	21.0	28.0	37.2
(3) Procurement by order	—	12.0	9.6
(4) Selective procurement	—	28.0	28.3
(3) + (4)	40.0	40.0	37.9

Sources: For 1980, Yu (1984, 373–74); for 1981, Liu (1982, 8); and for 1982, Zhou (1984, 488) and Ministry of Commerce (1984, 406).
  a. These different categories are described in the text.
  b. It is possible that this information refers to 1979.

gradually decreased from 93 percent in 1978 to 83 percent in 1982 (Ministry of Commerce 1984, 405). By 1982, the figure was below the 1957 level (there had been a gradual increase from then until 1978). Moreover, within commercial procurement the share of purchases directly by retail commercial units more than doubled from 5 percent in 1978 to nearly 12 percent in 1982. The bulk of these were probably on a voluntary basis.[10] Finally, the figures do not reflect procurement by wholesale commercial units based on mutual agreement with industrial producers (table 3.5).

Overall, taking into account direct retail sales by industrial firms and retail and wholesale procurement that occurred on a voluntary basis, the share of voluntary, market-oriented transactions in total sales of industrial consumer goods and industrial inputs into agriculture by producers was in the neighborhood of 50 percent in the early 1980s. Roughly one-sixth of total sales of industrial consumer goods and agricultural inputs occurred outside the commercial system (ibid., 406). This consisted primarily of direct marketing by industrial enterprises. Adding this to voluntary procurement by the commercial system (from table 3.7), assumed to include all procurement by retail commercial units, the resulting figure is equivalent to 49 percent of total commercial procurement plus sales outside the commercial system.

Somewhat later than in the case of producer goods, open wholesale markets for industrial consumer goods emerged, most notably in cities like Chongqing, and total transactions have grown rapidly. Wholesale markets appear to be quite flexible in terms of the kinds of entities allowed to participate. Private wholesalers, who operate almost entirely outside of the administrative allocation system, also have begun to appear, whereas the private sector had previously been

Table 3.6

Share of Industrial Enterprises in Total Retail Sales, 1952–87

Year	Total retail sales of industrial goods[a] (billion yuan)	Direct sales by industrial enterprises[b] (billion yuan)	Share of direct marketing (percent)
1952	11.44	3.79	33.1
1957	20.90	3.39	16.2
1965	31.20	2.42	7.8
1970	43.94	2.74	6.2
1972	52.60	4.10	7.8
1975	67.14	6.16	9.2
1978	84.80	7.32	8.6
1979	97.61	10.36	10.6
1980	114.19	16.50	14.4
1981	124.01	19.54	15.8
1982	131.86	21.68	16.4
1983	142.98	24.97	17.5
1984	169.27	31.41	18.6
1985	210.46	40.07	19.0
1986	237.71	45.76	19.3
1987	277.62	53.71	19.3

Sources: State Statistical Bureau (1982, 335; 1983, 373; 1984a, 66, 72; 1984b, 351; 1985a, 464, 466, 468; 1986b, 445, 447, 452; 1987a, 483, 485, 490; 1988b, 684, 686, 691); *China Economic Yearbook* Editorial Committee (1981, IV-121, 122).

a. Estimate based on the total value of retail sales, minus retail sales of food and the value of retail sales by the catering industry. There may be some overlapping of the two, in which case these totals are too low because of double-counting in the subtraction.

b. Including sales by state, collective, individual, and other enterprises.

largely limited to retail commerce. Still another indicator of the role of markets in the allocation of industrial consumer goods and inputs into agriculture is transactions at rural and urban free markets. These were dominated by agricultural products in the past, but sales of industrial goods have become more important in recent years. Total transactions at urban free markets have risen sharply, while those at rural markets increased steadily from the late 1970s (see table 3.7).

Micro Data at the Enterprise Level

Available information from a number of samples of Chinese industrial enterprises further supports the assertion that the market mechanism has come to play a substantial role in the allocation of industrial goods. Direct marketing by a small sample of twenty state-owned industrial enterprises is discussed in chapter 4 (see table 4.4). These data show that as of 1982–83, the share of the market in

Table 3.7

Transactions at Urban and Rural Free Markets, 1965–87
(billion yuan)

Year	Urban markets		Rural markets	
	Number of markets	Value of transactions	Number of markets	Value of transactions
1965	—	—	37,000	6.8
1974	—	—	32,000	11.4
1975	—	—	31,238	10.55
1976	—	—	29,227	10.2
1977	—	—	29,882	10.5
1978	—	—	33,302	12.5
1979	2,226	1.20	36,767	17.1
1980	2,919	2.37	37,890	21.17
1981	3,298	3.40	39,715	25.3
1982	3,591	4.52	41,184	28.79
1983	4,488	5.14	43,515	32.79
1984	6,144	7.52	50,356	38.17
1985	8,013	12.07	53,324	51.16
1986	9,701	24.44	57,909	66.21
1987	10,908	34.71	58,775	81.08

Sources: State General Bureau of Industrial and Commercial Administrative Management (1982, 59); State Statistical Bureau (1985a, 477; 1986a, 93; 1987a, 510; 1988b, 709).

allocation of enterprise output varied greatly, but overall it was significant, even dominant in some cases.

Information from a sample of state-owned industrial enterprises in Qingdao Municipality (Shandong Province) in 1984 indicates that the substantial share of the market reported at more aggregate levels is indeed reflected in high market shares for individual firms. The thirteen enterprises in the sample for the most part are medium-sized and include producers of numerous different consumer goods and producer goods. As can be seen from table 3.8, mandatory planning was negligible for production decision making in most of the sample firms; it was important in the sales activities of a few enterprises (though far from a majority) and accounted for a substantial portion of raw material input purchases by most of them. The low shares of market allocation for inputs are somewhat misleading, since "indirect planning" includes exchange of goods for each other in tied transactions, many of which were arranged by enterprises on a voluntary basis. If indirect planning and market allocation for raw materials are combined, the average share in total supply rises to nearly 40 percent. On the sales side, the share of the market even narrowly defined was over 31 percent on average.

Table 3.8

Plan and Market Shares for Qingdao Sample Enterprises, 1984
(percent)

Enterprise	Mandatory plan	Indirect plan[a]	Market allocation
Production			
1	0	73	27
2	0	100	0
3	0	85	15
4	0	67	33
5	0	100	0
6	0	0	100
7	0	55	45
8	100	0	0
9	0	91	9
10	0	94	6
11	0	95	5
12	2	0	98
13	94	0	6
Overall average[b]	15.0	58.5	26.5
Sales			
1	0	90	10
2	0	100	0
3[c]	40	37	15
4	0	80	20
5	0	0	100
6	0	0	100
7	0	93[d]	7
8	0	93	7
9	95	0	5
10	0	0	100
11[c]	31	51	28
12	79	0	21
13	90	0	10
Overall average[b]	25.8	42.8	31.4
Raw Material Supply			
1	19	75	6
2	62	0	38
3	66	16	18
4	79	1	20
5[c]	56	6	43
6	77	23	0
7	93	0	7
8	76	24	0
9	75	2	23

(continued)

10[c]	85	10	0
11	90	2	8
12	0	100	0
13	0	70	30
Overall average[b]	60.8	25.3	13.9

Source: Zou et al. (1986, table 3-1, 153).

    a. This category specifically refers to "guidance planning" in production, "selective purchase by units" for sales, and "allocation and cooperation [exchange]" in material supply.

    b. Weighted average by enterprise actual production and transactions.

    c. Computational error is preserved from the original source because there is no way of knowing the correct percentages.

    d. Source gave 95, which was corrected to 93 in view of the percentages for raw material inputs.

Data on plan and market shares are also available for a much larger sample of 429 industrial enterprises in 27 Chinese cities, with a broad coverage of different industries, sizes, and forms of ownership (CESRRI 1986a, chap. 2). As table 3.9 indicates, the share of output sold outside of both mandatory and guidance plans was substantial for many firms. The share of market purchases in total input supplies was over 40 percent for nearly one-quarter of the enterprises in the sample in 1984, for 30 percent of them in the first half of 1985. Another 17 percent of sample firms relied on the market for a substantial 20–40 percent of their input supplies in 1984, 22 percent in the first half of 1985. The picture is even more striking on the sales side: in 1984 close to half of the enterprises in the sample directly marketed over 40 percent of their total output (34 percent directly marketed 80–100 percent). In the first half of 1985, 56 percent of sample enterprises directly marketed over 40 percent of their output, 38 percent 80–100 percent.

These figures are all the more significant because 56 percent of the enterprises in the sample were large or medium-sized, 65 percent state-owned. Even assuming that state enterprises and large and medium-sized firms uniformly had lower shares of market transactions than the others, this means that close to half of all the state enterprises in the sample and nearly 40 percent of the large and medium-sized firms directly marketed at least 20 percent of their output in 1984. Some larger state-owned enterprises rely heavily on the market on both the input and the output sides, so this is a highly conservative estimate.

The share of direct marketing in total sales for the sample as a whole was 33 percent in 1984, slightly less in the first half of 1985. On the input side, the corresponding figures were 27 percent and 44 percent, respectively, showing a sharp increase (ibid., 16). Reportedly 51 percent of sample firms had at least a degree of independent authority in the three areas of production, supply, and marketing. Seventy-seven percent had to take the market into account in planning their production, 90 percent purchased a significant share of their total input supplies on the market,

Table 3.9

Shares of Market Input and Output Transactions for a Sample of Industrial Enterprises, 1984–85 (percent of total purchases and sales)

Share of market transactions in total purchases or sales	Share of total number of sample enterprises	
	1984	First half 1985
Input purchases		
0	9.6	6.5
0–20	49.6	41.9
20–40	16.8	21.5
40–60	9.1	10.3
60–80	3.2	4.7
80–100	11.7	15.0
Output sales		
0	14.9	16.2
0–20	20.1	15.7
20–40	16.4	12.0
40–60	6.7	10.7
60–80	8.2	7.2
80–100	33.7	38.2

Source: CESRRI (1986a, tables 1.1 and 1.2, 46).
Notes: Data are from a sample of 429 industrial enterprises in 27 cities. Of the sample, 279 were state-owned, 131 were urban collectives, and 19 were township and village enterprises. Of the sample, 241 enterprises were classified as large or medium-sized, 188 as small.

and 97 percent had direct marketing authority (ibid., 16–17).[11]

Other fragmentary data provide further support for the assertion that markets are playing a substantial, increasingly important role in the allocation of inputs and outputs of industrial enterprises. Incomplete statistics for 1985 suggest that the share of the market in consumption of key producer goods by locally owned industrial enterprises was as follows: rolled steel 38 percent, timber 46 percent, and cement 61 percent (*China Economic Yearbook* Editorial Committee 1986, V–32–33).

Summary

The evidence presented in this section shows that the share of the market mechanism, as defined by Chinese analysts, in total transactions of industrial goods is relatively high and has been growing in recent years. This is true of a wide range of producer and consumer goods, at both aggregate and micro levels. The market appears to have penetrated to many different types of firms, including those that would be expected to be under tighter plan control, such as large and medium-sized enterprises and state-owned firms.

There is, however, a major question that has not yet been answered: When Chinese articles and statistical compendia talk about the "market," are they referring to genuine markets with voluntary, self-interested transactions? Is it possible that what in China are termed markets are really a form of locally directed allocations, perhaps less strictly controlled and more flexible than formal central planning but not entirely voluntary from the point of view of the transactors?

Market Functioning

This section attempts to grapple, in a preliminary and tentative fashion, with the question of market functioning in Chinese industry. Are Chinese markets actually functioning in a way that is more or less similar to markets in industrialized capitalist economies, or are there major differences that invalidate such a conclusion? In-depth empirical research, including extensive fieldwork, would be necessary to answer this question definitively. Here all that can be done is to examine certain aspects of market functioning where problems might be expected, making some preliminary observations based on available data. Based on interview information and fieldwork (see chapter 4), there is no reason to believe that Chinese discussions of industrial markets are systematically biased or distorted. They are sometimes overly cursory or brief, leaving out important details on how markets operate. But the more detailed information that occasionally emerges can be used, with confidence that positive statements accurately reflect reality.

Market Pricing

The degree of flexibility and responsiveness of market prices may tell a great deal about how well markets are functioning. A detailed examination of market price trends and patterns is made in chapter 8. Here some basic topics are looked at briefly: the existence of market prices, their fluctuations, the incentives and opportunities for local authorities to exercise informal price controls, the likely extent of these, and their adverse impact.

Existence and fluctuations of market prices. Data on market prices are published widely in China, which leaves no doubt about their existence and shows that they are widely used for reference and transactions within China. The earliest available set of market price data are for thirteen different industrial producer goods at the Shanghai Market for the Means of Production in 1979–80 (Byrd 1985a, table 5, 16–17). Though the interpretation of price movements for different goods is sometimes ambiguous, prices in general differed considerably from official state prices, and there were wide price fluctuations. More stringent price controls imposed at the end of 1980 and in early 1981 caused market transactions to decline sharply, however.

Much more extensive market price data for industrial producer goods were regularly reported in various local newspapers during most of 1985, and in the newspapers *Jingji cankao* (Economic information) and *Wuzi shangqing* (Materials market situation) since then. Market price data cover a number of industrial producer goods and numerous large and medium-sized Chinese cities. Most different types of industrial producer goods are included, ranging from several varieties of steel products to pure nonferrous metals, basic chemicals, cement, coal, timber, and trucks.

Available price data indicate, first, that market prices differ greatly from state plan prices in virtually all cases (see chapter 8, tables 8.1 and 8.2); second, that market prices vary significantly across cities; third, that market prices fluctuate considerably over time (sometimes in different directions for different cities); fourth, that except in a few cases there is no evidence of strict, longstanding price controls imposed at the city level; and finally, that reported prices seem to have the characteristics of list prices (posted by would-be sellers or by the material supply system), not formed through an organized commodity exchange mechanism.[12] The existence of what appear to be genuine market prices for Chinese industrial products provides strong evidence that there are functioning markets at which these goods are traded on a voluntary basis.

Retail and wholesale prices for industrial consumer goods have occasionally been reported for different cities, albeit much less frequently than in the case of producer goods. There is considerable variation in prices across cities but relatively little over time. Retail prices in any case have been subject to somewhat greater control than prices of industrial producer goods, and this has also narrowed the margin of fluctuation for wholesale prices. Nevertheless, prices of many "minor" commodities have been progressively decontrolled. Finally, the 1986 decontrol of prices of a number of consumer durables suggests that market pricing has become more ubiquitous.

Incentives and opportunities for informal price controls. The existence of "market" prices does not necessarily mean that they are determined solely by market forces. But why would local government authorities want to impose price controls for goods whose prices have been officially decontrolled by the central government? Fear of local inflation may be one reason. Another is that if local "extra-plan" prices are held below market-clearing levels, local authorities' control over goods allocation is enhanced, perhaps providing certain benefits to them. Even more important is the obvious incentive local authorities have to hold down input costs to local enterprises, whose profit tax payments form an important part of local budget revenues. They also have an incentive to hold down prices of investment goods purchased by local entities, since this increases the amount of "real" investment that can be financed with a given nominal amount of local funds. Still another possible motivation for local government intervention in market pricing is simply to smooth market adjustments and avoid excessive, possibly unnecessary fluctuations in market prices over the short run. This last type of intervention is likely to be supportive of market functioning rather than constituting a hindrance.

Thus, local authorities have ample motivation and incentives to intervene in market price determination. Moreover, they retain considerable formal and informal control over local industry and trade. The system of state-owned industrial enterprise administration still involves a quasi-hierarchical subordination of firms to designated supervisory agencies. Moreover, the bulk of state-owned industrial enterprises under central or provincial control devolved to municipal administrative subordination in the mid-1980s. Wholesale commerce also is vulnerable to local government interference. Hence there are ample opportunities for local authorities to exercise informal price controls over "market" or "above-plan" transactions in industrial goods.

The extent to which they can hold prices far below equilibrium levels is severely limited, however. The larger the gap between local controlled prices and the market equilibrium level, the greater the incentives for producers to try to get around them. Authorities may be able to get individual producers to accept lower prices through pressure or by offering them needed goods at low prices in "exchange." On the other hand, goods cannot easily be attracted from outside the jurisdiction for below-market prices.

The impact of price controls. The deleterious effects of price controls can be divided into two main categories: the opening and indeed positive encouragement they give for administrative control over the allocation of resources, and the drying up of market transactions, as one side—the seller if the controls are holding prices below the equilibrium level—increasingly refuses to participate.

Subequilibrium prices mean that the goods carrying them have to be allocated by nonmarket means. But allocation in whatever form brings with it well-known associated inefficiencies and rigidities. At their worst, informal local price controls could lead to ad hoc local planning and allocation hardly less inefficient than such activities carried out at the provincial or national level.

Much depends, however, on the degree to which locally controlled prices deviate from market-clearing levels. A very small gap would not lead to strong demand pressures on available supply and moreover would generate only weak incentives to get around the controlled price. In this situation local government allocation would be more like a form of "management" to ensure orderly flows of goods. On the other hand, if the gap is large (as it often was between early 1981 and late 1984), the adverse effects could be much worse. Thus, a distinction should be made between informal price controls that only "manage" price adjustments and strive to avoid severe fluctuations, and stronger controls that strive to hold prices substantially below their equilibrium level for a long period of time.

The impact of price controls in drying up market transactions is evident from Chinese experience. This happened at the Shanghai Market for the Means of Production after price controls were more stringently enforced in late 1980 and early 1981. More generally, open market transactions drastically declined or even stopped for many industrial producer goods in 1981–83. In the face of price controls, transactions outside of plan channels can take a number of forms: they could simply stop completely; they could become subject to local government allocation control; they might be driven underground, in which case they would become illegal transactions on the "black" market; or they could take the form of exchange of goods for each other in tied transactions consummated at low plan prices. All of these result in problems and inefficiencies as compared with a smoothly functioning market mechanism.

With price controls, even transactions that nominally go through markets may become distorted. They may no longer be truly voluntary on the part of both sides, but even if they are, they could involve side payments or related favors in addition to the (controlled) quoted prices. It would be a gross oversimplification to assume that in a situation of severe price controls, something like a genuine market could be operating, with the short side determining the level of transactions and the overhang of excess demand not having a debilitating effect on market functioning.

This all suggests that for many Chinese industrial producer goods with artificially low prices, functioning markets, after operating for a short period of time in the late 1970s, were not very effective in 1981–83 due to imposition of stringent price controls. But with the general decontrol of prices for industrial producer goods outside the plan in 1984–85, the situation must have improved greatly.

The extent of ad hoc local price controls. Given the incentives and opportunities for informal price controls by local authorities, how prevalent are they? There is some qualitative evidence that local market prices indeed are "managed" by local governments. For instance, in transactions outside the plan, the Shashi Municipal Material Supply Bureau set prices "slightly" below the market level (Kui and Liu 1986, 13). An unmoving reported market price for copper in Jilin City for nearly three months in early 1985 and in Guangzhou City during the middle of 1985 are suggestive of local government intervention, though in the case of Jilin the price was a bit above the level in other cities in the same region, perhaps to attract inflows of copper. Instances of constant prices over periods of several months are exceptional, however—frequent relatively small fluctuations are the norm.

The true extent of local government interference in price determination remains uncertain. But whatever their role, local governments could not move local market prices far away from their equilibrium levels, in view of the difficulty and cost of enforcing below-equilibrium prices for a long period of time. Thus, all in all, local government involvement in setting market prices does not appear to have been a major phenomenon dominating market functioning.

Impact of Other Local Government Interventions

Even if market prices are not subject to controls, or are subject only to a certain degree of "management" to smooth fluctuations, local authorities may intervene to divert goods that otherwise would be sold on the market to other channels under their control, often at below-market prices. One Chinese source states that a considerable portion of the industrial goods decontrolled by the state and permitted to be sold on the market have not actually entered the market and instead have been used to exchange for other goods in short supply at low prices (Wang et al. 1986, 205).

This diversion is often made in the interest of other local firms, particularly those that cannot fend for themselves because their products are not in great demand in the marketplace or because they are in poor financial shape. Appropriating the products of better-off local enterprises and using them to exchange for low-priced inputs for other local firms can help the latter hold down costs and avoid becoming a financial burden that would require local government subsidies. But this, of course, has an adverse effect on the more efficient firms.

Chains of transactions may be necessary to use goods produced by one local enterprise to satisfy the needs of another. This can be costly and inefficient, and inappropriate transport patterns may result as well. One example is a local industrial bureau that needed rolled steel for some of its enterprises. Among firms under this bureau, the only one with "exchangeable" output was a producer of specialized motor vehicles. Forty of these vehicles, which were part of the enterprise's above-plan production, were diverted for sale to a unit in Qinghai Province at the state price; the Qinghai unit in return provided twenty *Jiefang* (Liberation) brand trucks, also at the state price. These trucks were then sold to some local units that needed them, who in return were required to turn over to the bureau their plan allocation quotas for 145 tons of rolled steel and 40 tons of aluminum ingots. Quotas for 40 tons of rolled steel were given to the vehicle producer as a reward for its sale of the forty vehicles at the state price, while the rest of the allocation quotas were given to other enterprises under the bureau (ibid., 205). No profiteering was occurring in these transactions—the bureau only charged standard service fees, and its main objective was to arrange necessary supplies for "its" enterprises.

The extent of this kind of diversion is hard to gauge. The need to resort to barter-like exchange deals should have been greatly reduced after price controls were lifted, but established channels for these transactions, inertia, and possibly uncertainty about the longevity of liberalization measures could allow them to persist for a certain period of time.

Some Chinese observers assert that the proportion of production and supply of key industrial goods exchanged at submarket prices is relatively large. Although more than half of China's total output of rolled steel was outside the central plan by the late 1980s, much of this was allocated through exchange transactions rather than at market-determined prices. On the other hand, at the micro level, many enterprises (including producers of eminently exchangeable heavy industry goods in short supply) reported that they obtained the bulk of their inputs not allocated through the plan in transactions at market prices. Moreover, the opposite problem—diversion of key materials from plan allocation channels to market channels by government agencies as well as enterprises intent on reaping the windfall profits—has received great attention in the Chinese press and media. Overall, this latter behavior may be more important than diversion in the other direction.

Unreformed Aspects and Enterprise Motivation

For various reasons, Chinese industrial enterprises also in at least some cases seem to prefer to continue engaging in exchange transactions at below-market prices. This appears to stem mainly from enterprise motivation and incentives in a largely unreformed, still compartmentalized financial accounting and control system. By selling their outputs at below-market prices, even when there are no price controls, enterprises can gain access through exchange to low-priced goods that they need. But more important, some compartmentalization in the accounting system or some other constraint may mean that the gain from getting these inputs at low prices is greater than the (net after-tax) loss suffered from selling the outputs at a below-market price. Profits from sales cannot automatically be transferred to whatever use the enterprise wishes. Moreover, in the state sector profits from sales are heavily taxed, whereas funds used for various kinds of workers' welfare benefits may be left untaxed. Many exchange transactions appear to be motivated by the desire to improve such workers' benefits.

One example of this type of behavior is the sale of above-plan output by a firm for the state price (60 percent below the market price), in return for which it received at the state price rolled steel it needed for investment projects. This allowed the enterprise to hold down its nominal investment budget and thereby build additional housing for its workers (which was included in the enterprise's total investment quota). Thus, the fundamental motivation in this case was a combination of investment hunger and the desire to increase workers' benefits, while the key constraint was an investment budget or quota fixed in nominal terms. Another example concerns a firm that sold its output at a low price, losing over 1 million yuan in revenues annually, in return for which it got liquefied natural gas for its workers, also at a low price. In this case there was the further incentive that by selling this portion of output at the state price, the enterprise was permitted to count it as part of state plan output target fulfillment (Wang et al. 1986, 208).

Again, it is impossible to ascertain the quantitative significance of this kind of enterprise behavior. It depends on having an "exchangeable" output to sell and finding a suitable barter partner, which is not easy. On the other hand, once established, such relationships may become longstanding. In any case, as long as there is such a degree of compartmentalization in enterprise finances and controls over nominal expenditures on particular items (especially those involving worker benefits), the incentives for firms to rely on exchange transactions will remain.

Enterprises may also not be averse to having price ceilings imposed on their sales outside the plan. If product quality is a choice variable and it is a characteristic valued by the demand side, then price controls may actually increase enterprise profits, by permitting firms to offer goods of lower quality. This result has been demonstrated analytically by Raymon (1983); it requires a cost-quality trade-off and certain assumptions as to how quality enters the utility functions of consumers. More important, the result only holds for "local" price ceilings, which are not much below market equilibrium prices. But as we have seen, this may actually be the situation for market prices of many industrial producer goods in China.

Overall Evaluation of Market Functioning

This section has tried to come to grips with the issue of how markets actually function in China. Several features of the situation that have an adverse impact on market functioning have been identified. Price controls generate tendencies for a return to administrative allocation and may also dry up transactions or drive them into other, less efficient forms. Local governments may intervene to divert goods from the market to controlled channels even in the absence of formal price controls. Enterprises themselves may have incentives to continue the practice of exchanging their outputs for goods they need, at below-market prices.

These problems undoubtedly impair market functioning to some extent. The extent and adverse effects of price controls have greatly diminished with formal decontrol, however. Similarly, cases of local government intervention and enterprise willingness to engage in "exchanges" rather than commodity market transactions must be weighed against the evidence that markets have indeed been established and that at least some transactions are occurring at uncontrolled prices. Moreover, incentives to divert commodity flows from plan to market channels may be even greater than the reverse tendencies. None of the problems discussed in this section is severe enough to bring into question the existence of functioning markets in Chinese industry, though they may result in relatively "thin" markets that are weak, fragmented, and vulnerable to administrative intervention. Some of these problems may be at least somewhat ameliorated over time as more stable market institutions and practices become established.

4. The Impact of Markets on Chinese Industrial Enterprises

THE IMPACT of Chinese markets for industrial goods on enterprise behavior and performance is best seen through case studies. The following discussion relies on detailed interview information and quantitative data from a sample of twenty state-owned industrial firms (see table 4.1).[1]

Enterprise Response to Market Conditions

It is possible to formulate a simple classification system for enterprise response to market conditions, focusing on the difference in response patterns to a sellers' market and to a buyers' market.

Response to a Sellers' Market

Enterprise response to a sellers' market can be divided into four main types, in ascending order of difficulty and economic benefits. The first is passivity, which simply involves taking advantage of the secure market position to avoid any exertion, even that required to expand output to the limit of capacity.[2] There is no responsiveness to nonquantitative aspects of demand, such as quality, timely delivery, producing to user specifications, postsale service, and so on, since the enterprise is not even responding to the strong quantity signals of a sellers' market. Firms with a modicum of motivation or prodding from supervisory agencies generally act more positively than this, so it is not surprising that few in the sample exhibit this response, even temporarily.[3]

A second type of behavior is the expansion response—the enterprise vigorously increases output until it meets a physical or technical constraint it cannot overcome or a change in market conditions that imposes a demand constraint. But there is no attempt to cut costs, develop new products, meet customer needs, or otherwise respond to nonquantitative aspects of demand. Performance in these areas may even deteriorate as a result of the rush to increase output as rapidly as possible. A premier example of this kind of response is the Chongqing Clock and Watch Company during its "expansion phase" in 1979–81 (Byrd and Tidrick 1984, 38–44). Chongqing's response differed little in many respects from what

Table 4.1

Names and Abbreviations of Sample Enterprises

Full name	Abbreviation
Anshan Iron and Steel Corporation	Anshan
Baoji Nitrogen Fertilizer Plant	Baoji
Chengdu Locomotive and Rolling Stock Factory	Chengdu
Chongqing Clock and Watch Company	Chongqing
Jiangmen Nanfang Foodstuffs Factory	Jiangmen
Jinling Petrochemical General Corporation	Jinling
Mindong Electrical Machinery Corporation	Mindong
No. 2 Automotive Plant	N2 Auto
Nanning Silk and Linen Textile Mill	Nanning
North China Petroleum Administration	NC Petro
Northwest No. 1 State Cotton Textile Mill	NW Cotton
Qingdao Forging Machinery Plant	Qingdao
Qinghe Woolen Textile Mill	Qinghe
Qingyuan County Economic Commission	Qingyuan
Sanchazi Forestry Bureau	Sanchazi
Shanghai High-Pressure Oil Pump Plant	SH Oil Pump
Shanghai No. 17 State Cotton Textile Mill	SH Cotton
Shenyang Smelter	Shenyang
Tianjin Color Textile Corporation	Tianjin
Xiangxiang Cement Plant	Xiangxiang

Source: Tidrick and Chen (1987, table 2-1, 12).

would happen in a traditional centrally planned economic system when an enterprise is given priority access to resources and a mandate to expand output.

A third type of response is the technical response, often related to engineering priorities and solutions.[4] It may involve a focus on quality improvement, even beyond customer needs; acquisition and use of the most advanced technology, again disregarding cost considerations and customer needs; even an attempt to introduce new, more technologically advanced products; or, more rarely, cost cutting. One example is the Shenyang Smelter's production of copper whose purity won quality awards but exceeded the needs of most users (Byrd 1985b, 48). Since the technical response is undertaken without regard for the needs and preferences of the demand side, its benefits are often limited despite the considerable effort involved. Most of the enterprises in the sample facing a chronic sellers' market gravitated toward this response, particularly if they were supply- or capacity-constrained rather than financially constrained.

A final, rare type of response to a sellers' market can be termed the market-oriented response. Sometimes it occurs in enterprises that have gone through a period of facing a buyers' market and have learned lessons that "stick" when market conditions revert to excess demand. Some firms may try to enhance their prestige by demonstrating the ability to export, while others may focus on long-term expansion or strive to increase domestic market share by enticing customers away from other producers. The most notable example of the market-oriented response is the No. 2 Auto Plant, which became more responsive to customers during a period of excess supply of trucks in 1981 but then continued this pattern even when the market again tightened in 1982–83. No. 2 has been striving to increase its market share (it recently became the largest truck producer in China); to develop exports; and to expand into regional markets previously served by the No. 1 Auto Plant.

Response to a Buyers' Market

The first response to a weak market on the output side tends to be neglect and disbelief. The enterprise is slow to recognize that market conditions have changed; it may maintain an inward, technical orientation similar to the third response to a sellers' market, or it may continue rapid expansion. Once perception of the new situation sinks in, the first reaction may be one of dependency. The enterprise hopes to rely on help from authorities, in the form of subsidies or protection from competition, to stay in business. It may hope that commercial units will continue to procure its products even if they are not in demand on the market. Well-managed firms are unlikely to maintain this posture for long, and government supervisory agencies have proven unwilling to allow them the luxury of this option for more than a limited period of time.

A good example of this brief stage of passivity is the Qingdao Forging Machinery Plant's initial reaction to the sharp fall in demand resulting from the investment cutbacks of 1979–80 (Chen et al. 1984, 80). The plant at first did very little, in the expectation that it would be bailed out by orders for its products by the First Ministry of Machine Building, but these were not forthcoming. Then it went on a sales promotion blitz, which moved it into the next type of response, discussed below.

A second stage of response to a buyers' market involves vigorous sales promotion. The enterprise increases its sales staff; sends out people to drum up business; engages in advertising; and takes other related measures to expand sales. Price reductions may be part of this strategy, but there is no effort to raise quality, improve products or develop new ones, cut costs, or otherwise respond to demand. For firms like the ones in the sample, which generally produced goods of relatively good quality, this response could be at least temporarily effective in opening up new markets and stimulating sales. Nearly all sample firms facing a buyers' market engaged in sales promotion, but most of them also took other actions.

The second type of response to a buyers' market naturally comes to be supplemented by a third, the intensive response. This involves a genuine attempt to meet customer needs, through a combination of shifting product mix, improving quality, developing new products or varieties, cutting prices (both directly and by selling a better product for the same price), and providing better warranties and postsale service. In many cases, firms have been able to shift most of the burden of lower revenues onto the government by lowering profit remittances, so the pressures for cost reduction may be relatively weak. Otherwise the benefits of this response in generating goods better suited to demand, at least at the micro level, are obvious. A key distinction between the second and third types of response is that the former does not involve the sphere of production, whereas the latter does.

An example of this type of response is again the Qingdao Forging Machinery Plant. It drastically shifted its product mix from large friction presses used primarily by state enterprises to small ones used mainly by collective firms, in response to changes in the source of demand for its products. This change in product mix took place despite the much lower profitability of small presses.

There is one more radical response to a buyers' market, that of exit into new lines of products. This involves a wholesale change of orientation and is a positive, active response (rather than an administratively imposed shift in product lines as might occur for firms persisting in the first type of response). Though no sample firms have fully engaged in this type of response, some were on the verge of exit from producing one of their main products (clocks in the case of Chongqing), while others strove to develop completely new products to employ underutilized factors of production (usually labor, but sometimes also land or capital).

Market Conditions and Enterprise Response

The crucial impact of market conditions on enterprise behavior is evident from the above typology. Table 4.2 shows the differing responses of sample firms to buyers' markets and sellers' markets for their outputs, based on a careful examination of interview information, which broadly agrees with statements by the enterprise managers themselves. Output market conditions were defined for the purposes of the table as those faced by the industry concerned in 1982–83. Moreover, they refer to the supply-demand situation at official state prices, leaving open the question of whether prices for goods sold outside the plan cleared the market (if any such market existed).

At least four of the eight sample firms facing a sellers' market ended up in the third, technically oriented behavior pattern; only one exhibited the market-oriented response. More important, there appears to be no dynamic within the confines of a sellers' market that leads enterprises to more positive actions. At most there is an evolution from the second to the third response. Firms facing a capacity constraint will, if possible, invest heavily in expansion, and if they then meet a raw-material constraint they may turn to a focus on quality, technology, and so forth.

Table 4.2

Market Conditions, Product Characteristics, Technology, and Enterprise Response, 1982–83

Market conditions for output[1]	Enterprise response[2]	Nature of product[3]	Type of product[4]	Production technology[5]	Market conditions for main inputs[6]
Sellers' market					
NC Petro	1–2	H	R	X	ED[7]
Sanchazi	1–2	H	R	X	ED[7]
Anshan	3	H/D[8]	M	P	ED[9]
Baoji	2[10]	H	M	P	ED
Jinling	3	H	M	P	ED
Shenyang	3	H	M	P	ED
Xiangxiang	3	H	M	P	ED[9]
N2 Auto	4	D	I	E	ED
Buyers' market					
Mindong	7	D	M/I	E	ED
Qingdao	7	D	I	E	ED
SH Oil Pump	6(3)	D	M	E	ED
Chongqing	7	D	C	E	ES
Jiangmen	7	H/D	C	P	ED
Nanning	7	D	M/C	T	ES
NW Cotton	6–7	H	M	T	ED
Qinghe	7	D	M	T	ED
SH Cotton	5(3)	H	M	T	ED
Tianjin	7	D	M/C	T	ES(?)
Neither category					
Chengdu	3	D	—	E	—
Qingyuan	7	—	—	—	—

Source: Information gathered as part of the collaborative research project on Chinese state-owned industrial enterprise management, conducted by the Institute of Economics of the Chinese Academy of Social Sciences and World Bank.

1. Full names of enterprises are presented in table 4.1.

2. 1 = passivity; 2 = expansion response; 3 = technical response; 4 = market-oriented response; 5 = neglect/dependency; 6 = sales promotion; 7 = intensive response.

3. H = homogeneous product; D = differentiated product; H/D = enterprise produces both.

4. R = raw material; M = intermediate good; I = investment good; C = consumption good; M/I = enterprise produces both intermediate and investment goods; M/C = enterprise produces both intermediate and consumption goods.

5. X = extractive; P = continuous process; E = engineering (including assembly line operations); T = textile industry.

6. ED = excess demand (sellers' market); ES = excess supply (buyers' market).

7. These enterprises in extractive industries have their own source of inputs. Both petroleum reserves and forestry resources, however, are in very short supply in China.

(continued)

8. Rolled steel can be considered a differentiated product with many varieties, while pig iron and unprocessed steel can be considered homogeneous products. But this distinction is somewhat arbitrary.

9. These enterprises "own" mines producing their main material input and are therefore to a large extent insulated from the general shortage situation for these inputs.

10. It was difficult to ascertain this enterprise's response from the information provided.

The response to a sellers' market may depend on the cause of the shortage situation, however. If the primary constraint is insufficient capacity in the industry, producers, if given access to financial resources, will engage in the expansion response; this may lead eventually to a shift in market conditions to excess supply. If the main constraint is material inputs or energy, firms are likely to move into a technical response since the scope for output expansion is limited. Finally, if input and output prices that make production unprofitable are the primary cause of a persistent sellers' market, producers will attempt to exit. Firms unable to exit (such as mines) will in any case not be able to expand with internally generated funds, and low profits may also deter entities with funds available (banks, local governments) from providing them.

A buyers' market, on the other hand, generates strong pressures for enterprises to respond in ways that are beneficial to the demand side. Most sample firms facing a buyers' market have moved into the intensive response pattern. The negative responses (the first and second) are at most temporary stages in a natural sequence that leads to more positive actions. As long as production remains profitable, the proximate cause of the buyers' market does not appear to have a major effect on enterprise response. In particular, producer-goods firms facing a buyers' market because of a government-mandated cutback in investment exhibit a mode of response similar to that of producers of high-priced consumer durables in excess supply due to industrywide overexpansion. The Chongqing Clock and Watch Company is an example of the latter, the Qingdao Forging Machinery Plant of the former.

Market Conditions and Inventories

Kornai (1980, 117–19) argues that in a chronic shortage situation, enterprises' normal input stocks comprise a relatively large share of total inventories, whereas normal output stocks have a relatively small share; furthermore, stocks of usable outputs will be close to the minimum possible level. On the other hand, in a buyers' market, input stocks are a relatively small proportion of the total, while output stocks are relatively large.

Table 4.3 gives ratios of year-end input and output inventories to sales and to each other for sample firms in 1982. These data support Kornai's hypotheses or confirm the assessments of market conditions in 1982–83.[5] On average, output inventory/sales ratios of enterprises facing a buyers' market were over six times

Table 4.3

Input and Output Inventories of Sample Enterprises, 1982

| | Ratio to sales revenue | | |
Enterprise	Input inventories	Output inventories	Ratio of input to output inventories
Sellers' market			
NC Petro	0.157	0.040	3.890
Sanchazi	0.059	0.029	2.061
Anshan	0.155	0.007	20.840
Baoji	0.257	0.014	18.571
Jinling	0.097	0.015	6.598
Shenyang	0.105	0.005	20.754
Xiangxiang	0.097	0.010	9.334
N2 Auto	0.179	0.012	14.346
Average[a]	0.126	0.013	9.319
Buyers' market			
Mindong	0.362	0.588	0.615
Qingdao	0.417	0.054	7.725
SH Oil Pump	0.170	0.010	17.179
Chongqing	0.260	0.075	2.460
Jiangmen	0.130	0.047	2.794
Nanning	0.226	0.147	1.542
NW Cotton	0.149	0.050	2.961
Qinghe	0.106	0.023	4.659
SH Cotton	0.060	0.006	9.964
Tianjin	0.115	0.056	2.063
Average[a]	0.171	0.048	3.579
Other			
Chengdu	0.206	0.002	94.256
Qingyuan	0.236	0.053	4.430
Overall average[a]	0.155	0.025	6.247

Source: Tidrick and Chen (1987, table 2-17, 29; table 2-18, 30).
   a. Geometric average.

as large as those for firms facing a sellers' market. No enterprise facing a sellers' market had an output/sales ratio above 4 percent. There was greater variation among those facing a buyers' market, but some of the low observations can be explained by enterprise- or locality-specific factors.[6] In other cases, the shift to a buyers' market had been relatively recent and may not have penetrated to the sample firms by 1982. Thus, while a sellers' market on the output side invariably meant low output inventories, a buyers' market did not necessarily generate high inventory levels immediately, though the tendency was there.

    Input/output inventory ratios also support Kornai's contentions or the observations on market conditions in table 4.2. The average ratio for firms facing a sellers' market was more than twice that for enterprises facing a buyers' market, but this is entirely explained by the differences in output inventory/sales ratios.

The impact of market conditions for inputs is more problematic. In fact, the average ratio of input inventories to sales for enterprises facing a buyers' market was considerably higher than for firms facing a sellers' market. Moreover, the corresponding ratios for the three enterprises facing a buyers' market on the input side were very close to the average for all enterprises facing a buyers' market.[7] Lags in adjustment may partly explain these patterns: the emergence of a buyers' market may initially lead to a buildup of input inventories if production declines while the flow of inputs to the firm temporarily remains high.

The evolution of inventories over time also sheds some light on changing market conditions. A good example is the Anshan Iron and Steel Company, whose output inventory/sales ratio jumped from 0.4 percent in 1979 to 1.1 percent in 1980 and to 1.2 percent in 1981 as a buyers' market emerged for steel, only to fall back to 0.7 percent in 1982 with the return of the sellers' market. The No. 2 Auto Plant's output inventory/sales ratio rose from 2.7 percent in 1980 to 6.6 percent in 1981 due to the buyers' market for trucks, then fell sharply to 1.2 percent in 1982 with the resurgence of demand. For five of the eight firms facing a buyers' market in 1982–83, output inventory/sales ratios showed a rising trend over time, in most cases quite sharp. The declining trend in the other three firms can be explained by enterprise-specific factors.[8] There was a general downward trend in input inventories between the late 1970s and early 1980s, with the average input inventory/sales ratio falling from 0.444 in 1975 to 0.265 in 1978 and to 0.177 in 1982. This may reflect improvements in inventory management, which had been extremely lax in the Cultural Revolution period, more than changing market conditions.

Factors Influencing Enterprise Response

This section looks at aspects other than output market conditions that can affect enterprise behavior and performance in response to market forces. A detailed consideration of these factors is beyond the scope of this chapter; moreover, the sample of twenty enterprises is too small to support any solid conclusions. Nevertheless, there are some intriguing patterns.

Product Characteristics and Production Technology

There are a number of dimensions, shown in table 4.2. Most producers of homogeneous goods faced sellers' markets, whereas those making differentiated products generally faced buyers' markets. Excluding the two firms making gray cloth (which has, somewhat arbitrarily, been classified as homogeneous), the only producer of homogeneous goods facing a buyers' market was the Jiangmen Nanfang Foodstuffs Plant, which made noodles (considered homogeneous) and candy and soft drinks (differentiated). The only producer of differentiated products facing a sellers' market in 1982–83 was the No. 2 Auto Plant.

The relationship between market conditions and classification of goods as raw materials, intermediate products, investment goods, or consumption goods is more complex. The only producer of final goods facing excess demand was the No. 2 Auto Plant. Enterprises facing a buyers' market, on the other hand, included producers of both intermediate and final goods, most of the latter consumer goods. Another interesting pattern concerns production technology. Except for the two firms in extractive industries and the No. 2 Auto Plant, in engineering, all of the firms facing a sellers' market used continuous-process technology. On the other hand, except for the textile plants (whose classification in this schema is somewhat fuzzy anyway), all of the enterprises facing excess supply used batch-production techniques.

A full consideration of causal relationships between technical aspects and market conditions is beyond the scope of this study. Some of the superficially strong associations in the sample are misleading. The linkage between product homogeneity and sellers' markets is most likely spurious. Similarly, the lack of producers of final goods facing a sellers' market is in part illusory. Cement, timber, and much steel are direct inputs into the construction industry and hence do not differ as greatly from machinery (which must be installed before it unambiguously becomes a final good) as the classification system used in table 4.2 would suggest.

Aside from the direct or indirect effects they may have on market conditions, technology and product characteristics constrain an enterprise's response to market forces. In the case of homogeneous products, scope for new product development is limited, and new products may have only a small effect in stimulating demand anyway. The fixity of the capital stock in many continuous process industries, which are characterized by asset specificity in Williamson's (1985) terminology, may make exit difficult and uneconomical. Moreover, it may be very costly to slow down or stop production. Thus, firms producing homogeneous products with continuous process technologies may find it hard to respond in quantitative or qualitative ways to the demands of a buyers' market, which means that most or all of the burden of adjustment has to be taken up by price changes. But in China price controls hindered downward as well as upward adjustments in prices. In this context it is interesting to note that all of the enterprises of this type in the sample faced a sellers' market and hence did not have to make difficult adjustments to a buyers' market in the absence of price flexibility.

Another important technical factor is the degree of ease with which product mix can be altered. This is particularly important for multiproduct firms facing different market conditions for different outputs. At one extreme, the Shenyang Smelter had virtually no control over the amounts of various kinds of by-products it recovered from ores during the smelting process, which were determined by the mineral composition of the ores it received. Reducing production of by-products was not a viable alternative since this would increase pollution. The enterprise therefore could not respond to excess supply by cutting output, while the homogeneity of its products (pure nonferrous metals) rendered other forms of response ineffective as well. In the end, the smelter dealt with severe excess supply of the by-product cadmium by tying sales of it to those of zinc, one of the enterprise's main products for which demand was strong.[9]

The Chongqing Clock and Watch Company represents both an intermediate case and the opposite extreme. Though workers could be shifted from clock production to watchmaking, scope for shifting equipment was restricted, and it was hard to shift product mix between clocks and watches without substantial new investment. On the other hand, the company could alter the grade of watches it produced merely by redesigning the face and changing the brand name. Parts and components for all grades of men's watches produced by Chongqing differed only in the quality standards to be met in postproduction testing. Hence, the enterprise could raise or lower average quality by changing brands and by using components of higher than minimum standards for the grade of watch produced (Byrd and Tidrick 1984, 55).

While technical aspects do have an impact on enterprise response to market forces, they do not appear to be as important as market conditions themselves. Whether a firm is facing a sellers' market or a buyers' market for its output has a much greater impact on its behavior and performance than the technology and product characteristics of the industry it is a member of, though these can shape and constrain enterprise response.

Direct Marketing

The share of enterprise direct marketing[10] ("self-sales") in total sales varied predictably with changing market conditions, as can be seen from table 4.4. Except for No. 2 Auto and Anshan Steel, both of which had faced excess supply in 1981, none of the sample firms facing a sellers' market directly marketed more than 10 percent of total output in 1980–82. On the other hand, some enterprises facing a buyers' market sold the bulk of their output on their own, and the overall average share of self-sales was roughly 33 percent. Thus, sample data support the hypothesis that a buyers' market was a precondition, though not necessarily a sufficient condition, for a high share of enterprise direct marketing in the early 1980s.

The qualitative role of direct marketing also varied systematically with market conditions. In a sellers' market the right to sell part of output directly is a valued privilege, conferred on producers often over strenuous objections from commercial organizations and supervisory agencies. Under these circumstances, self-sales for sample firms have been closely tied to enterprise-specific reform packages or even "special favors." The benefits to producers from direct marketing in a sellers'

Table 4.4

Direct Marketing and Exports, 1980–82 (percent)

Enterprise	Share of self-sales in total sales[a]	Share of exports in total sales[b]	Share of direct exports in total exports[c]
Sellers' market			
NC Petro	0.2[d]	—	0
Sanchazi	0[e]	0.3	0
Anshan	12.0[d]	1.1	45.4
Baoji	very small[f]	0	0
Jinling[g]	very small[f]	15.3	0.1[h]
Shenyang	1.8[i]	—	0
Xiangxiang	8.6[j]	0	0
N2 Auto	41.6[d]	0.4	92.7
Buyers' market			
Mindong	82.5[k]	31.3	74.0[k]
Qingdao	90[l]	1.7	0
SH Oil Pump	—	39.2[m]	0
Chongqing	30[n]	3.1	0
Jiangmen	39.3[o]	8.3	0
Nanning	26.6[p]	28.1	0
NW Cotton	12.6[q]	23.2	0
Qinghe	3.9[r]	36.8	0
SH Cotton	very small[f]	10.7	0
Tianjin	10.5[s]	47.0[t]	0
Other			
Chengdu	0	0	0
Qingyuan	high	low	0

Source: Collaborative Research Project on State-Owned Industrial Enterprise Management.

a. Ratio of revenues from product sales on a voluntary basis outside of mandatory plans to total sales revenue, unless otherwise indicated.

b. Share of revenues from sales for export (including sales to foreign trade departments and direct exports) in total sales revenue, unless otherwise indicated. Export sales are valued at prices actually received by the producer. Note that exports and self-sales do not overlap, except for direct exports.

c. Direct exports are defined as those undertaken by the enterprise on its own account, as opposed to sales to foreign trade departments.

d. Share of physical output accounted for by self-sales (crude oil in the case of the North China Petroleum Administration, rolled steel in the case of the Anshan Iron and Steel Company, and trucks in the case of the No. 2 Auto Plant).

e. Before 1980, the enterprise had some self-marketing rights, which were taken away in that year. Subsequently, all sales outside the plan apparently had to be approved by the Jilin Provincial Forestry Bureau. Some timber was exchanged with PLA units in return for road construction services, while some was provided to "owners" of some of the afforested land and to units that tended forests under contract.

f. Precise figures were not given, but the enterprise indicated that the share of self-sales was very small.

(continued)

g. For 1981–82 only (since the Jinling Petrochemical General Corporation was established only in 1981).

h. Rough estimate based on ratio of tonnage of direct exports to tonnage of total exports.

i. Not including self-sales of the main nonferrous metals produced (copper, lead, zinc), which reportedly were relatively small.

j. Quantity of self-sold cement divided by total sales of cement in 1981–83.

k. Since 1981, all production has been marketed by the enterprise itself and all exports have consisted of direct exports.

l. Rough estimate.

m. Ratio of exports to output of plunger pumps (the value of plunger pump output accounted for about 98 percent of gross industrial output value of the factory).

n. Share of self-sales for watches in 1982.

o. Share of value of output of candy and noodles sold to units other than the two "official" commercial intermediaries (the Jiangmen Municipal Candy Company and Jiangmen Municipal Foodstuffs Company). Even sales to these organizations have been largely on a voluntary basis, though linked to provision of raw materials.

p. Share of self-sales was 18 percent in 1981, 49 percent in 1982, and 82 percent in 1983.

q. Share of total physical output of cloth sold directly by the enterprise in the second half of 1982 and in 1983, not including cloth sold to commercial departments on a voluntary basis.

r. Share of self-sales rose from 0.8 percent in 1981 to 7.7 percent in 1982.

s. Very rough estimate of the share of self-sales of cloth in total physical output of cloth.

t. Share of cloth exports in total cloth output.

---

market include the ability to exchange products for needed goods; the ability to capture part or all of the commercial margin through sales at the wholesale or retail price; room for manipulation of product mix and direct sale of the most profitable goods and varieties; and, where permitted, the ability to charge a higher price. (Sample firms generally could not freely raise prices in 1980–82.)

Not surprisingly, within-plan distribution agencies tended to oppose enterprise direct marketing in a sellers' market situation, and lengthy bargaining over its share often occurred. For example, the right to directly market 10 percent of total output was formally granted to the Baoji Chemical Fertilizer Plant only in 1982 and was not implemented even at that time. Self-sales of goods in short supply could be eroded by various authorities forcing firms to sell goods to them (or to designated customers) outside the plan. At the Xiangxiang Cement Plant the share of direct marketing crept upward year by year, rising from 8.0 percent of total sales in 1981 to 11.9 percent in 1984. But a considerable part of directly marketed output in fact was allocated by government agencies or virtually "requisitioned" by powerful organizations like the railways and power bureaus.[11]

On the other hand, direct marketing in a situation of excess supply is a burden on enterprises, which tend to resist it, at least initially. Though there was often a lag while perceptions of market conditions changed and bargaining took place, in the end most sample firms were forced to take on substantial marketing responsibilities. Since self-sales allowed the impact of market forces to be felt directly by producers, the mechanism by which a buyers' market came to be associated with a high share of enterprise direct marketing is very important. If most or all of output had continued to be allocated by plans or administrative directives even when there was excess supply on the market, the pressure on enterprises to become more responsive to customer needs would have been much weaker or even absent.

Exports

There is also a superficially close relationship between market conditions and the share of exports in total sales (table 4.4). Except for the Jinling Petrochemical General Corporation, firms facing a sellers' market exported only a small proportion of their total output in 1980–82, whereas export shares for firms facing excess supply on the domestic market ranged as high as nearly 50 percent. For some enterprises, the linkage between the buyers' market and high exports was at least in part a causal one. One response to a weak domestic market is to expand exports. This strategy was followed by the Jiangmen Nanfang Foodstuffs Factory, whose share of exports in total sales rose from 2.7 percent in 1978 to 10.6 percent in 1982; the Mindong Electrical Machinery Plant, whose export share rose from virtually nil before 1976 to 38.2 percent in 1978 and stayed above 30 percent thereafter; and the Nanning Silk and Linen Textile Mill, whose export share jumped from 21.5 percent in 1983 to 44.9 percent in the first ten months of 1984.

This relationship, however, is to a large extent spurious. Many firms facing a buyers' market in 1980–82 also had high export shares earlier when facing chronic excess demand. Moreover, export shares for some firms facing a buyers' market, like the Qingdao Forging Machinery Plant, declined rather than increased. The fact that, on average, the share of enterprise direct exports in total exports was higher for firms facing excess demand than for those facing excess supply raises more doubts.[12]

Exports may be very important in providing firms with experience in competitive international market conditions. The Mindong Electrical Machinery Corporation, for example, captured the Singapore market for small electrical generators from a Japanese firm in the late 1970s by successively matching price reductions; after the competitor exited, Mindong was able to raise prices somewhat. There was virtually no difference in quality standards between Mindong's products made for domestic sale and those produced for export, to the obvious benefit of domestic users. The authority to export directly and establish direct contacts with foreign customers has been crucial in this respect. For most sample firms there has been considerable insulation between domestic and export production.

Financial Considerations

Perhaps somewhat surprisingly, financial aspects have not played a dominant role in shaping enterprise response to market forces. This is broadly true of overall profitability, profit remittances (direct taxes) and indirect taxation, and investment financing. As can be seen from table 4.5, profit rates on sales for sample firms in 1980–82 ranged from a low of 5.5 percent of sales to a high of 51.4 percent. Variation in the profit rate on capital was even greater, from 3.8 percent to 101.6 percent. (Asset valuation is distorted because of low depreciation rates on the one hand and failure to revalue existing assets on the other.) There were no substantial differences in the profit rate on sales as between firms facing a sellers' market and those facing a buyers' market, but the average profit rate on capital of the former was only 20 percent compared to 35 percent for the latter. Most of this difference is explained by the five textile plants, whose average rate of profit on capital was 71 percent. The modest difference in indirect tax rates between the two groups of enterprises is entirely explained by higher average tax rates for consumer goods (14 percent) than for other goods (6 percent).

More important than the lack of any systematic relationship between market conditions and profitability is the fact that profitability seems not to have influenced enterprise response, at least in the short run. Even the least profitable of the firms facing a buyers' market, the Jiangmen Nanfang Foodstuffs Plant, engaged in highly positive responses. Similarly, there is no indication that for firms facing a sellers' market, higher profits led to different response patterns. High profits, however, do allow managers to indulge their desire for high technology, high quality, or large investment projects (see Byrd and Tidrick 1987).

The onset of a buyers' market not surprisingly tends to have a negative effect on producers' profitability. Only in one sample firm, Jiangmen, was there a sustained rise in the profit rate on sales during a period when it was facing a buyers' market. In other factories the deterioration in profitability attributable to a buyers' market was sometimes spectacular. The Nanning Silk and Linen Textile Mill's profit rate on sales dropped from 31 percent in 1981 to 17 percent in 1982 and about 10 percent in 1983. Overall, in sixteen out of twenty-three "observations" (years in which a sample firm faced a buyers' market), profitability dropped. These declines were only partly due to falling prices; costs also tended to rise, due to reduced production and higher unit overhead costs as well as increased expenditures on sales promotion, quality improvement, product differentiation, and so forth.

Table 4.6 shows investment-capital ratios for sample firms. Investment rates were considerably higher for firms facing a buyers' market, perhaps due to their lower capital intensity and the larger proportion of old enterprises with undervalued capital stocks. The average share of externally financed investment in total investment also was higher for firms facing a buyers' market, but by a smaller margin. Hence, larger absolute amounts of external funds have gone to firms in a buyers' market situation than to those facing a sellers' market. This may be partly related to the fact that the investment figures cover the period 1980–82, and buyers' markets emerged close to the end of that period for many sample

Table 4.5

Financial Indicators, 1980–82 (percent)

Enterprise	Profit-sales ratio[a]	Profit-capital ratio[b]	Tax rate on sales[c]
Sellers' market			
NC Petro	37.7	26.4	6.1
Sanchazi	24.3	15.4	6.0
Anshan	35.1	20.7	6.9
Baoji	19.5	11.4	3.0
Jinling	19.7[d]	27.5[e]	10.8[d]
Shenyang	9.2	30.2	5.7
Xiangxiang	35.8	25.3	13.2
N2 Auto	18.9	11.1	5.0
Average[f]	22.9	19.7	6.5
Buyers' market			
Mindong	11.3	21.2	5.2
Qingdao	10.8	9.2	4.0
SH Oil Pump	51.4	82.1	5.1
Chongqing	23.4	28.7	27.2
Jiangmen	5.5	3.8	5.2
Nanning	26.5	46.9	15.3
NW Cotton	24.1	58.1	15.0
Qinghe	30.2	64.5	17.9
SH Cotton	21.8	101.6	14.6
Tianjin	27.8	97.7	4.9
Average[f]	19.8	35.3	9.2
Other			
Chengdu	30.2	27.0	5.0
Qingyuan	14.8	17.9	10.2

Source: Tidrick and Chen (1987, table 2-14, 26; table 2-21, 33; table 2-22, 34; table 2-23, 35).

a. Ratio of administrative profits to sales revenue.

b. Ratio of administrative profits to total value of fixed assets valued at original purchase price.

c. Ratio of indirect taxes to sales revenues.

d. For 1981–82 only, since the Jinling Petrochemical General Corporation was established only in 1981.

e. For 1982 only. The assets of two large plants under Jinling were only "certified" and included in the inventory of fixed assets in that year, though they already were in operation in 1981. This distorts the figure for 1981.

f. Geometric average.

firms. The textile plants also contribute to the differences in investment rates, but they differ widely among themselves, with the Northwest State No. 1 Cotton Textile Mill and the Shanghai No. 17 State Cotton Textile Mill having very low investment rates and shares of external financing.

Table 4.6

Investment Rates, 1980–82 (percent)

Enterprise	Ratio of gross fixed investment to total fixed assets[a]	Ratio of externally financed fixed investment to total fixed assets[b]	Ratio of externally financed to total fixed investment[c]
Sellers' market			
NC Petro	11.6	5.4	46.6
Sanchazi	10.2	2.1	20.6
Anshan	5.0	2.0	40.0
Baoji	12.8	0.2	1.6
Jinling[d]	5.5	2.8	50.9
Shenyang	15.1	1.3	8.6
Xiangxiang	10.3	8.5	82.5
N2 Auto	4.7	0.3	6.4
Average[e]	9.4	2.8	32.2
Buyers' market			
Mindong	—	—	—
Qingdao	5.6	0.7	12.5
SH Oil Pump	8.2	3.2	39.0
Chongqing	28.4	16.3	57.4
Jiangmen	22.7	2.7	11.9
Nanning	15.2	10.2	67.1
NW Cotton	2.4	0	0
Qinghe	24.4	20.3	83.2
SH Cotton	8.8	2.1	23.9
Tianjin	41.5	29.8	71.8
Average[e]	17.5	9.5	40.8
Other			
Chengdu	5.8	2.3	39.7
Qingyuan	12.4	7.7	62.1

Sources: Byrd and Tidrick (1987, table 4-2, 86–87); Tidrick and Chen (1987, table 2-14, 26).

a. Ratio of total fixed investment to total value of fixed assets at original purchase price.

b. External financing basically consists of government grants and bank loans, as contrasted to internal financing which is primarily from retained profits and depreciation funds (including the major repairs fund). In some cases, relatively small amounts of investment from particular, enterprise-specific sources had to be somewhat arbitrarily classified as either external or internal financing.

c. Ratio of second to first column.

d. For 1981–82 only, since Jinling was established only in 1981.

e. Simple arithmetic average of column above. Hence, the average in the third column is not generally equal to the ratio of the averages for the first and second columns.

Overall, financial aspects did not play a determining or even a highly influential role in enterprise response to market conditions. The pervasiveness of bargaining and negotiations in the system, combined with sharp differences in profit rates due to price distortions, meant that the relationship between financial performance and what the enterprise could do in responding to market forces was relatively weak. The decline in profitability naturally associated with the onset of a buyers' market did not appear to inhibit firms from making highly beneficial responses, perhaps because of their ability to negotiate the necessary resources for themselves.

Input and Output Markets

There is a clear relationship between market conditions for outputs and those for main material inputs, as can be seen from table 4.2. All of the sample firms facing excess demand on the output side used raw materials that also were in short supply. Four of the eight had their own source of raw materials, however, and were therefore to some extent insulated from the sellers' market on the input side.[13] The majority of enterprises facing excess supply on the output side were in the unenviable position of facing a sellers' market on the input side, at least in 1982–83. Thus, a sellers' market for output appears to be invariably associated with a sellers' market for main inputs, but a shift to a buyers' market does not necessarily mean that a corresponding change will occur immediately on the input side.[14]

This lack of relationship between a buyers' market for outputs and input market conditions at first sight seems puzzling. A weak market should cause producers to cut input purchases, since they cannot build up inventories indefinitely. Part of the explanation may be administrative obstacles: firms may still have been forced to buy inputs through customary administrative channels, which were slow to reflect changes in market conditions. In some cases there may have been perceptual or other lags, so that a buyers' market for inputs emerged only after a buyers' market for output had been established for a certain period of time. Relative price structure in China, where profits at each stage of processing of a given raw material tend to be higher than at the previous stage, also may contribute to a situation where there is overinvestment in downstream stages of processing and hence excess supply, but underinvestment and shortage in upstream stages.

But the main reason for a continuing sellers' market for inputs in the face of a buyers' market for outputs is the multiple uses many inputs have. Heavy demand by some users of an input would take up any slack caused by other users reducing their orders, preserving shortage for everyone. The metal products used by the Mindong Electrical Machinery Corporation, the Qingdao Forging Machinery Plant, and the Shanghai High-Pressure Oil Pump Plant could also be used for other purposes. The sugar required by the Jiangmen Nanfang Foodstuffs Plant could be consumed directly as well as used in production of candies and soft drinks.

Shortage on the input side makes the producer's task more difficult and diverts attention to arranging supplies or imposes other constraints on response. A sellers' market for inputs also makes it more difficult to reduce costs. None of these factors, however, prevents firms from engaging in the intensive response.

For the most part, the various technical, financial, and other aspects examined in this section were dominated by the overall dichotomy between a buyers' market and a sellers' market in their impact on enterprise response. Though they could shape and constrain response in certain ways, they did not change its basic thrust. Hence, the shift from the chronic sellers' market typical of the traditional centrally planned economy to a buyers' market was crucial in improving efficiency and enterprise responsiveness to the demand side in the early 1980s.

Government Response to Market Forces

The response of government authorities to market forces and changing market conditions can crucially affect their impact on enterprises, enterprise response, and dynamic trends. Government actions can range from decisions on how much to invest in different projects using budgetary funds to controls over production or investment decisions of firms, price controls, controls over transactions, or other attempts to affect the market directly. Considerable analytical work has been done on government response to a sellers' market, or the impact of shortage on government behavior (see in particular Kornai 1980, chaps. 9, 10, and 21). Government response to a buyers' market in centrally planned economies is much more uncharted terrain.

Sellers' Market

In China, government response to chronic shortage has exhibited both similarities and differences compared to patterns in other socialist countries. The government has usually tried to avoid price increases for the entire supply of a shortage good, particularly if producers are already earning adequate profits. But in recent years, "parallel markets" for transactions outside the plan have emerged, with higher, flexible prices. As a result, a "two-tier system" has become prevalent for goods with low plan prices (see chapter 9). The pressures from a strong sellers' market are accommodated by letting some supply at the margin be allocated through the market, while retaining plan allocation and plan prices for the rest.

Increasing imports or cutting back exports is a relatively simple short-term response to shortage. In China, however, this response has been notably lacking in a number of instances; for example, high coal and especially petroleum exports were maintained in the face of a severe energy shortage. Increasing investment in industries whose products are in short supply may lead to improvements over the long run. But in China, investment has been at least somewhat responsive to profitability, leading to underinvestment in low-profit industries such as coal. The decentralization of control over a large share of investment and its financing in the 1980s probably increased its responsiveness to profitability (see Byrd and Tidrick 1987). Another problem in China is that the budgeting process makes it difficult to change investment shares in different industries drastically.

An almost universal response of governments to shortage is imposition of rationing to ensure that high-priority users receive adequate supplies. China had widespread rationing of consumer goods prior to the late 1970s. Rationing of producer goods occurred through the state material supply plan, but its coverage was uneven and incomplete for many commodities (see chapter 5). Moreover, such rationing in China suffers from the same problem as investment budgeting: shares of different industries and subsectors have been "sticky" and hard to adjust. This makes rationing an unsatisfactory tool for improving economic efficiency through ensuring adequate supplies to priority users.

Buyers' Market

The buyers' markets that have emerged in Chinese industry since the late 1970s elicited an interesting government response. The following discussion focuses on three main spheres: marketing policies, price adjustments and controls, and controls over production and investment.

Government response has been most striking in the area of marketing: the government planning and distribution systems essentially abdicated responsibility for procurement of enterprise output in the face of a buyers' market, forcing producers to fend for themselves and sell their own products. This response by the system was a crucial link in the chain of causation leading from a buyers' market to positive enterprise response. It appears to have been missing in the Soviet Union, where surpluses of some consumer goods were not unknown.[15] The process by which this passive but arguably very beneficial government response occurred differed somewhat as between consumer goods and producer goods, but the end result was the same.

In the case of consumer goods, the impact of an emerging buyers' market is first felt as a buildup of inventories in the warehouses of wholesale commercial units procuring the goods from industrial producers.[16] For a while these commercial units may continue to purchase the goods concerned, but as inventories grow to immense proportions, pressures for change increase, due to the financial costs of carrying large inventories or even limitations on warehouse space. An interim response might involve storage of some goods at the factory site, or possibly imposition of production ceilings, with all output still purchased by the commercial system. But eventually the commercial system refuses to continue to procure all output, and the burden of marketing is put on the producer. It is not surprising that Chinese commercial enterprises would want to stop buying consumer goods when sales are slow and inventories are accumulating. What is interesting is that this desire has generally been realized, both for sample firms and more generally in Chinese industry as a whole.

Refusal by commercial units to purchase an enterprise's output makes the latter responsible for sales, feeling the direct impact of market forces. This in turn puts the whole area of marketing largely out of government control and stimulates competition among producers and between producers and commercial units (which still have large inventories to sell off). One reason why the government allowed this to happen may have been that forcing enterprises (particularly large, successful ones) to cut production, which could solve the inventory problem while maintaining the monopoly of the "official" commercial system, would have been contentious and difficult. It may have been "politically" easier to force firms to make joint decisions on production and sales in response to market forces, which were more impersonal than production ceilings imposed by the government on a case-by-case basis.

Commercial reforms may have been an important factor, since they had the objective of making the commercial system more profit-oriented, concerned about inventories, and independent in its decision making. This made it more difficult for authorities to order commercial units to purchase industrial goods already in serious excess supply.[17] But commercial reforms got fully underway only several years after industrial reforms. Reform policies promoting enterprise direct marketing may also have played a role, but this link was tenuous in the early 1980s.

In the case of producer goods, the impact of excess supply on marketing can be even more immediate, since so many transactions take place directly between producers and users. When users' production or investment plans are cut, they simply make no new plan-based orders and even cancel existing purchase contracts if necessary, leaving producers to face the full brunt of the buyers' market almost right away.[18] Indeed, machinery producers were the first major group of industrial firms in China to feel the impact of a buyers' market in 1979–80, as material-supply organs and users refused to purchase ordinary types of machinery and equipment in excess supply.

Demand for producer goods is very sensitive to the level of investment. Sharp cuts in budget-financed investment in 1980 and 1981 generated temporary buyers' markets for most producer goods. Another factor in the case of machinery was the proliferation of producers in the 1970s, many of them small, backward, and inefficient. This created a large "overhang" of potential supply that could respond to increases in demand (though by providing low-quality, obsolete goods). As a result, the buyers' market for ordinary types of machinery has been more resilient than for other producer goods.

Government response in the area of pricing has been rather passive, but at least in some cases it served to intensify enterprise response. Complete decontrol of prices has rarely been the initial response chosen. Downward adjustments in government-set prices have been common, but invariably too late and too small to restore equilibrium. A good example is the series of reductions in watch prices in the early 1980s (Byrd and Tidrick 1984, 45). Sometimes limited downward floating of prices by producers within certain limits was permitted, as in the case of certain machinery and electronics goods in 1979–80. Slow and uneven downward adjustment of prices intensified competition among producers.

The difficulty of imposing ceilings on production by factories and regions has already been alluded to. This did occur in the case of textiles, but not in any other industries represented in the sample. The central government tried to impose limits on investment in capacity expansion for a number of consumer durables like watches (ibid., 44–45, 68–69), as well as for textiles. Controls did not cover all investment in the industries concerned, particularly by small factories outside the state plan. Moreover, existing firms were allowed to increase production by utilizing slack capacity or improving efficiency, which may have permitted some disguised capacity-increasing investment. Investment controls may even have encouraged "preemptive" investment by enterprises and localities to increase their long-term market share.

Another possible government response to a buyers' market is to force some producers to exit. In China, sizable state-owned firms are virtually never closed down. Hence, those under pressure to leave an industry suffering from excess supply invariably were small rural collective enterprises. A policy of forced exit can be applied for numerous reasons other than market conditions, including concerns about efficiency, energy consumption, and financial considerations. When strictly implemented, as in the case of small cigarette plants, it has been effective at least in preventing further entry by small firms. Success in other industries has been mixed. In any case, closure of firms has at most been able to ameliorate the trend toward a buyers' market but not reverse it.

The inability to use exit as a major part of industrywide response to a buyers' market makes patterns of adjustment more rigid and inefficient. Even if all enterprises are making strong efforts to improve their products and become more responsive to demand, this may not be sufficient if the least efficient and competitive producers really should exit from the scene. In fact, in a situation where exit is impeded, positive enterprise response at the micro level may be inconsistent with efficient industrywide response. For example, by responding as best it can, a firm may unduly prolong its life and make it more difficult for authorities to close it down. This may have occurred in the case of the Shenyang Smelter, which faced a sellers' market rather than a buyers' market, however (Byrd 1985b, 85–86).

Another local government response to a weak market has been protection of producers from outside competition. This is most commonly implemented by ordering local users and commercial units to buy only from local producers, even if these cannot meet outside competition in terms of price, quality, and so forth. Sample firms have benefited little from this kind of protectionism, but in a number of cases they suffered from protectionist behavior by local governments, their own or others. The Mindong Electrical Machinery Corporation faced severe difficulties in expanding its sales network to other provinces or even to other parts of its home province of Fujian. The No. 2 Auto Plant faced resistance from some local governments to mergers it proposed with smaller truck factories. In addition to being pressured to buy spindles and textile equipment from local sources rather than from Shanghai, the Northwest No. 1 State Cotton Textile Mill for a time was ordered not to ship any gray cloth out of Shaanxi Province, to ensure that local printing and dyeing plants would run at close to capacity.

Internal protectionism places obstacles in the path of dynamic, expanding firms trying to move into regional markets outside their home area and holds back enterprises in backward regions by forcing them to buy high-priced, poor-quality locally made goods. Protectionism also impedes backward enterprises by insulating them from competition that would force them to make improvements in order to survive and develop. More generally, it results in fragmented markets with consequent loss of efficiency gains from free trade and economies of scale. Finally, protectionism slows adjustment to market forces and exit of inefficient producers.

All in all, government intervention for the most part has not succeeded in transforming a buyers' market back into a sellers' market. In some respects, government responses have served to intensify the situation (e.g., slow and insufficient price adjustments); in others, they have dampened the impact (production or investment controls, internal protectionism). But one type of government action can immediately reverse a buyers' market situation: a sharp increase in government-financed investment or in government approvals of investment projects can cause a buyers' market for investment goods and intermediate inputs to be rapidly eliminated and replaced by a brisk sellers' market. This happened in China in 1982 and especially in 1983–84. Easing of credit policy, by increasing effective investment demand, also can quickly cause a buyers' market to revert to a sellers' market. Loose credit policy was a driving force behind the investment boom of late 1984 and early 1985. Government-mandated increases in investment activity, however, are not necessarily a direct response to the buyers' market. There may be some linkage, but it is rather tenuous: the government may see the buyers' market for investment goods as evidence that the economy can absorb increased investment without overheating, or, less likely, investment may be increased partly as a means of easing the difficulties of producers hard-hit by the buyers' market.

Patterns of Market Competition and Price Adjustments

In China in the early 1980s, overt price competition in many industries was restricted by price controls, even though in buyers' markets there was downward pressure on prices. Price discrimination based on demand features was taboo, though price differentiation based on supply considerations (cost of production, within-plan versus above-plan output, and so on) was often permitted. Despite these obstacles, firms facing a persistent buyers' market had strong incentives to find ways to reduce the "effective price" of their output in order to compete successfully, commonly by offering improved quality for the same price. (This contrasts with the disguised quality deterioration that is pervasive in a persistent sellers' market.) Changing brand names may accomplish the same result, as in the case of the Chongqing Clock and Watch Company (Byrd and Tidrick 1984, 55). Illegal price reductions may also be resorted to, sometimes with the connivance or at least tacit agreement of local authorities. These kinds of activities are hard to prevent, particularly if producers can pass the burden of lower prices on to the government through lower profit taxes or profit remittances.

Chinese enterprises have become increasingly free to engage in nonprice competition, which can be beneficial in improving the efficiency and flexibility of the economic system. Many sample firms made substantial improvements at the micro level in responding to the exigencies of a buyers' market with nonprice competitive measures. The Jiangmen Nanfang Foodstuff Plant's development of new products and varieties, the Qingdao Forging Machinery Plant's major shift of product mix, and the Chongqing Clock and Watch Company's new product development and quality improvement are particularly striking examples but by no means the only ones.

Competition in International Trade: The Parallels

Interregional competition may well be the most important form of competition in Chinese state-owned industry. Local competition between major firms situated close to each other is likely to be severely limited. In the first place, local governments would generally not set up or encourage more than one major producer of the same commodity within a small area. If there are several producers, they are probably under different government agencies, so their distribution channels may be compartmentalized and largely insulated from each other.[19] Finally, if there are a number of potentially competing producers in a single province or region, all under provincial or lower-level jurisdiction, authorities can intervene to limit competition by dividing up the market. The strength of any competition between state enterprises and local, small, nonstate firms depends on the degree to which technical and other conditions are suitable for small-scale production.

A second major feature of the landscape is that local and provincial governments maintain considerable control over industry and trade in their jurisdictions. Their objectives include fostering local or regional industrialization and increasing revenues.[20] To further these goals, they have tried to protect "their" industry from outside competition. This protection can influence investment decisions as well, since governments will be tempted to invest in high-profit industries in protected local markets.

Given these features of China's economic system, the main form of competition in Chinese industry (interregional competition) may be more akin to competition in international trade than to competition within well-integrated national markets. This has some interesting implications. Barriers to interregional trade erected by local and provincial governments may have been the most serious obstacle to the development of competition and resulting benefits. The danger of collusion and anticompetitive arrangements by firms was probably relatively small in the early 1980s.

Another similarity with competition in international trade is the importance of establishing distribution networks in "foreign" markets, particularly in the case of differentiated products. The Mindong Electrical Machinery Corporation had to do this to expand sales in other provinces and even in other parts of its home province of Fujian. Mindong's retail outlets in different parts of the country typically involved a joint venture or association with a commercial unit located in the market area being penetrated. Local governments in these areas understood what was happening and often tried to disrupt Mindong's establishment of sales outlets.[21] Other kinds of joint ventures and associations, including those involving production, often had the objective of gaining footholds in new markets or maintaining position in existing markets.[22]

Still another analogy with competition in international trade is the difficulty of exit from industries where the country or region suffers from a comparative disadvantage. Exit from an entire industry as a result of international competition may be more strongly resisted than exit of some firms from an industry in the process of domestic competition. If some but not all local producers are shut down, there may be no loss of local government revenue or local employment if the rest of them take up the slack, but shutting down the only local producer means "export" of the local government revenues earned by it and loss of local employment opportunities. In China there is more often than not only one major local producer, so its exit from the scene would imply the eradication of the local industry and hence would be resisted by the local government. Finally, local government control over industry and trade implies at least some ability to protect local enterprises, particularly those in extremis.

While the similarities between competition in Chinese industry and competition in international trade lead to pessimistic conclusions in many respects, there are some grounds for hope, based on the possibility of growing intra-industry trade involving competition among producers of differentiated products, leading to changing niches and market shares rather than widespread specialization by region and industry. This type of competition has important benefits and would appear to be feasible in China. Of course it is more appropriate for some products than for others, and it cannot work for commodities where differential regional resource endowments play the critical role (e.g., in coal mining or nonferrous metals production). The analogy with international trade suggests that mutuality in lowering barriers to interregional trade in China is quite important; there may be room for gradual, coordinated lowering of barriers to allow local and regional adjustments to take place reasonably smoothly.

Price Pressures and Adjustments

The interaction among market forces, price determination, and enterprise response is crucial. One issue is the degree of responsiveness of Chinese state-owned industrial firms to changing output and input prices. Sample firms facing a sellers' market were very responsive to relative profitability considerations in decisions on product mix, to the extent that they were not constrained by product mix targets.[23] Reforms emphasizing the importance of profits and weaker external controls over product mix undoubtedly strengthened this tendency. The Xiangxiang Cement Plant stopped producing lower grades of cement, which were less profitable. The Shenyang Smelter, given the freedom to produce grade 1 or grade 2 electrolytic zinc, produced only the former, since it carried a higher price and unit costs were about the same. Insufficient price differentials for quality led other firms to avoid production of better-quality goods.

Lack of responsiveness to input prices also is evident. Though many sample firms complained about price increases for key inputs obtained outside the plan, they were not easily deterred from such transactions. With distorted prices, production was often profitable even with higher prices for inputs. Moreover, firms could to a large extent avoid the impact of high input prices by exchanging their products for the inputs required, valuing both at low state-set prices. But enterprises did turn down chances to buy high-priced inputs on the market if they would incur losses as a result.

When market conditions shifted from excess demand to excess supply, enterprises became much more responsive to quantity signals on the output side. But at the same time they remained sensitive to relative profitability. Indeed, since reforms emphasizing profits occurred roughly at the same time as the emergence of buyers' markets, enterprise responsiveness to both price and quantity signals on the output side probably increased.

When price and quantity signals conflicted (products in demand were less profitable ones), the degree to which firms gave priority to profitability considerations depended on the tautness and firmness of their profit targets as well as the degree of ease with which they could sell their more profitable products. If the enterprise had to sell the bulk of its output on the market, and if its profit targets were not strictly enforced, quantity signals would tend to dominate price signals in decisions on product mix. For example, the Nanning Silk and Linen Textile Mill was forced to shift production toward more profitable varieties only in 1983, when its profit target became very firm after two successive sharp yearly declines in realized profits.

On the input side, if there is continuing shortage, price responsiveness may remain weak, as long as production continues to be profitable. If the market for inputs has also turned weak, enterprises naturally will strive to obtain lower prices. The Chongqing Clock and Watch Company intended to force suppliers of components for its products to accept lower prices, hoping by this means to increase its own profits.

The extent and speed with which government authorities adjust prices in response to changing market conditions is an important factor. There has been some responsiveness of government-set prices to market conditions, but only with a lag, which in some cases was very long. Watch prices were reduced a number of times in 1980–84, but the reductions were too late and too small to prevent growing excess supply at the national level. The textile price adjustment of early 1983 occurred at least a year after industrywide problems with excess supply of synthetic textiles became apparent. Instituting official price increases for goods in excess demand has been even more difficult. Prices of many "basic goods" have been held down, and examples of administrative price increases that completely cleared the market are rare indeed.[24] Even the 60 percent increase in state cement prices in January 1986 may not have cleared the market (see chapter 9).

Government resistance against price reductions for goods in excess supply has been based mainly on fears about the effect on budgetary revenues. Reduced enterprise profits due to lower output prices would mean lower profit tax payments or profit remittances to the government, through reductions in profit taxation, adjustments in indirect taxes, etc. Resistance against price increases has been sparked by similar fears about the impact on users (in the case of producer goods) and concerns about inflation (in the case of consumer goods or inputs into consumer goods). Price increases could easily get passed on, and in the case of investment goods would also have a harmful impact on the budget—the amount of "real" investment possible with given nominal budget funds would be reduced. Inevitable leakages would mean that the government could not, for example, recoup its revenue losses due to a price reduction from the higher profits of users of the good concerned.

All sample firms produced goods subject to price control, yet most of them formally or informally had some role in setting prices.[25] But enterprise pricing decisions, even when freely made, could be a source of rigidity. Willingness to lower prices depended largely on the perceived ability to have profit remittance targets lowered to compensate for the loss of enterprise revenue. On the other side, some firms did not raise prices or did not raise them by the full amount allowed, even in a strong sellers' market, perhaps in part due to a desire to avoid criticism for price gouging.

There has been a basic asymmetry in price pressures and adjustments as between a buyers' market and a sellers' market, particularly in the scope of changes. In the face of excess supply, buyers exerted downward price pressure on the total supply of the good concerned. Buyers could almost always refuse purchases if they considered the price too high, since they could get the goods at a lower price from another source. In the case of consumer goods, an individual's choice not to purchase is usually entirely free. But even in the case of producer goods, firms for the most part could refuse to buy items they did not need, which could often be a cover for refusal on the grounds of excessively high price.[26] On the supply side, as has been seen, producers were often willing to cut prices in order to sell their products, provided that they could also reduce profit taxes and remittances to the government.

Price pressures in a situation of excess demand were felt differently. There was no pressure from buyers with access to supplies to raise prices; on the contrary, they strongly preferred that prices be held down. Would-be purchasers without access to supplies at the controlled price or with insufficient plan allocations were willing to pay market prices, however. Thus, buyers did not mind a dual-price system when there was excess demand at the plan price, though there must have been conflicts over which ones obtained supply allocations at the plan price.[27] Producers would prefer that the price of total supply be raised but nevertheless felt that a dual-price system was better than being forced to sell all output at the controlled price. Under these circumstances, a two-tier pricing system has emerged. The two-tier system, its impact, and its evolution are discussed in chapter 9.

In sum, upward pressures on prices could be partly accommodated by maintaining low within-quota prices and higher (often virtually market-determined) prices at the margin, whereas downward price pressures usually could be relieved only by a general price reduction. Indeed, in the sample there are no examples of differentiation between plan and above-plan prices for goods in excess supply. On the other hand, even before 1984–85 nearly all sample firms facing a sellers' market were in industries with multiple pricing. Larger enterprises, however, commonly were forced to sell all of their output at the low state price, while smaller plants could get a higher price for all output (based on their higher costs).

Dynamic Trends and Performance

So far this chapter has looked primarily at static patterns of response and interactions. It remains to analyze the dynamic adjustments that have occurred. Changes in market conditions may be caused by government and/or enterprise actions; the new market situation in turn affects enterprise behavior; the two together (new market conditions and enterprise response) may then engender a response by the government; this will have an impact on market conditions and on firms' response; and so on. Dynamic aspects are crucial since they determine whether a prevailing sellers' market can be transformed into a buyers' market, and whether a buyers' market will be longlasting or only temporary.

Consumer Goods

One kind of dynamic adjustment pattern is exemplified by the Chinese watch industry in 1979–83, and by the Chongqing Clock and Watch Company in particular. In a highly profitable industry given priority access to investment resources and for which raw material constraints are relatively unimportant, producers, supported by local governments and supervisory agencies, will engage in the expansion response. New producers may also enter the industry. As a result, total supply will grow rapidly, meeting and then surpassing demand. Even if material inputs are in short supply, as in the case of grain and sugar for the Jiangmen Nanfang Foodstuffs Plant, their diversion from other uses may allow the expansion response to occur anyway.

The government's response to the emerging buyers' market is crucial. In the case of watches, despite some lagged downward adjustments, prices remained too high to stimulate demand sharply or to discourage producers; investment ceilings also were only partly successful. Most important, producers were not insulated from the market; commercial units were not forced to procure all watches produced, which put the burden of making sales on producers, at least at the margin. Under these conditions, firms became very responsive to customer needs and competition became heated, including both price competition (to some extent overt but largely disguised in the case of watches) and various kinds of nonprice competition.

This pattern was followed in many consumer-durables industries, though perhaps not in as extreme form as in the case of watches. In 1984–85 these industries were commonly characterized by incipient or actual oversupply of ordinary, low-quality brands, alongside severe shortages of a few of the best national brands and imports. In quantitative terms, the bulk of domestic production faced a buyers' market.

Dynamic adjustment in the textile industry followed a broadly similar route. Prices of synthetic textiles were very high at the outset; moreover, the textile industry received priority allocation of resources in line with national policies promoting rapid growth of consumption. In 1982 a nationwide buyers' market emerged, which was felt to varying degrees by all sample textile plants. After building up enormous inventories, commercial units were allowed to refuse to purchase all or part of factory output. Attempts to impose production ceilings on different localities and factories did not eliminate the buyers' market. In early 1983 a major adjustment in the prices of textiles and textile raw materials was instituted, which appears to have been successful in largely eliminating the great differences in prices and profitability between synthetics and cotton textiles. But even after 1983 there was still a buyers' market for most textiles, with discriminating customers choosing on the basis of quality, color, styling, and other attributes rather than solely on availability and price.

These examples suggest that adequate profitability and access to financial resources may be prerequisites for the emergence of a buyers' market in consumer goods. The impact of market conditions for material inputs is harder to gauge. In the case of textiles, chemical fiber production was very profitable, and large imports were permitted. Large imports of cotton also occurred, but even more important, cotton prices were raised sharply in the late 1970s to stimulate domestic production. The textile firms in the sample had great difficulties in obtaining raw materials of the right quality and specifications, however, in part because of continuing administrative control over cotton and synthetic fiber supplies. These problems did not prevent them from moving into an "intensive" response to the new market situation.

Investment Goods

The transition to a buyers' market for investment goods and intermediate inputs typically resulted from a reduction in demand due to a cutback in government budgetary investment. This caused a decline in orders for capital goods from users with plan allocations and from the material supply system. The impact of the buyers' market on producers was felt more quickly than in the case of consumer goods. The sharp cutback in central government budgetary investment in 1981 temporarily generated excess supply of certain goods which have been chronically in short supply before and since, such as copper.

Initial government response was the same as in the case of consumer goods: producers were left to fend for themselves. Many machinery plants, such as the Qingdao Forging Machinery Plant, had to sell the bulk of their output directly. The Mindong Electrical Machinery Corporation became responsible for virtually all sales. Even the Anshan Iron and Steel Company had to sell 14 percent of its rolled steel output directly in 1981. For machinery and electrical equipment as a whole, the bulk of procurement by the material supply system occurred outside of directive plans in the early 1980s.

The government may have been somewhat more willing to let prices of producer goods float downward. Lower prices did not mean automatic government revenue losses, since lower profits for producers could be offset by higher profits for users or lower costs of investment goods paid for by the state budget. But perhaps sensing that demand was fairly price-inelastic, firms have been reluctant to cut prices as a means of stimulating demand in a weak market. If the cause of the buyers' market was a cut in government-financed investment, price reductions alone were unlikely to clear the market.

A major factor in market trends for intermediate goods and investment goods was the emergence of new sources of demand that partly offset the decline in budget-financed investment. The dynamic rural nonstate industrial sector had a large thirst for investment goods as it expanded rapidly in the late 1970s and early 1980s. The products needed by these smaller firms usually had different specifications and characteristics from those sold to state enterprises earlier, so producers often faced excess supply for their "old" products and had to adjust product mix to produce goods in demand.[28]

The staying power of a buyers' market for investment goods and intermediate inputs depends greatly on central government investment demand and on money and credit policies. After major cutbacks in 1980–81, capital construction investment started to revive in late 1981, as investment by enterprises and local authorities increased rapidly; budgetary investment then rose sharply in 1983, which more than offset stabilization of decentralized investment through administrative controls. In 1984, budgetary and other investment both increased greatly, due in part to looser credit policy.

The revival of investment demand had an almost immediate effect on market conditions for basic intermediate goods, which had briefly suffered from excess supply in 1981. The sellers' market for rolled steel had returned in full force by 1983, while the Shenyang Smelter had major problems with excess supply of copper for only a few months in 1981. In engineering industries, experience has been more varied; the sellers' market for trucks returned quickly in 1982, but machinery producers in the sample still faced a rather weak market in 1983. The number of producers of ordinary machinery remained so large that even a sharp increase in demand could be accommodated. Higher profits on machinery and equipment than for many basic process industries may also have been a factor. With the gradual liberalization of policies on imports of machinery and equipment, users often preferred to buy imported equipment because of its superior quality and reliability, despite much higher prices. Machinery markets probably strengthened considerably with continuing inflationary pressures and high investment demand in the mid-1980s.

Conditions for Emergence and Durability of Buyers' Markets

Under what conditions does a buyers' market emerge, and under what conditions is it sustainable over the long run? The former seems to require that production be reasonably profitable and that resources be made available for expansion (which happened in the case of consumer durables), or that demand be cut back enough to match or fall short of supply (intermediate goods in 1981), or a combination of both (possibly machinery).

Sustainability of a buyers' market does not appear to have been a serious problem for many industrial consumer goods; demand is to some extent inherently limited by goods' characteristics and consumers' preferences. Moreover, consumer goods continued to receive some priority in resource allocation, and profits on many goods remained high enough to attract new entrants. Wage inflation in the mid- to late 1980s, however, may have put considerable pressure on markets for consumer goods.

On the other hand, a revival of investment demand, financed by the budget, credit, enterprise retained funds, or all three, can quickly cause reversion to a sellers' market for investment goods and intermediate inputs into investment goods. The sharp decline in investment demand of 1980–81 was simply not sustainable.

Thus, the buyers' market for investment goods and intermediate inputs is much more fragile than the buyers' market for consumer goods. In the twenty-firm sample there is no clear-cut case of a buyers' market for consumer goods reverting back to excess demand, but this happened for two producers of intermediate goods (the Shenyang Smelter and the Anshan Iron and Steel Company) and one producer of investment goods (the No. 2 Auto Plant). Sharp cutbacks in investment are likely to be only temporary, part of cyclical swings. Nevertheless, it may be possible for a buyers' market to "stick," particularly if there are large numbers of producers with slack capacity and if entry is relatively easy (as in the case possibly of ordinary machinery).

Do some of the beneficial behavior patterns "learned" by enterprises facing a buyers' market stay with them even when conditions revert to excess demand? A similar question can be asked about institutional arrangements like direct marketing by producers. Not surprisingly, when market conditions revert to excess demand, commercial agencies or material supply authorities try to retake control over product sales from firms. But enterprises resist this tendency, since direct marketing in a sellers' market confers important benefits. Because of inertia, their existing high share of self-sales, and stated reform objectives of greater enterprise autonomy, firms have been in a better position to do so than they were in trying to expand direct marketing in the original sellers' market situation. The Anshan Iron and Steel Company's share of self-sales of rolled steel dropped only from 14 percent in 1981 to 10 percent in 1983, when it amounted to a substantial 540,000 tons. The No. 2 Auto Plant was able to hold onto the right to market directly about one-sixth of its total truck output in 1983, despite a series of bitter disputes with the State Material Supply Bureau over this issue. This partial retention of direct marketing rights by firms even after the return of a sellers' market is probably typical of Chinese industry as a whole.

It is more difficult to ascertain whether there has been continuity in enterprise behavior patterns. The No. 2 Auto Plant continued to exhibit customer-oriented behavior even after 1982. But this factory is among the most entrepreneurial in the sample and not typical of Chinese state-owned industry as a whole. The Anshan Iron and Steel Company, on the other hand, closed its "retail shop," at which steel had been sold in small quantities, primarily to smaller firms. It also stopped engaging in sales promotion, whereas in 1981 it had sent people all over the country to find buyers.

Given the "investment hunger" characteristic of centrally planned economies dominated by state ownership, for investment demand to be restrained—thereby preserving the buyers' market for investment goods and intermediate inputs into investment goods—central planners must exercise great self-discipline in limiting their approvals of large new capital construction projects, restricting total budgetary spending on investment, and controlling investment by lower levels in the economic system. To a considerable degree, Chinese central planners and policy makers made the shift in orientation from production and growth to efficiency and consumption starting in 1979. At the national level, production and investment plans have generally been quite slack and have been overfulfilled by large margins.

There were also strong forces limiting budget-financed investment spending in the early 1980s. The commitment to increase consumption levels was implemented largely through wage increases, which reduced enterprise profit remittances to the budget, and subsidies, which constituted a prior claim on the budget. There was also a great aversion to budgetary instability, shown by sharp reductions in expenditures and budget deficits in 1980–81. These factors combined to generate strong built-in limits on budgetary investment expenditure, at least through 1982. Concerns about the price and availability of investment goods led to imposition of direct controls over investment financed by local governments and enterprises. Tight credit also played a major role in this regard. The net result was to maintain a buyers' market for many investment goods in China through 1982.

After 1983, however, budget-financed investment once again boomed, as revenue constraints were eased by enhanced control over subsidies and a 10 percent (soon raised to 15 percent) levy on extrabudgetary incomes of firms and local governments. Weak control over credit in late 1984 and early 1985 was even more important in exacerbating demand pressures. The rapid growth of industrial production in 1983–85 tightened market conditions for intermediate goods and investment goods. Another problem was that the cost of capital to enterprises remained low (Byrd and Tidrick 1987). As a result, firms had little financial incentive to economize on their use of capital and hence maintained high latent demand.

Even if strong at the outset, the self-discipline of central planners is likely to be eroded over time. This is particularly true if, as in the case of China, tight control over budget-financed investment is largely nullified by an investment boom undertaken by local governments and firms. Thus, central restrictions only reduce the central share of total investment, creating even greater difficulties in controlling aggregate investment in the future.

One interesting feature of the situation in China is that the "suction" effect, whereby excess demand for investment goods pulls resources away from production of consumer goods, exacerbating shortages of the latter (see Kornai 1980, chap. 21), has been limited and kept within bounds. Buyers' markets for many types of consumer goods were rather robust even in a situation of strong investment demand. Aside from the continuing priority given by authorities to expanding production of consumer goods, the high profitability of many consumer goods and the orientation of enterprises toward promoting workers' interests may in part explain this phenomenon. Another factor has already been mentioned: inherent limitations on demand for many specific varieties of consumer goods.

Socialist Markets and Economic Performance

How important is the buyers' market in improving economic efficiency and performance, and what obstacles impede it from fully playing the role ascribed to well-functioning markets in a capitalist economy? The problems of measuring efficiency at the enterprise level are formidable, while linking changes in performance to different possible explanatory factors is even more difficult. Moreover, the relationship between enterprise performance and industrywide or economy-wide performance is by no means unambiguous. Measured performance is likely to deteriorate when a firm faces a buyers' market, even though it may be taking strenuous measures to respond to demand and maintain sales. Prices may be soft in a buyers' market, but in any case the enterprise's efforts to promote sales, alter product mix, develop new products, and improve quality will almost certainly raise costs. Burgeoning inventories as producers take on commercial roles are another factor causing deterioration in performance.

Not surprisingly, profitability has declined for most sample firms facing a buyers' market. But quantitative indicators by no means tell the whole story. The strong measures by many enterprises to respond to nonquantitative aspects of demand, strikingly different from the behavior of firms facing a sellers' market, must weigh heavily in any evaluation. The benefits to consumers and users are far greater in a buyers' market, starting with ready availability of the goods concerned but also including improved quality, a closer match of product characteristics with customer needs, better warranties and postsale services, and downward pressures on prices.

Set against these advantages are certain costs. The most obvious one is the cost of excess capacity and forgone production. This has been exacerbated in China by the slow, even perverse, adjustment of production structure to a weak market—exit is impeded, while profitability continues to attract new entrants who may not have been aware of the situation when investment decisions were being made or who hope to operate in protected local markets. But excess capacity in industries facing a weak market does free up supplies of intermediate goods in short supply (steel, electricity, etc.) for use in production of other goods that enjoy a sellers' market.

The problem of excess capacity may be symptomatic of more serious difficulties with medium-term adjustment to a buyers' market. As noted in chapter 2, capitalist firms in industrialized market economies typically maintain a certain level of inventories and even excess capacity as part of a competitive strategy that puts high priority on always being able to meet customer demand. In China's buyers' markets, on the other hand, industrywide excess capacity has been largely the unintended result of numerous investment decisions by "investment-hungry" investors. The magnitude of excess capacity and high inventories in some industries in China may well be a sign of inefficient, slow adjustment to market forces, as opposed to a moderate, "normal" degree of slack to meet unexpected surges in demand.

A number of obstacles that weaken the beneficial impact of buyers' markets in a centrally planned economy can be identified. The extreme difficulty of closing down state-owned enterprises is a critical one, which is damaging to incentives, efficiency, and economic performance. Just as harmful are the government behavior patterns engendered: cartel-like market sharing or investment control arrangements instituted by the central government, easing of credit to enterprises in trouble to keep them in business, or "internal protectionism" by local governments. If adjustment to a buyers' market has to occur subject to a binding constraint that no state enterprise can be closed down, it will be slow, inefficient, and wasteful.

Another feature of the Chinese situation has been the lack of pressure on firms to reduce costs, even in a buyers' market characterized by vigorous competition in other spheres (including price cutting). This is due to weak enterprise financial discipline—the burden of declining profits has usually been passed on to the government budget in the form of reduced profit remittances. A squeeze on profits, therefore, may not generate much pressure to cut costs, and a major benefit of well-functioning markets in a capitalist economy is lost.[29] This suggests that a combination of buyers' markets and relatively firm enterprise profit targets may generate better incentives than weak markets but slack and manipulable profit targets.

Finally, lags in price changes inhibit industrywide adjustment to a buyers' market, though they may "intensify" response at the enterprise level. If output prices are high enough for most firms to earn substantial profits, in a shortage situation price and quantity signals are mutually consistent in calling for increases in production. If a buyers' market emerges and prices are not adjusted downward, price and quantity signals become contradictory. Existing firms will be encouraged to expand, and new entrants will be attracted to the industry by high prices and profits, but quantity signals will accurately reflect the weak market situation. This may lead to uneven, slow, and possibly perverse industrywide adjustment.

A general picture of what happens in buyers' markets in a centrally planned economy can now be drawn, based on the experience of Chinese industry and that of the twenty sample firms in particular. The situation is unambiguously better than in the case of chronic sellers' markets. Customers are better served, product quality is improved, and new products become available over time. But the improvements associated with buyers' markets are limited in important ways by certain features of the institutional environment. These obstacles prevent many advantages of well-functioning markets from being realized, even if buyers' markets could be preserved for a long enough period of time to have an impact. The very survival of buyers' markets is in doubt for investment goods and intermediate inputs.

5. The Redistributional Role of Chinese Economic Planning

THE MODERN, predominantly state-owned sector of China's economy exhibits many similarities to the traditional model of a centrally planned economy. The Chinese system, however, departed somewhat from this model even before the late 1970s. Subsequent reforms have accentuated and transformed these differences, to the point where the Chinese system took on some unique features with rather different implications for economic behavior and performance. This chapter examines the Chinese production planning system and the closely associated systems of compulsory procurement of output and administrative allocation of material inputs and energy—the heart of a traditional centrally planned economy—where the Chinese system exhibits some profound departures.

It will be argued that Chinese planning has come to play only a limited role in the direct allocation of resources and in mobilizing resources and effort through plan-based incentive schemes. Markets have become important in directing resource allocation (see chapter 3), and profit incentives largely independent of production planning have come to the fore. Chinese planning remains important primarily because it generates and redistributes large rents embodied in goods subject to administrative allocation through the planning and material supply and commercial systems at low, state-set prices. The primarily redistributional role of planning, the multiple pricing practices that have emerged, and the increasing importance of the market mechanism and profit motive have some interesting implications.

The Chinese Planning System

China's industrial production and product distribution planning system has the following main features:[1]

1. It is not comprehensive at any level of government; substantial portions of the total supply of nearly all goods are produced and allocated outside the central plan. Different levels of government have their own compartmentalized, insulated plans, as part of the fragmented, "cellular" structure of economic administration (Donnithorne 1972; Lyons 1986).

2. It is also not comprehensive in terms of its coverage of industrial products.

The bulk of goods, accounting for a substantial share of industrial output, are not subject to plan control by the central government.

3. Chinese planning is highly aggregated, covering a much smaller number of products than in the Soviet Union. Plan targets and quotas hence must be disaggregated into operational directives for production.

4. Planning is a bargaining process, with strong tendencies toward "planning from the achieved level" or similar bureaucratic compromises.

5. Planning is subject to a number of timing problems which, for example, force some input allocations to be made before production plans are set. Final targets are often promulgated late in the plan year, by which time production is largely determined.

The Chinese planning system differs from those of other real-world centrally planned economies in the degree to which these features are present. In the Soviet Union as well, planning has been a bargaining process, targets are relatively aggregated, and there are channels for obtaining inputs outside the plan. "Market" transactions in the USSR, however, appear in most cases to have involved diversion of goods originally produced within the plan to extra-plan channels. In China, by contrast, most goods transacted outside the plan are produced outside of plan channels as well. Though undoubtedly there have been timing and bargaining problems in the USSR, these appear to have been more serious in China, where the "command system" had taken hold much more weakly.

As in other centrally planned economies, production planning in China has been closely linked to compulsory procurement of output at low administratively fixed prices, for subsequent allocation through the state material supply and commercial systems. In the traditional central planning system, all output is procured in this manner and hence the distribution plan only implements or operationalizes the production plan. But in China the system has evolved differently. Production planning is multilevel, with the central plan covering only a fraction of total production of most goods (see table 3.1). A considerable share of the centrally planned portion of supplies is turned over to provinces and ministries for further, detailed allocation.[2] Partial central government control over the distribution of outputs means incomplete control over the allocation of key inputs to users. Allocation authority is held by a number of separate, often competing organizations, ranging from the State Planning Commission to central ministries, provinces, local governments, and enterprises. Mandatory production planning thus has become linked with compulsory allocation of output and is profoundly influenced by the latter, while the two are generally (though incompletely and with considerable uncertainty) linked to allocation of low-priced inputs through the supply plan. So the order of importance of production planning, output distribution, and input allocation is profoundly different from what it is in the traditional centrally planned economy.

Multitiered production planning in China is accompanied by multiple pricing. By the early 1980s only a small number of goods, such as standard lathes, watches, and certain kinds of high-quality steel, had one price set by the central government that applied to all output.[3] Some goods, such as coal and electricity, had prices set by the national government, but with different prices for different parts of the country. For most important producer and consumer goods the price set by the central government only covered a part of total supply, often surprisingly small. The relatively low state-set price of cement, for instance, applied to only about ten large plants in the early 1980s. The state price of caustic soda covered only thirty-odd large factories; that of soda ash, only five producers. Pricing of the remainder of total supply of most producer goods ranged from strict control at the provincial level to looser control at lower levels and to market pricing at the margin. Occasionally, attempts were made to institute stricter price controls for certain important producer goods, but these failed or were superseded by subsequent liberalization, or were subverted by exchange and other similar arrangements.

The linkage among production plan targets, compulsory delivery of output, allocation of inputs, and price controls is often tenuous and uncertain. Price controls for some goods may cover a larger proportion of total supply than is allocated through the central plan, while some goods produced under "local" control may be brought into the central plan through purchases and resales at high prices. All the linkages are subject to bargaining.

The number of goods allocated through the central plan in China has been small as compared with the Soviet Union. In 1981 the number of Category I goods allocated directly by the State Planning Commission and State Material Supply Bureau was only 256; combined with the 581 products subject to allocation by central ministries (Category II), the total was only 837 (Zhu Rongji 1985, 291). Yet this was the highest figure ever achieved in the history of the People's Republic of China; in 1957, at the height of the First Five-Year Plan period, the total number of Category I and II goods was only 532. In the 1980s, the number of industrial producer goods actually allocated by the central government fell sharply. In 1985, reportedly only 23 of the 256 Category I products were actually subject to material balancing and allocation through the central plan (Ling 1986, 2).

The relatively small number of centrally planned goods in China partly reflects narrower coverage by the plan, but it is also due to a higher degree of aggregation in planning. The most extreme example is coal, which is allocated through the central plan as a single commodity, even though there are numerous types, grades, and specifications of coal with different uses. Rolled steel also counts as a single commodity for central planning purposes, though it is divided into fifteen subcategories when targets are given to enterprises.[4] This relatively high degree of aggregation of plans is also evident at the enterprise level. The Chongqing Clock and Watch Company had two physical output targets, one for total output of watches, one for total output of clocks. There was no attempt through the production planning mechanism to influence product mix choices by the enterprise within these two very broad product categories. Other enterprises also had rather aggregated production plan targets (see Tidrick 1987).

Product mix tended to be specified more finely by commercial or material supply agencies procuring an enterprise's output under the plan, but this typically involved bargaining between producers and users or commercial intermediaries rather than a hierarchical formal planning process. Moreover, finer specification of product mix by procurement agencies has become increasingly related to market influences, since commercial intermediaries have become more concerned about their ability to sell the goods they purchase.

Because production planning and particularly the allocation of key inputs to users are subject to pervasive bargaining, with planners appearing to rely heavily on "planning from the achieved level," planning has become a blunt instrument for affecting resource allocation. Planning based on past performance can become virtually irrelevant in a situation where enterprise production is highly variable. An example of how ridiculous this can be when the market situation faced by a firm is changing rapidly is the Chongqing Clock and Watch Company. In 1983 it made its own plans to produce 1–1.2 million watches and no more than 300,000 clocks, based on the market situation. Authorities, planning largely on the basis of previous performance, assigned it targets of 900,000 watches and 500,000 clocks, which it ignored (see Byrd and Tidrick 1984, 27).

Central plan allocations to major users appear to be very scattered, resulting in higher transport costs and great inconvenience. For example, twenty-four of China's twenty-nine provinces were supposed to provide Anhui Province with rolled steel through the central plan in the first half of 1982. Only 50 percent of the total supplied was to come from factories within Anhui Province or from nearby provinces (compared to 75 percent in 1981). Some distant suppliers were supposed to send Anhui tiny shipments of one ton or so, whereas the major steel plant located in the province was to send large amounts of output to other provinces in accordance with the central plan (Zhu and Wen 1983). The only reasonable explanation for this highly inefficient distribution pattern is that central planning has been a bargaining process with distribution rather than optimization or efficient production as its main focus.

The Shenyang Smelter provides another illuminating example. A large user of copper, the Shenyang Cable Factory, was located almost next door to the Shenyang Smelter. Yet the smelter supplied virtually no copper to the cable factory as part of the central plan. Instead, the latter received large plan shipments from distant Yunnan Province, while the smelter sent large amounts of plan-allocated copper to Heilongjiang Province as well as even more distant locations. Apparently the reason behind this irrational spatial pattern was the desire of planning authorities to achieve a "fair" distribution of transport costs among major copper users (interview information, June 1987).

Another problem concerns timing. Production and profit plan targets are often promulgated well into the plan year, much later than initial material supply allocations, which must be set well before the beginning of the year. The latter therefore become mere guesses as to future needs—or, as will be argued later, the mechanism for redistributing rents embodied in low-priced goods—while the system runs for a good part of the year without any formal production plan in place. Some input plans also come in late, like the Shenyang Smelter's allocations of imported copper ore and blister, aggravating supply management problems (see Byrd 1985b, 8).

Prereform Antecedents and Evolution

China's multitiered planning, supply, and distribution system already existed in embryonic form in the 1960s and developed considerably in the 1970s. The emergence of a substantial locally run industrial sector was related to the Cultural Revolution "industrial province" policy and the development of the "five small industries" (iron and steel, chemical fertilizer, cement, agricultural machinery, and hydropower), which were largely under county jurisdiction (see Wong 1986, 574–76). Production planning, supply, and output distribution for these plants increasingly came to be controlled at the provincial or subprovincial level, though there was a substantial infusion of central government investment financing during much of the Cultural Revolution decade.[5]

A key development was the practice of letting goods be subject to allocation by the government entity that established, financed, and controlled their producer, which came to apply even to the most important producer goods. As a result, central government control over flows of these goods was weakened, and local governments gained considerable power, as well as strong incentives to build up local producer goods industries. Though multilevel production planning and allocation control did not change the administrative character of industrial management in prereform China, they did loosen the system somewhat from central control.

Another major source of decentralization in the Chinese planning system was the transfer of administrative jurisdiction over most large, nationally important enterprises to provincial and local control in the early 1970s. These included the Anshan Iron and Steel Company, Daqing Oilfield, the No. 1 Motor Vehicle Plant, and the Shenyang Smelter. But for many of these firms, administrative decentralization of control meant very little except in the financial sphere—profits previously remitted to the central government were instead turned over to local or provincial governments. Their supply problems were too complex for local or provincial authorities to handle, and in any case the central government wished to retain control over the allocation of their output. Hence, production, input allocation, and output distribution remained to a large extent under the control of central ministries.[6] Nevertheless, the decentralization of administrative and financial control over large enterprises must have enhanced provincial and local government access to their products somewhat.

Weakening of central government price controls appears to have accompanied the decentralization of planning and allocation. Cost-based multiple pricing emerged as a response to widely differing unit costs among firms of different sizes, which used different technologies to make the same product. This allowed small, backward, and high-cost producers, which had proliferated, to make profits or at least break even, while the profits of the larger, more advanced enterprises could be held within limits. Provinces were permitted to institute higher "temporary" prices for the output of local factories, which were supposed to be based on their higher production costs and in practice remained constant over long periods of time.

Another, more innovative multiple pricing practice was for local firms to charge higher prices for goods sold outside the locality than to local customers, benefiting the latter. The coal industry provides some good examples. At the Dongshan Coal Mine in Taiyuan, Shanxi Province, as early as 1965 the price for local sales (11.20 yuan per ton) was somewhat lower than that for outside sales (13 yuan per ton). In 1975 the price for outside sales was increased by 20 percent to 15.60 yuan per ton, while that for local sales remained unchanged (Tian and Pi 1981, 16, 17). Fifteen small commune and brigade coal mines surveyed in Shanxi Province were forced to sell coal to local industrial users at 8.04 yuan per ton and for local civilian use at 6.77 yuan per ton, compared with an average production cost of 8.88 yuan per ton. Sales to outside customers, however, were at over 27 yuan per ton (He 1982, 42).

A related prereform innovation was interprovincial and interlocality "exchange," occurring outside the central plan, which began in the early 1970s and expanded in the late 1970s (see chapter 3). This provided some much-needed flexibility to the system and enabled certain provinces to grow much more rapidly in the 1970s than otherwise would have been possible.

The impact of these departures from traditional central planning was limited before the late 1970s. They introduced an element of territorial autarchy to complement the ministerial-autarchic tendencies of the Soviet-type system. But material and financial incentives were limited, and local authorities and firms were probably still responsive to central directives. There were no profit-retention schemes for firms, no bonuses for workers, and only limited revenue-sharing incentives for local governments. Local governments did not greatly enhance price flexibility. Differential prices were primarily based on differing production costs, and prices in general were not flexible. Moreover, decentralization did not reach down to the enterprise level but rather stopped at local government bureaus.

Changes during the Period of Reforms

The Chinese planning system changed, and new planning policies and mechanisms were developed, in response to day-to-day pressures on it from the economy, buffeted by reform and adjustment starting from the late 1970s. Thus, the Chinese planning system in the mid-1980s did not represent the result of conscious, well thought out, and consistent reforms but rather was mainly the result of a series of ad hoc responses to the evolving economic situation, combined with a general desire on the part of reformers to reduce the scope and importance of short-run directive planning.

Some of the most important changes since the late 1970s include a sharp reduction in the number of commodities subject to central planning and allocation; reductions in the shares of output of virtually all producer goods subject to allocation through the central plan; loosening of product mix targets, leaving planning more aggregated than previously; greater independence for the state commercial and material supply systems, especially in terms of ability to refuse to buy unmarketable products from producers; increasing scope for enterprises to arrange activities and sell output outside the plan; and a related shift in the focus of planning from production to distribution of inputs and outputs, now distinct from the former because of the growing market portion. These developments accelerated the weakening of central planning in Chinese industry. Unlike in the prereform period, much of the more recent decentralization reached the enterprise level.[7]

A major influence on planning in the 1980s was the expanding role of market forces, combined with great differences and wide swings in market conditions. The 1980–81 investment cutbacks generated buyers' markets for many capital goods and material inputs. Other buyers' markets emerged because of high prices in relation to low and declining costs, which caused a strong supply response by existing producers and widespread new entry. The response of the system in this situation tended to be a gradual breakdown of planning, which eventually left output primarily subject to market allocation (see chapter 4). The revival in investment demand starting in 1982, however, caused a return to excess demand for most investment goods and intermediate inputs. The sytem's response to excess demand has typically been to maintain price controls for the bulk of output while letting marginal production and incremental production be sold freely on the market. Thus, a two-tier allocation and pricing mechanism has emerged. Since 1984 there has also been an increasing dose of "forced" expansion of market allocation by reformers, which strengthened the tendency toward a two-tier system for goods in short supply. The two-tier system, its impact, and its likely future evolution are discussed in chapter 9.

What Chinese Planning Does Not Do

Command planning[8] in China does not play a dominant role in the allocation of resources; does very little to facilitate central government control over the economy; and has to a large extent lost its incentive and effort/resource mobilization functions. A fiscal mobilization role may remain, but it is much attenuated.

Roles of Planning

Mandatory production planning and administrative allocation of goods, like any resource-allocation mechanism, can have a number of different functions. In the traditional centrally planned economy, planning is the primary means of guiding the allocation of resources, through directives passed down by government agencies to enterprises and enforced through compulsory procurement of outputs and administrative allocation of inputs. This type of planning facilitates tight, detailed control over the economy. Another important role of planning in the traditional framework is to mobilize effort and hidden enterprise resources through plan-based incentive schemes, often involving "taut" plans—high targets in relation to the available resources of the enterprise concerned. Fiscal mobilization occurs through high turnover taxes and enterprise profit remittances to the government budget. Planning in an economic system like that of the USSR is not geared toward promoting redistributional goals, which are furthered by other instruments like wage controls, nationalization of assets, taxes on luxury goods, and so on. But in many countries, planning, price controls, and compulsory allocation of goods are used to influence the distribution of income and wealth.

Slack and Loose Production Planning

Production planning in China has been slack and loose, as opposed to taut and firm in the traditional model of central planning (see Tidrick 1987, 182–84). If firms chronically exceed their production plans, then neither the plan targets themselves nor plan-based incentives determine the level of output.

Available evidence on fulfillment of gross output value targets by the sample of twenty state-owned industrial enterprises analyzed in chapter 4 is summarized in table 5.1. Though most firms had little trouble fulfilling their output value plans even in the prereform period, the margin of overfulfillment increased greatly after the late 1970s, when more than 80 percent of the time, the plan was overfulfilled by at least two percent, and nearly 20 percent of the time by over 20 percent. Table 5.2 provides similar information on the fulfillment of physical output plans by the same sample. The margin of overfulfillment also increased considerably after 1978, though there were fewer cases of extreme overfulfillment of targets.

Short-term plans for firms are loose in addition to being slack. When there was a danger that a firm would not be able to fulfill its plan, the plan target could be and frequently was lowered so that it could be achieved. In some cases this even involved ex post adjustment of targets after the end of the year. The Shenyang Smelter had its 1982 profit target adjusted downward after the end of the year so that it would still meet the target (interview information, October 1984). This is by no means an exceptional case.

The evidence in favor of considerable slackness and manipulability in Chi-

Table 5.1

Plan Fulfillment by Chinese State-Owned Industrial Enterprises, 1965–84[a]

Percent of plan fulfilled	1965–78		1979–84	
	Number of observations	Percent of total[b]	Number of observations	Percent of total[b]
<90	8	13	0	0
90–98	4	6	0	0
98–100	1	2	3	4
100–102	9	15	8	12
102–110	19	31	22	33
110–120	13	21	20	30
120–150	7	11	13	19
>150	1	2	1	1
Total	62	100	67	100

Source: Collaborative research project between the Institute of Economics of the Chinese Academy of Social Sciences and the World Bank on Chinese state-owned industrial management.

a. From plan targets and realized values of gross industrial output value for a sample of twenty state-owned industrial enterprises. Each enterprise/year for which targets and actuals are available is treated as one observation. Plan fulfillment ratios are based on final plan targets; where there was no final plan target reported, the initial plan figure was used. The ranges include the top but not the bottom value, except that exactly 100 percent plan fulfillment is included in 100–102 rather than 98–100.

b. Percentages may not add up to 100 due to rounding.

nese industrial planning is fairly strong, but the proposition itself is a relatively weak one. It does not say anything about the role of allocation of material inputs or energy in determining short-run resource allocation. Production planning may have essentially lost its role in short-term resource allocation, but control conceivably could be maintained through administrative allocation of certain key inputs. An argument along these lines is made by Naughton (1986a, 684), who asserts that government control over resource allocation has been maintained through control over energy and particularly electricity supplies.

Diversion of Managerial Attention from Plan Fulfillment

Managerial attitudes toward the importance of plan fulfillment have changed during the period of reforms. Enterprise managers appear to have become much less concerned about achieving plan targets per se. In fact, many of them seem to have striven for high rather than low targets, presumably because they are still easy to fulfill given slack in the system and because higher output targets carry increased allocations of low-priced inputs through the plan.[9]

Table 5.2

Fulfillment of Production Targets by Chinese State-Owned Industrial Enterprises, 1965–84[a]

	1965–78		1979–84	
Percent of plan fulfilled	Number of observations	Percent of total[b]	Number of observations	Percent of total[b]
<90	16	12	5	3
90–98	8	6	5	3
98–100	1	1	3	2
100–102	35	25	37	20
102–110	50	36	67	36
110–120	22	16	43	23
120–150	5	4	16	9
>150	2	1	10	5
Total	139	100	186	100

Source: Collaborative research project between the Institute of Economics of the Chinese Academy of Social Science and the World Bank on Chinese state-owned industrial management.

a. From plan targets and realized physical output of main products for a sample of twenty state-owned industrial enterprises. Each product for each enterprise in each year was treated as one observation. Plan fulfillment ratios are based on final plan targets; where there was no final plan target reported, the initial target (if one was given) was used.

b. Percentages may not add up to 100 due to rounding.

Direct evidence on managerial attitudes is provided by a 1985 survey of 1,386 managerial personnel in industrial firms, which asked them to rank the most important constraints affecting their decision making. As is shown in table 5.3, state plan targets were only fourth in importance (among eight possible choices), after the market, the enterprise's own potential, and workers' desires.[10] This is a logical consequence of slack planning and the growing importance of the market mechanism.

The "Marginal" Role of the Market Mechanism

Since the late 1970s, markets have begun to play a significant role in the distribution of most industrial goods, as was documented in chapter 3. The role of the market mechanism in resource allocation can be magnified beyond its share in total production and supply, under certain conditions. Profit-maximizing firms respond to conditions at the margin in determining their level of production; if every firm is engaging in market transactions for each of its inputs and outputs, production decisions will be based solely on the market situation, rather than being determined by plan parameters.[11]

Table 5.3

Constraints on Chinese Industrial Enterprise Decision Making, 1985[a]

Item	Overall rating	Rank
Pressure of market	71.0	1
Enterprise's own potential	65.4	2
Workers' demands	48.9	3
State plan targets	36.5	4
Methods of other firms	33.2	5
Peer support or opposition	24.1	6
Risk borne by the manager as an individual	12.9	7
Shortage of funds	3.8	8

Source: CESRRI (1986a, 288).

a. The question posed was: "In your actual experience, which aspects do you perceive as having the greatest impact on your decision making?"

The two critical questions hence relate, first, to the enterprise objective function and, second, to the extent to which all firms interact with the market at least at the margin. A case can be made for both profit maximization and near-complete market penetration at the firm level, though undoubtedly these do not hold strictly for all enterprises. If they hold "approximately" for a sufficiently large number of firms, industrial output as a whole may behave as if plan targets do not influence the level of production.

Market Penetration at the Enterprise Level

The second question is in principle a straightforward empirical issue, but it would require in-depth research to reach reliable conclusions. Nevertheless, some suggestive evidence is available. Information from a survey of 429 industrial firms (see table 3.9) indicates that over 90 percent of them relied on the market for some of their input purchases in 1984, 93.5 percent in the first half of 1985. On the sales side, over 85 percent of them sold at least some output on the market in 1984, slightly less in the first half of 1985. This does not necessarily mean that firms were engaging in market transactions at the margin for all of their inputs and outputs, but it does show that there has been considerable penetration of the market to large numbers of enterprises. The figures are particularly significant because over 56 percent of the sample firms were large and medium-sized, and 65 percent of them were state-owned (CESRRI 1986a, 7).

The respective shares of plan and market varied greatly by size and ownership of firms (table 5.4). But this does not mean that a substantial number of large, state-owned enterprises had no involvement with the market, as is sometimes

Table 5.4

Plan Shares for Different Types of Enterprises, 1984

	Share of plan in total transactions (percent)				
Type of plan	State enterprises	Urban collectives	Township and village enterprises	Large and medium-sized enterprises	Small enterprises
Production	29.5	12.2	4.1	28.4	3.6
Sales	71.1	4.4	1.7	84.5	4.5
Supply	86.8	6.5	3.1	68.0	3.0

Source: CESRRI (1986a, 65).

suggested. Even if it is assumed that state enterprises and large and medium-sized firms invariably had lower shares of market transactions than other types of firms, 88 percent of the latter and 90 percent of the former were involved in some market transactions on the input side in the first half of 1985.[12] The corresponding figures on the output side were 71 percent for large and medium-sized firms and 75 percent for state enterprises. Since some large state enterprises had substantial shares of market transactions as early as 1982–83 (see chapter 4), market penetration to large and medium-sized firms has been even greater than these calculations would suggest.

One question that naturally arises is whether some key inputs are not transacted on markets at all; administrative control over their distribution could then be used as a "lever" to direct resource allocation in the industrial sector as a whole. The most obvious candidate for this status is electricity. But a case can be made that the market mechanism both directly and indirectly has been playing a significant, growing role in the allocation of electricity. Widespread self-generation by small township and village enterprises using diesel generators (Xue 1985a, 20) represents a high-cost alternative source of supply, which carries something close to a market-determined price, since fuel for generation typically is bought on the market. There are also many different kinds of compensation trade and barter arrangements for electricity. Enterprises, for example, could directly invest in power-plant development in return for electricity supplies (*GWYGB*, no. 17, June 30, 1985, 531–34). Higher prices increasingly have been charged for electricity consumed above plan quotas or for electricity produced by power plants burning high-priced coal or other fuel. All in all, a "market" for electric power has been belatedly emerging.

Enterprise Objectives

If the enterprise objective function is something other than maximizing profits, then planning may have an impact on short-run resource allocation even if the assumption of complete market penetration is satisfied. There is considerable evidence, however, that Chinese enterprise decision makers have been taking profits more and more seriously as the main goal of their firms' activities. A major tendency in the various enterprise financial incentive schemes implemented since the late 1970s has been to enhance the relative importance of profits and reduce the number of other targets (Byrd 1983b, 330). The income tax system for state-owned firms accentuated this trend, as has the slackness of output plan targets. Profit incentives are important not so much because of their elevation in the incentive system as because of the benefits that accrue to enterprises, their workers, and their managers through profit retention. Firms are allowed to use their retained profits for investment in expansion, bonuses for workers (and increasingly for managers as well), and workers' welfare expenditures, including housing. Guidelines on the proportions of retained profits that can be used for different purposes have often been ignored in practice.

There is also some direct evidence on managers' attitudes. A survey of 359 factory directors (from the sample of 429 firms) asked them to rank fourteen possible reasons for engaging in cooperative relationships with other enterprises. "Improving economic results" received the highest overall rating, ahead of "expanding production," "obtaining modern technology," "improving raw material supplies," and other alternatives (CESRRI 1986a, 178).[13] Direct interviews with numerous managers also generally indicated an increasing focus on profits as opposed to physical output.

This does not mean that Chinese state-owned industrial enterprises, any more than large corporations in other countries, are "pure" profit maximizers. The fact that expanding production scale (capacity) received the second highest rating in the above-cited survey is suggestive and not surprising considering the endemic "investment hunger" of CPEs. The real question is whether firms essentially act "as if" they are maximizing profits, since this is often consistent with rapid expansion of production and capacity.

Strong evidence that major enterprise decisions and actions have been inconsistent with increasing profits would be required to refute convincingly the "as if" profit maximization hypothesis. It is hard to find such instances in the twenty-firm sample analyzed in chapter 4, except those that involved sacrificing profits to increase worker benefits. This was a common phenomenon, which in the context of China's rigid factor-allocation system is not necessarily inconsistent with profit maximization (see below). On the other hand, the positive evidence available is not sufficient to demonstrate convincingly that enterprises always have acted to maximize profits.

One test for profit maximization is whether firms engage in loss-making activities at the margin. If they do so they are not maximizing profits. Most enterprise decisions on whether or not to participate in the market appear to be based primarily on financial considerations, however. If a firm cannot make a profit producing goods outside the mandatory production plan, it will generally not engage in such activities. The Shenyang Smelter refused to buy scrap copper supplies on the open market because the price was bid up by other smelters and copper users who could afford to pay higher prices and still make a profit, either by selling output at a higher price or by processing it into high-profit downstream products. Price controls prevented Shenyang from raising its own output price, and it was not allowed to engage in downstream processing (Byrd 1985b, 29).

If factor allocation is rigid, profit maximization is in any case consistent with a number of other enterprise objective functions. If a firm's total wage bill is fixed and subject to external control, then it would make the same short-run resource allocation decisions whether it is maximizing profits or "total net product," a maximand postulated by Byrd and Tidrick (1984, 30–32). If the number of workers in the enterprise is fixed exogenously, then it will behave in the same way whether it is maximizing profits or average net product per worker, a maximand often assumed in models of the Yugoslav-type labor-managed firm. Even if there is a discretionary element in wages, as long as the labor force is fixed exogenously, firms maximizing profits, average product of labor, and total net product will behave in the same way, except that profit-maximizing firms will hold down wages to the extent possible whereas the other two types will be indifferent as between wages and profits. Thus, rigidities in factor allocation make short-run profit maximization a more plausible maximand. And since labor in the state sector of China's economy has been administratively allocated, rigidity of enterprise employment is not an unreasonable assumption.

More broadly, enterprises may have a kind of "schizophrenic" objective function, acting to maximize profits in activities outside the mandatory plan but pursuing somewhat different objectives (and subject to more external constraints) in activities within the plan. With complete market penetration, activities and transactions outside the plan determine a firm's total level of production, and these appear to be based primarily on profitability considerations, so the result is the same as if the enterprise were maximizing profits in all of its activities. The various objectives pursued in within-plan activities would reduce profits if they cause deviation from profit-maximizing behavior, but they would not otherwise affect firms' short-run decisions.

An important group of enterprise objective functions, widely used in the analysis of centrally planned economies and of capitalist firms, has rather different implications from profit maximization. The firm is assumed to maximize the quantity or gross value of output or sales, subject to a "resource" or profit constraint. This approach was developed by Baumol (1959) in the study of capitalist firms and later used by Ames (1965) and Portes (1969) in the analysis of Soviet-type economies.[14] Firms with this type of objective function produce more than profit-maximizing firms and make negative profits on goods produced at the margin. Moreover, they are subject to "income effects" analogous to those in consumer theory (see Portes 1968), unlike profit maximizers. As a result, their activity is influenced by changes in production targets, input allocations, and plan prices for inputs and outputs, because these affect the financial resources at their disposal (Portes 1969, 205–6).

The Baumol/Ames/Portes objective function may be a reasonable approximation of reality in economies where the planning system is comprehensive and well developed and profit and resource-use targets are an integral part of production planning. But in China this has not been the case; given the existence of a parallel market where involvement is based primarily on profit considerations, output maximization subject to a profit constraint would appear to be more unrealistic than the conventional profit-maximization assumption, at least for activities and transactions at the margin.

It is also not clear that Chinese industrial enterprises have generally been subject to meaningful financial resource constraints in their production activities, much less that these constraints were determined by profits. Though firms were encouraged by government authorities to use retained profits to meet working capital requirements, they preferred to use these funds for workers' benefits or fixed investment. Hence, they relied on bank loans to finance nearly all purchases of production inputs.[15] Controls over bank loans for circulating capital have been weak and in any case were based on norms for the level of circulating capital in relation to production rather than on enterprise profits or profitability. Moreover, in practice, bank loans for working capital may still have been based largely on the "real bills principle" and hence freely granted as long as they were covered by goods in stock.[16] Thus, working capital loans do not seem to have been a binding constraint on production and in any case have been tied much more closely to the level of production than to profits. Even if short-run production activity is subject to financial resource constraints, these are not closely tied to profits.

Finally, given the attitudes of enterprise managers mentioned earlier, switching around the maximand and constraint to come up with profit maximization subject to the constraint that plan targets have to be met would appear to be an interesting alternative to the Baumol/Ames/Portes model. If plan targets are slack and can be fulfilled without abandoning profit-maximizing behavior, this objective is identical to profit maximization.

Numerous other objective functions can be envisaged, including various combinations. Among them are maximization of output or firm size and similar quantity-oriented goals. Output maximization, either physical output or an indicator like gross output value, is superficially attractive, since output has often been the focus of enterprise incentive schemes and the "quantity orientation" of firms in centrally planned economies is well known. These economies suffer from chronic shortages, and firms would seem to be constrained by availability of material inputs and energy rather than by financial resources to purchase them.[17] Firms under these conditions may well maximize output, up to the point where materials, energy, capacity, or labor become binding constraints.

But in its pure form, output maximization implies behavior that is not observed in China. An output-maximizing firm would expend arbitrarily large amounts of resources and incur arbitrarily large losses to increase production in the short run, until it hits a binding capacity constraint. Chinese enterprises, on the other hand, have become increasingly oriented toward profits rather than output or gross output value, particularly in activities outside the plan. Though lower levels of government are concerned about local gross output value and may have put pressure on enterprises to fulfill gross output value plans, they are also concerned about their budget revenues, dependent on enterprise profits to a considerable extent, and have become increasingly unwilling to subsidize losses.

The existence of markets for most producer goods in China, with flexible prices responsive to supply and demand, is inconsistent with the hypothesis that firms maximize output subject only to physical constraints in the short run, except under certain conditions: (1) enterprises hit capacity constraints before material supply constraints become binding, or (2) output maximizing firms (i.e., state enterprises) are not allowed to purchase inputs on the market, while the firms that do participate (perhaps mainly collective and private firms) behave more like conventional profit maximizers. Alternative 1 seems dubious in view of the widespread shortages of many producer goods, combined with excess capacity in a number of industries. Alternative 2 is no more palatable, since participation in these markets by state enterprises has been widespread, at least on the demand side.

Maximizing investment and the size of the firm would mean not diverting more than minimal funds to such ''nonproductive'' uses as workers' housing, bonuses, or welfare benefits. But this is contradicted by the massive spending of enterprise retained profits for these purposes. Thus, in its pure form maximization of firm size is not very satisfactory, either.

All in all, despite its flaws, profit maximization, subject to constraints set by the planning and administrative systems, may well be a more attractive hypothesis than plausible alternatives. It appears to be more realistic than output maximization subject to a profit-related financial-resource constraint. If the labor force is fixed it is consistent with other postulated maximands like total net product and average net product per worker. Finally, quantity or size maximization is not appealing except in combination with other objectives.

Summary: Resource Allocation, Control, and Mobilization

The argument that planning in Chinese state-owned industry has lost its resource allocation role has three central elements: (1) production planning has been slack and loose, and fulfillment of plan targets per se is no longer the central focus of managerial attention; (2) market penetration in the state-owned industrial sector has reached the point where most firms engage in at least some market transactions for most of their inputs and outputs; and (3) enterprises maximize profits, subject to relatively slack constraints imposed by the planning system, so the "income effects" of plan targets and plan prices do not affect their behavior.

If mandatory planning has little or no influence on the level of production in Chinese industry, its role in facilitating direct government control over economic activity also is very limited. Depending on how it is exercised and what rules enterprises are subject to, mandatory planning may affect a firm's choice on whether or not to participate in the market, which could have an effect on production (see chapter 6). But this is a far cry from the control that command planning is assumed to have in centrally planned economies. The widespread bargaining, negotiations, and target revisions endemic to Chinese planning, in which the lower level often has considerable bargaining power, also weaken government control over the economy.

Production planning and allocation of inputs and outputs have largely lost their function as a mobilization device to encourage greater effort and efficiency on the part of Chinese enterprises. With slack targets, tautness in plans has not been used as a means of mobilizing enterprise effort and resources.[18] Early Chinese reform efforts attempted to create a link between material benefits and plan fulfillment at both enterprise and individual worker levels, but this has remained tenuous in practice given the slackness and looseness of plans. In any case, the most common type of linkage between plan targets and financial incentives is of a threshold nature, with a certain level of benefits provided if the plan target is reached but no extra benefits related to the degree of overfulfillment. Given slack planning, these kinds of incentive schemes do not encourage higher production at the margin. Performance-related incentive schemes, in the form of profit-sharing systems, often had no relation to the profit plan, let alone the production plan. Hence, they should be regarded as profit-based rather than plan-based.

The Distributional Impact of Chinese Planning

The Chinese industrial planning, pricing, and goods-allocation system does have important distributional consequences. Given the atrophy of the other functions, redistribution has arguably become its most important role. A strong emphasis on income redistribution is a hallmark of socialism, but the redistributional aspect of production planning and administrative allocation of goods is not commonly emphasized.

Redistributional Mechanism

The redistributional mechanism of Chinese planning is the allocation of goods through the state plan at low prices. Thus, it involves redistribution of incomes among organizations and does not affect individuals directly. There may be strong secondary effects on the latter, however, if their material benefits depend on the profits of the organizations they work for.

Goods allocated through the plan are attractive to their recipients for two possible reasons: their availability, and the fact that they carry a lower price than alternative sources of supply. The first type of advantage is strictly applicable only if there is no other viable source of supply. To the extent that the market is effectively functioning and goods are available, albeit at a higher price, only the second type of benefit is relevant. Moreover, the financial advantages of plan-allocated inputs become quite obvious when a parallel market is in existence. The market also provides an outlet for sales or resales of goods subject to plan allocation.

By definition, a redistributional mechanism takes income away from certain organizations or individuals and transfers it to others. Producers of goods subject to compulsory procurement through the plan lose potential income, since they presumably could sell their output on the market at a higher price. These same producers usually gain substantial benefits from receiving plan allocations of inputs needed for production. There is generally at least in principle a close linkage between plan output targets and input allocations, which sharply reduces "net" redistribution.

Compulsory procurement and administrative allocation of goods at low prices is a major form of redistribution akin to enterprise-specific indirect taxes and subsidies. There is also "direct" redistribution of the incomes of state enterprises through the profit distribution system (transformed into a still ad hoc, negotiated profit tax system in 1983–85). This plays an important role in determining the ultimate destination of the rents obtained through access to low-priced plan allocations. For instance, a firm could convert plan-allocated inputs into output sold on the market at a high price, earning substantial profits, but these could be taxed away by the government. Or the enterprise might be forced to sell most of its output through the plan at low prices, in which case the benefit would be transferred to the purchaser and gross profits would be much lower. But whether the purchaser could appropriate these rents depends on its output plan and profit-sharing system.

Generation and Flow of Rents

In the Chinese context, rents can be thought of as abnormally high returns to production or trading units.[19] Substantial rents are generated by the low controlled prices for goods subject to allocation through the state material supply plan and for certain basic consumer goods. These rents are carried from seller (producer) to buyer (user) as the goods are traded at the low prices. Who in the system actually benefits from these rents depends on the whole system of plan prices, input and output allocations, and profit distribution. Embodied rents can be carried through the entire chain of production and distribution, in which case they accrue to final consumers or investors. For investments financed by the government budget, low-priced investment goods translate into lower budgetary requirements, or more "real" investment for the same nominal budgetary resources. In the case of consumer goods, rents go to consumers, but indirectly they may benefit the government budget as well. If the government has a commitment to maintain a certain standard of living for the urban population, then low-priced consumer goods allow lower nominal wages, which in turn would mean higher enterprise profits and profit remittances to the budget.[20]

Given the weakness, territorial and administrative decentralization, and fragmentation of Chinese planning, the movement of embodied rents through the chain of production and commercial transactions is uneven and subject to diversions and alterations. Though in principle rents could be carried all the way to purchasers of final goods, the process is more complicated than this and subject to incessant bargaining and negotiations.

The situation where plan prices are higher than equilibrium prices on the parallel market is conceptually possible but is not likely to be stable over any length of time. In this situation, goods carry economic penalties or "negative rents" for those who purchase them. As noted in chapter 4, however, under these circumstances downward pressure is exerted on the price of the entire supply of the good concerned, and two-tier systems have not in practice emerged. Exceptions could occur when the "negative rent" involved is covered directly by government budget, as in the case of the state procurement system for grain.

Magnitude of Rents

Embodied rent is the saving to the purchaser from buying the good concerned through plan allocation rather than on the market. The total value of embodied rents carried by an industrial good can be roughly estimated by comparing the market price and the state plan price and multiplying the difference by the amount of the good concerned that is subject to state plan allocation. This measure can be inaccurate because if every agent actually tried to appropriate rents by selling the good on the market, the market price might fall. But existing market prices at least can provide a rough indication of the magnitude of embodied rents.

Table 5.5 shows some illustrative calculations of the 1985 value of embodied rents for centrally allocated coal, rolled steel, timber, cement, and trucks. The estimates are rough because state and market prices vary by region and transportation costs have not been netted out. Moreover, these figures do not include embodied rents carried by goods subject to allocation at below-equilibrium prices by provincial and local governments, so they are conservative estimates. Even so, the estimated total value of embodied rents for these five products alone is over 40 billion yuan, close to 5 percent of China's gross industrial output value or 10 percent of heavy industry output value in 1985. The share of embodied rents in the value of specific products can be very high, for example 47 percent for rolled steel.[21] The magnitude of rents is certainly significant enough to attract

Table 5.5

Illustrative Calculations of Embodied Rents, 1985 (billion yuan)

	Goods (amounts in million tons unless otherwise indicated)				
	Coal	Rolled steel	Cement	Timber[a]	Trucks[b]
Total output	872	36.93	145.95	63.23	360[c]
Central plan					
amount	441	21.0	28.3	19.4	150[c]
(share)	(50.6)	(56.9)	(19.4)	(30.7)	(41)
State price[d]	40	700	60	170	30,000
Market price[d]	80	1,600	120	300	42,000
Embodied					
rents[e]	17.6	18.9	1.7	2.5	1.8

Estimated total embodied rents for these goods: 42.5

Sources: Table 3.2; Xia (1985, 4); State Statistical Bureau (1986a, 55, 56, 57).

a. Million cubic meters.

b. Thousand units.

c. The total output figure is an early forecast of total production of trucks (presumably not including automobiles) which is probably an underestimate. The figure for centrally allocated trucks, however, is the state mandatory plan target for the year and hence is likely to be accurate.

d. These prices are only illustrative, given the wide range of concrete goods included in each product category and the lack of detailed price data. Nevertheless, they are broadly in line with available information on state and market prices.

e. Amount of centrally allocated production multiplied by the difference between market and plan prices.

"rent-seeking behavior"[22] by producers and traders as well as by others in the system.

Distinctive Features of the Chinese Situation

Rent generation and redistribution through the planning system in China has a number of distinctive features. Since they are embodied in goods, rents accrue to purchasers or consumers. In market economies, on the other hand, typically restrictions against entry permit higher prices and hence rents for existing producers. The latter requires barriers to entry by new producers, whereas the former is based on segregating consumers or users as well as goods flows. Another difference between rents in China and in market economies is that in the latter they tend to get capitalized over time as factors are attracted by high returns, whereas in China such adjustment tends to be slow and incomplete due to system rigidities. Much of what occurs in Chinese state-owned industry is the flow of embodied rents along the chain of production and trade (perhaps with leakages) rather than their appropriation by the particular agents who first purchase the goods concerned. Rents embodied in low-priced inputs generally carry a quid pro quo in the form of appropriation of rents through compulsory procurement of the output generated.

The domain and aggregate value of rents as well as their distribution are subject to bargaining within the hierarchy of industrial administration and supervision. Though prices may be fixed in the short run, there is usually considerable room for variation through changes in product mix, new product development, etc. Bargaining occurs between an enterprise and its immediate supervisory agency rather than as competition among numerous agents striving to appropriate rents. The supervisory agency must simultaneously try to limit the requests of subordinate firms and bargain with higher levels for more rents or allocations.

Possible Objections

Two main objections can be raised against the assertion that the Chinese planning system plays an important redistributive role. It could be argued that rents obtained by enterprises through low-priced inputs are offset by appropriation of rents through compulsory purchase of output at controlled prices, and therefore that "net" rents accruing to particular firms are always very small. A related point is that there are theoretical and practical limits to the amount of redistribution that can occur through indirect taxation (Sah 1983), and hence also to the amount of redistribution that could occur through the Chinese industrial planning system.[23] A second possible objection is that even if large embodied rents are generated and redistributed by the Chinese planning system, these have only a minimal impact on agents. It could also be argued that with wage and bonus controls, the appropriation of rents by individuals is extremely difficult, so "organizational rents" do not influence individual behavior significantly.

Earlier in this chapter some rough calculations showed that there are substantial rents embodied in goods allocated through the plan (table 5.5). The large "gross rents" in the system must provide a potent incentive for rent-seeking behavior. Official price relativities generate great differences in profit rates between different industries. For example, in 1984 the ratio of profits and indirect taxes to total assets for state enterprises ranged from a low of 2.6 percent in the coal industry to a high of 59 percent in the petroleum industry and 56.7 percent in food processing (State Statistical Bureau 1985a, 379–80). There is also wide variation in profitability within these broad subsectors, even for different varieties of the same product. Low-profit industries like coal generate substantial rents embodied in coal allocated through the state plan, while in high-profit industries, substantial rents are earned by producers because of low input prices and/or relatively high output prices.

Enterprise profit retention rates differ markedly, but they do not offset differences in gross profitability. For the sample of twenty state-owned industrial

Table 5.6

Profitability and Retained Profits in Twenty State-Owned Industrial Enterprises

	Ratios 1980–82 average (percent)			Unit profits (yuan/employee)	
Enterprise[a]	Profit/total assets[b]	Retained profit/ assets[b]	Profit retention rate	Profit/labor force	Retained profit/labor
Anshan	30.8	2.9	9.4	7,029	658
Baoji	14.0	3.1	22.0	2,950	650
Chengdu	29.5	3.0	10.0	3,293	329
Chongqing	22.1	7.6	34.3	3,220	1,103
Jiangmen	21.2	14.8	70.1	1,343	941
Jinling[c]	40.4	3.6	9.0	10,740	965
Mindong	8.9	2.3	25.6	1,141	292
N2 Auto	10.3	2.5	23.9	3,342	799
Nanning	34.9	5.1	14.5	3,624	527
NC Petro	39.7	0.4	0.9	6,697	60
NW Cotton	77.4	9.8	12.6	4,292	542
Qingdao	6.4	0.5	8.0	1,148	92
Qinghe	47.1	8.0	17.1	5,379	920
Qingyuan	17.4	4.6	26.6	1,153	307
Sanchazi	19.4	5.0	25.6	1,554	397
SH Cotton	149.8	11.3	7.5	5,679	428
Shenyang	27.1	2.1	7.7	8,110	621
SH Oil Pump	64.9	5.9	9.0	6,690	605
Tianjin	75.9	9.4	12.4	4,213	522
Xiangxiang	30.9	2.5	7.9	8,477	674
Total[d]	29.3	2.7	9.0	6,191	560

Source: Tidrick and Chen (1987, table 2-11, 23; table 2-12, 24; table 2-16, 28; table 2-19, 31; table 2-23, 35).

a. For full names of enterprises, see table 4.1.

b. The denominator is net value of enterprise fixed assets plus value of quota circulating assets.

c. For 1981–82 only.

d. Based on total profits, assets, and labor force of sample firms.

firms, differences in profit tax and remittance rates did not offset differences in pretax profitability, and there was great variation in both. As is shown in table 5.6, there is not a great degree of "nivellation," unlike in Hungary (see Kornai and Matits 1984). The ratio of profits to assets is significantly positively correlated with that of retained profits to assets ($R = 0.54$). Some highly profitable enterprises retained a relatively large share of their total profits. Similarly, profits per worker are positively though weakly correlated with retained profits per worker ($R = 0.30$).

For the much larger sample of firms in the China Economic System Reform Research Institute study, the ratio of retained profits to capital exhibits almost as much variation as the ratio of pretax profits to capital, though there may have been some evening out overall (Hua et al. 1986, 21). The correlation between growth of total profits and that of retained profits was 0.57 (CESRRI 1986, 16). If some of the growth of profits was due to appropriation of rents, then at least part of the rents appropriated by firms probably was not siphoned off by the profit-sharing system.

Even if there was some leveling of highly unequal profit rates through the profit-retention system, differences remained, and there was ample room for enterprises to gain possession of rents through bargaining for "special deals" of various kinds.[24] Though "net" rents may have been much smaller than "gross" rents, they were still substantial enough to influence the behavior of firms and other entities. Particular firms could always try to appropriate additional rents at the margin through bargaining over targets, allocation quotas, and to a lesser extent prices.

The second argument can be dealt with by showing that the existence of substantial rents influences the actions of firms and other decision-making bodies. In the first place, firms with high retained profits do spend large proportions of them on workers' benefits—housing and welfare facilities if not bonuses and other forms of cash payment. Thus, individuals do benefit from appropriation of rents. One example is the construction system in Henan Province, where retained profits per worker in 1981 were 547 yuan, compared with 171 yuan in the rest of the province's industry, and average bonuses per worker were 166 yuan, compared with 96 yuan in the rest of industry (Byrd 1987b, 231). Even if direct managerial rewards are limited, the responsiveness of managers to workers' interests means that the former have a strong incentive to engage in rent-seeking activities on behalf of their units.

State enterprises in China put significant time and effort into rent seeking. Attempts to get more inputs through the plan are pervasive, involving repeated requests, stationing procurement agents at major suppliers, and provision of side payments or other benefits to suppliers or to authorities responsible for planned distribution. Overreporting of input requirements is ubiquitous as it is in other centrally planned economies; this constitutes a potent form of rent-seeking behavior. Similarly, firms use various means to try to maximize the share of their output sold on the market at high prices. "Lobbying" for better profit-retention arrangements, extra investment funds, more bonuses or welfare for workers, and "special deals" in other spheres of finance is universally practiced by enterprises.

Implications of Planning as Redistribution

The Chinese planning system as it has evolved since the late 1970s has some distinct advantages, which are reviewed in this section. The redistributional role of planning is problematic, however.

Redistribution as Process Rather than Objective

Redistribution in Chinese economic planning involves organizational units rather than individuals, but "better" income distribution among organizations does not appear to be appropriate as an ultimate economic goal. Income distribution among individuals, households, communities, and regions is obviously important, but redistribution among organizations may not be a suitable or effective vehicle for promoting these legitimate objectives. Concern about income distribution among organizations is relevant only if this affects income distribution among individuals in ways that cannot be mediated by other policy instruments, like wage controls.

In any case, planning in China is not promoting specific, enunciated redistributional goals. Instead, it is very much a bargaining and balancing process among different organizations promoting their own benefits and those of their members. In this situation the central planning apparatus can do little more than serve as an arbiter of competing claims for resources. Egalitarian allocations emerge as the easiest and often the only viable method for planners to deal with competing claims. But this means that planning is not promoting any widely held or compelling redistributional objectives; hence, if its redistributional role has significant costs, there is probably little on the benefit side to offset them.

Redistribution occurs as part of the process of planning and is not one of its explicit objectives. To a large extent, redistribution is aimed at offsetting or ameliorating the effects on incomes of distortions which themselves were introduced by government actions or controls. This is similar to indirect taxation in China, where rate variation is defended as compensating for distortions generated by the administered price system. But it would be simpler and more effective to eliminate the original distortions rather than try to compensate for them with offsetting distortions.

Given that "planning as redistribution" is not furthering any explicit national objectives, its only rationale can be as a transitional practice on the path from prereform planning to allocation by the market. Huge existing distortions were inherited from the prereform period, and it is understandable that these could not be eliminated right away. Thus the final evaluation of Chinese industrial planning should be based primarily on whether it promotes or hinders the transition toward a full-blown market system.

Advantages of Planning as Redistribution

The main advantages of the Chinese planning system of the late 1980s are, first, that to a large extent it avoids problems of inconsistency and inflexibility that have plagued comprehensive directive production planning in centrally planned economies; second, it generates better price signals that are more flexible and responsive to supply-demand conditions than administrative prices; and third, dynamic pressures are generated for further expansion of the role of the market. (This last benefit is discussed in chapter 9.)

Consistency and flexibility. A major advantage of the Chinese system is that it to a large extent finesses the inflexibility and inconsistency problems that plague traditional central planning. Because of the weakness and fragmentation of Chinese planning and industrial administration, the large number of firms, and the large size of the country, these problems would likely be even greater than in other centrally planned economies.

In China, shortfalls in input allocations can be made up by going to the market, where goods are increasingly available, albeit at higher prices. This not only permits greater flexibility (and, presumably, efficiency) in production activities but also weakens considerably the impact of planning mistakes on economic performance.[25] On the output side, the Chinese system permits enterprises to turn to the market if their output targets are low in relation to capacity. This also can compensate for planning mistakes, and, as long as output targets are relatively low, at least partly for artificially low prices of output allocated within the plan.

These benefits ascribed to the Chinese planning system are similar to those attributed to the "second economy" in centrally planned economies,[26] but there are some important differences. The multilevel Chinese planning system gave extra-plan or loosely locally planned activities and transactions a greater aura of legitimacy and open recognition than has been the case in a country like the Soviet Union. This reduces the costs of extraplan transactions to transactors, improving their efficiency. Moreover, in China transactions outside the central plan comprise a high and growing proportion of total supply. Finally, the parallel market extends to primary distribution (from the point of sale by producers), rather than merely involving secondary redistribution by users who have received the goods concerned as part of their plan input allocations. The Chinese pattern thus may have considerable benefits in exposing producers more directly to the market.

Market price signals. The Chinese system also generates more accurate price signals at the margin, and these may have a disproportionate influence on enterprise decision making. Regardless of the distortions in Chinese markets, both natural and administratively imposed, market prices provide a better reflection of underlying supply and demand conditions than state plan prices, since they adjust in response to changes in market conditions. (Chapter 6 demonstrates with the use of a formal model that under certain conditions the efficiency properties of a market economy are duplicated.)

To the extent that markets and market transactions are considered legitimate in the system, a major source of distortions is removed. In analyses of black markets, it is typically assumed that there are costs to participating in the black market, that these costs are higher for sellers than for buyers, and often that the marginal cost of involvement in the black market is an increasing function of the share of total transactions taking place in the black market. These assumptions generate the well-known result that the equilibrium price in the black market is higher than the market equilibrium price would be with all restrictions abolished (Michaely 1954). But if market transactions are assumed to be no more costly than transactions within the plan, prices for the former are much more likely to be close to what they would be in competitive market equilibrium. Even if engaging in free market transactions does carry some costs, costs of distribution through the planning system also must be high from the viewpoint of purchasers.

Dynamic pressures and trends. Perhaps even more important than any static efficiency benefits of the Chinese planning system are the strong dynamic pressures induced. These are explored in chapter 9, where it is suggested that the inherent dynamic tendencies of the system lead to continued expansion in the share of market allocation in total output and shrinkage in that of planning.

Drawbacks of Planning as Redistribution

Among the most serious difficulties associated with planning as a redistribution-oriented process are the diversion of resources to redistributional (rent-seeking) activities; the attitudes and practices fostered in the planning system; the impact on investment patterns; and hindrances to the development of well-functioning markets.

Diversion of planners' time and attention. A major problem with planning as redistribution is that planners and government agencies spend a great deal of time and effort redistributing rents. Time, effort, and resources spent on sorting out redistributional issues (by planners) and in seeking redistributional gains (by enterprises and organizations striving for plan allocations and high profit retention rates) divert attention from more important policy issues in the case of the former and from productive activities in the case of the latter. The diversion of managerial resources from cost reduction to bargaining for a higher share of profits is especially striking when an enterprise or organization faces a decline in its revenues due to changes in its environment (or "objective circumstances").

Attitudes and behavior patterns. Perhaps even more important than the resources expended on redistribution are the attitudes and behavior patterns fostered. Planners may become accustomed to redistributing resources, so that they see this as the principal role of planning. Enterprises are even more likely to view the planning mechanism as simply a distributor of rents. As these attitudes become ingrained, it may become more difficult for mandatory short-term planning to exit from the scene, even though this was the general direction of reforms in the mid- and late 1980s. Not only may the organizations gaining benefits from the existing flow of rents strongly resist the loss of these benefits, but the planning system itself may become accustomed to its redistributional role and therefore may impede reform.

Impact on competition. The size of the parallel market in a dual-price system is much smaller than when all output is allocated through the market mechanism, but the number of competitors may not be small. A more potent hindrance to effective competition may be the perceived possibility of gaining access to plan allocations, which could distract competitors from the market and toward activities that permit them to get goods through the plan. The most severe problems, however, arise from the actions government organizations may take to obtain or hold onto rents, most commonly through internal protectionism, which segments the domestic market (see below).

Market segmentation and protectionism. Rents and redistribution in Chinese planning may exacerbate a tendency toward separate and segmented markets and protection of local industry. Local governments have authority over local industry and trade and potent incentives to increase local industrial output and budget revenues (see chapter 4). Given the recent emergence and limited development of the market mechanism so far, all the ingredients for market segmentation and protectionism at the initiative of lower levels of government are present. This may severely hinder the development of effective competition in many industries, as well as eroding the static efficiency gains from reliance on the market mechanism. Segmented markets tend to be more amenable to local government control; hence, they may make it more difficult for firms to become independent from government involvement. Overall, market segmentation and local protectionism constitute a severe obstacle to China's market-oriented reforms.

The central government took a strong stance against internal protectionism in the early and mid-1980s. Probably more important, market forces themselves generate strong pressures against local protectionism—for example, profit-oriented local firms will strive to purchase inputs from outside suppliers if these are superior to local products in terms of quality and price. There appears to have been a reduction in outright protectionism by localities and provinces, especially since 1984–85. But the potential is still there; moreover, the decentralization of industrial administration to the city level, which started in 1983, may have increased protectionism by cities, even while possibly reducing protectionism by provinces. A particularly troubling example is what occurred when Shenyang Municipality was given autonomy in economic planning and management. Shenyang had previously relied heavily on shipments of steel ingots from the nearby Anshan Iron and Steel Company, which it rolled into steel products. After the separation, Shenyang immediately began to integrate backward into steel production, while the rest of Liaoning Province integrated forward into processing (interview information, August 1985).

Investment patterns. Planning as redistribution can have an adverse effect on the efficiency of investment. Rents carried by low-priced goods generate a distorted structure of profits. If these profits are used for inappropriate investments, distortions are compounded and passed on to the future. In principle, it should be possible to have an efficient system of financial intermediation that would direct plan-generated rents to the investments with highest returns. But the Chinese financial system is relatively undeveloped and still bears the burden of its traditional role as simply a supplier of funds to the production sphere. The problems of large rents flowing through the system and underdeveloped financial intermediation therefore reinforce each other.

Planning as Redistribution and Rent-Seeking Behavior

Rent-seeking behavior by agents is designed to gain benefits through appropriating rents caused by distortions in the economic system, rather than by engaging in economically productive activities to earn profits. Rent seeking can result in static efficiency losses because it uses up real resources, or because it induces distortions. On the other hand, rent seeking can have a positive welfare impact by getting around or removing a distortion, which may more than offset the cost of resources used in rent seeking.[27]

In China, a major form of rent seeking involves trying to obtain goods at low prices through the plan and then converting the embodied rents into financial gain. For firms outside the state planning and allocation system, such as rural enterprises, rent seeking may entail making oneself an attractive partner for a state enterprise or improving one's product so that it will be considered a candidate for inclusion in the plan. In a dynamic context, rent seeking may involve large investments which then "justify" additional provision of material inputs and energy through the plan. Still another form of rent-seeking behavior is widespread "lobbying" by different organizations for changes in prices of planned commodities, strengthening or weakening of price controls, or maintenance of the status quo.

One way in which embodied rents can be appropriated is by reselling them on the market at higher prices. In most cases this kind of action is very much frowned on if not outright illegal. Nevertheless, the temptation to engage in such behavior must be very great when the market price exceeds the plan price by a wide margin (see tables 8.1 and 8.2). In a situation where input allocations are not mutually consistent and producers must in any case rely on the market to purchase many inputs, diversion of goods from plan channels to the market may be hard to detect. Such diversion by commercial units may be even more common than similar actions by producers.

Sellers may also appropriate rents by demanding side payments or other kinds of favors. This kind of rent seeking could be widespread, without showing up in recorded transaction prices. Commercial agencies may charge numerous fees on various pretexts, with the extra costs included in the effective price to the purchaser. These activities are hard to detect; moreover, they sometimes verge on legality, since exchanges of goods for each other in tied transactions are considered legitimate activities.

A borderline activity involves using inputs allocated through the plan to produce goods that are then sold on the market for high prices. This is hard to detect and appears not to be considered wrongdoing as long as the firm concerned meets its mandatory output target. Still other activities can be more broadly construed as rent seeking. One is manipulation of the price system, for example, making a slight change in a product and then charging a higher price on the grounds that it is a "new product."[28] Another is investing in small-scale processing facilities to appropriate rents from locally produced, low-priced raw materials or agricultural goods by making high-priced downstream products. This has been a persistent, longstanding problem in the case of many cash crops. Productive investments also can be oriented toward taking advantage of high output prices for certain goods, like consumer durables.

A central question about rent-seeking behavior is whether and in what way it may destabilize the "two-tier" Chinese system of short-term resource allocation. This issue is addressed in chapter 9. The static impact of rent seeking depends greatly on the situation to which it is being compared. In China, comparing the existing situation with a first-best optimum is probably not appropriate; as has already been noted, this means that rent seeking could result in an improvement in economic welfare in the static sense. However, the diversion of time and attention of planners and managers induced by rent seeking is very hard to quantify yet may be the most important static cost. In any case, the dynamic impact of rent-seeking behavior almost certainly dominates static efficiency effects.

6. Plan and Market in the Chinese Economy: A Simple General Equilibrium Model

ECONOMIC reforms in Chinese industry have resulted in the emergence of a two-tier plan/market system (see chapters 3, 5, and 9). Industrial goods are subject to multiple allocation mechanisms, including various administrative channels (termed "planning" for the purposes of this chapter) and the market. Even for particular state-owned industrial enterprises, part of each input and output may be allocated administratively, part obtained or sold on the market. The same good can carry very different prices, depending on the allocation mechanism it is subject to. The share of the market in total supply and demand varies for different products and enterprises.

This chapter analyzes the Chinese state-owned industrial sector as it functions under the two-tier system, with the aid of a simple static general equilibrium model. The main purpose is to examine the impact of planning and the efficiency of the market mechanism in a stylized economy that is a hybrid of plan and market. The model represents a preliminary attempt to come to grips with some key "stylized facts" of the Chinese situation:[1] (1) the existence of functioning markets for most industrial goods, alongside the traditional system of administrative allocation and pricing; (2) market prices that are flexible and responsive to supply and demand; (3) relatively slack production plan targets in relation to capacity for most enterprises; (4) plan input allocations for most firms that are insufficient for full capacity production and often even to produce the level of output required by the output plan; (5) rigidity in allocation of factors of production (land, labor, and capital); (6) a strong profit orientation on the part of state enterprises; and (7) a planning system that appears to be very weak in enforcing priorities and instead serves primarily as a means of distributing plan allocations and associated benefits or "rents" to various claimants.

The key assumptions used in the model emerge naturally from these stylized facts. Each good in the economy can be distributed partly through the plan and partly through the market. Output plan targets and input allocations are modeled as minimum constraints on the flow of commodities from and to enterprises, while plan allocations of goods to final demand (consumption and investment) are minimum constraints on purchases of these goods by consumers and investors. Factors of production (including labor) are exogenously fixed. Enterprises maximize profits, subject to the constraint that they must fulfill their output plan targets.[2] Wage rates (and enterprise wage bills) are set exogenously in nominal terms.[3] Certain other assumptions made in order to generate key results of the model include segregation of final demand into two distinct components (consumption and investment), emanating from two distinct sources (consumers and "investors"); distribution of profits to investors; and "compensating" adjustments of wages and investors' profit shares in response to changes in plan parameters.

The model abstracts from reality in order to focus on certain issues, neglecting others. It is not suitable for analyzing the market *process* in China or more generally for looking at dynamic issues (for instance, the impact of different patterns of investment on growth). The model's simplistic assumptions about factor allocation make it an inappropriate tool for analysis of this sphere. It cannot be used for in-depth study of China's planning system, though its results are consistent with our understanding of Chinese planning (see chapter 5). Some parts of the economy have been left out of the model to keep it streamlined, like public finance (which could easily be incorporated, however). The modeling of investment decision making and financing also is simplistic.

Microeconomic Framework

There are h different homogeneous commodities in the model (indexed by k). It is assumed that all commodities can be unambiguously classified as investment goods, consumption goods, intermediate inputs, or some combination of these three categories.[4] Furthermore, the number of goods of different types is a fixed characteristic of the economy.

Part of total output, supply, and demand for each good is controlled by the planning system, while the rest is allocated through the market mechanism. Each good carries two prices, a plan price q_k, which applies to all transactions within the plan, and a market price p_k, which applies to market transactions. Plan prices are fixed by the planning system, whereas market prices equilibrate demand and supply on the "parallel market." Both plan and market prices are specified in terms of an accounting unit (which is not itself a commodity). In addition, the first commodity (which can be thought of as "money") serves as medium of exchange.[5] The first commodity is not subject to plan allocation and hence all of it carries the "market" price p_1. Plan prices are all fixed by the planning system in relation to the market price of the first commodity. That is, q_k/p_1 is a constant for all $k = 2, \ldots h$.[6] The vector of market prices is $p = (p_1, \ldots, p_k, \ldots, p_h)$, and the vector of plan prices is $q = (q_2, \ldots, q_k, \ldots, q_h)$.

Factors of production (land, labor, and capital) are not included in the list of commodities, since enterprise factor endowments are assumed to be fixed and are assigned to firms exogenously. They do affect the production possibilities of different enterprises, as reflected in their respective production sets (see below). Factors other than labor do not earn any explicit financial rewards; workers earn fixed nominal wages.

Producers

There are m producers (indexed by j), each of which has a production set Y_j. $y_j \in Y_j$ is a vector $(y_{j1}, \ldots, y_{jk}, \ldots, y_{jh})$, with inputs carrying negative signs and outputs positive signs. Total net production by all producers is $y = \sum y_j$,[7] and the aggregate production set is $Y = \sum Y_j$. The following assumptions are made on production sets:[8] (1) Y_j is closed and convex; (2) $0 \in Y_j$; and (3) $\{-R^h\} \subset Y_j$.[9]

Producers pay fixed positive wages w_{ij} to each worker in their labor force; to be consistent with the specification of prices, wages are in terms of the numeraire good.[10] Firm j's wage bill is $w_j = \sum_i w_{ij}$, and the total wage bill is $w = \sum w_j$. Zero production does not mean zero profits; the "floor" below which profits cannot fall (if the firm shuts down) is $-w_j$.

The jth producer faces a plan $v_j = (v_{j1}, \ldots, v_{jk}, \ldots, v_{jh})$, which is a vector of output targets and input allocations that must be fulfilled. Some coordinates of v_j can be positive (output targets), some negative (input allocations), and some zero (no plan). Net total plan targets/allocations for all enterprises are $v = \sum v_j$. Plan transactions all carry plan prices q, whereas transactions other than those specified by v_j occur on a voluntary basis through the market, at prices p. The plan thus sets minimum production and purchase requirements for each producer, limiting actual production to a subset Yj of Y_j: $Y_j = \{y_j \in Y_j / v_{j*} (y_j-v_j) \geq 0\}$.[11] Y_j is defined as the *plan-consistent* production set of the jth producer.

An enterprise is *plan-constrained* with respect to input or output k if $y_j \in Y_j$ but for $y_{jk} \neq 0$, $y_{jk} = v_{jk}$, and moreover, an infinitesimal reduction in the absolute value of v_{jk} would cause an equal fall in the absolute value of y_{jk}, so that $y_{jk} = v_{jk}$ still holds.[12] A firm is *unconstrained* if it is not plan-constrained for any input or output. Plan constraints are different from quantity constraints in disequilibrium theory, which involve absolute restrictions on levels of activity. Plan constraints here involve voluntary refusal by an enterprise to purchase an input on the market, or to produce and sell an output for the market. Plan-constrained firms are responding to market prices and their given vector of plan targets and allocations, rather than to binding restrictions. Refusal by a profit-maximizing enterprise to purchase an input on the market, for example, simply means that the market price is too high to elicit such a response. Similarly, refusal to produce an output for the market means that the market price is too low.

Given convexity of production sets, high output plan targets and input allocations are likely to discourage enterprises from participating in the market. The more output an enterprise produces for the plan, the higher the marginal cost of producing additional output (at least it is no lower), and hence the need for higher market prices to elicit production for the market. Sufficient reductions in output targets and input allocations always cause plan-constrained enterprises to become unconstrained. Plan constraints are in relation to the market price rather than the plan price, so changes in the latter do not determine whether or not a firm is plan-constrained.

The set V_j of different possible plans for enterprise j must satisfy certain conditions to ensure that plans indeed can be achieved. The output targets in the vector v_j (all $v_{jk} > 0$, or v_j^+) must together be in at least one element of Y_j. The same is true of input targets (all $v_{jk} < 0$, or v_j^-), though they need not be in the same element of Y_j as the output targets.[13]

Enterprises maximize profits (or surplus) subject to meeting all plan targets. Letting s_j be the jth producer's profits (also specified in relation to the price of the numeraire good), its maximization problem is:

$$\underset{y_j \in Y_j}{\text{Max}}\ s_j = p \cdot (y_j - v_j) + q \cdot v_j - w_j \qquad \text{s.t.}\ v_j * (y_j - v_j) \geqslant 0. \qquad (1)$$

An alternative way of stating the problem is Max s_j subject to $y_j \in Y_j$. Given the assumptions on plan targets, the plan-consistent production set Y_j is nonempty and convex, so a maximum level of profits does exist. Since plan targets are obligatory and resales of plan-allocated inputs are not permitted, enterprises must produce at least v_j^+, and must also accept their input allocations v_j^-. Hence, they will always use plan inputs that are not needed for production within the plan for production for the market. Some firms may be forced to purchase inputs on the market to achieve their mandatory output targets. Total net profits are $s = \sum_j s_j$.

Consumers

There are n consumers (indexed by i), with preferences $\geq^C_i$ and consumption sets X_i, whose elements are $x_i = (x_{i1}, \ldots, x_{ik}, \ldots, x_{ih})$. Total consumption is $x = \sum x_i$, and the total consumption set is $X = \sum X_i$. Consumers are also employees, assigned to enterprises with no freedom to change jobs. Consumer i (working at producer j) receives nominal wages w_{ij}, which he takes as given, and plan allocations c_i of consumer goods, at prices q. Total plan allocations of consumer goods are $c = \sum c_i$; the total wage bill is $w = \sum \sum w_{ij}$. Consumers have exogenously fixed resources of consumer goods e_i; total resources of all consumers are $e = \sum e_i$. Plan-allocated consumer goods cannot be resold, which means that $c_i \in X_i$ must hold. Consumers are assumed not to be able to sell their resources, either, though there is free disposal of commodities. Each consumer's purchases of consumption goods are $x_i^P = x_i - e_i \geq 0$. The ith consumer's plan-consistent consumption set X_i is $X_i = \{x_i \in X_i / x_i - e_i \geq c_i\}$.

The following standard (Debreu 1982, 711) assumptions are made on consumption sets and preferences: (4) X_i is closed, convex, and has a lower bound for $\geq {}^{C}_i$; (5) there is local nonsatiation in the possible consumption set X_i; (6) the set of all consumption bundles weakly preferred to a given $x_i \in X_i$ (i.e., $X_i = \{x_i' \mid x_i' \geq {}^{C}_i x_i\}$) is closed; (7) if x_i and x_i'' are two points in X_i with $x_i'' > {}^{C}_i x_i$,[15] and r is a real number in $]0,1]$, then $(1-r)x_i + rx_i'' \geq {}^{C}_i x_i$; and (8) there is an $x_i{}^{\circ} \in X_i$ such that $x_i{}^{\circ} \ll e_i$.

Under these assumptions, consumer preferences can be represented by a continuous, quasi-concave utility function, which the consumer maximizes subject to his budget constraint. Letting $u^C_i(x_i)$ be the utility function of the ith consumer, his maximization problem is as follows:

$$\underset{x_i \in X_i}{\text{Max }} u^C_i(x_i) \qquad \text{s.t. } w_{ij} \geq p \cdot (x_i^P - c_i) + q \cdot c_i. \qquad (2)$$

A consumer is plan-constrained for good k if $x_i \in X_i$ but $x_{ik} - e_{ik} = c_{ik} \neq 0$.[16] A consumer is unconstrained if he or she is not facing plan constraints for any goods.

Investors and the Flow of Surplus

"Investors" are left unspecified as to their precise identity, but they can consist of enterprises, the government, or other institutions. There are o investors, indexed by g, with preferences $\geq {}^I_g$, investment sets Z_g, and actual investment z_g. Investors receive plan allocations of investment goods d_g, at prices q; any purchases above d_g are made on the market, at prices p. Total allocations of investment goods to investors are $d = \Sigma \, d_g$. Each investor has resources of investment goods t_g; hence, his purchases of investment goods are $z_g^P = z_g - t_g \geq 0$. Investors receive financial "endowments" just sufficient to purchase the investment goods allocated to them through the plan, plus a fixed share of any profits left over once all investors have received their funds for within-plan purchases of investment goods. f_g is the total amount of funds accruing to investor g:

$$f_g = q \cdot d_g + a_g(s - q \cdot d) \qquad \text{if} \qquad s \geq q \cdot d$$

$$f_g = q \cdot d_g \qquad\qquad\qquad \text{if} \qquad s < q \cdot d. \qquad (3)$$

a_g lies on the closed interval between zero and one, with $\Sigma \, a_g = 1$. This is only one of many possible formulations for the flow of funds to investors, but it has the advantage that each investor always has sufficient funds at least to purchase the investment goods allocated to him through the plan.[17] Plan-consistent investment sets are $Z_g = \{z_g \in Z_g \mid z_g - t_g \geq d_g\}$. Investors also are not allowed to sell their resources or plan allocations.

Investors' preferences satisfy the same kinds of assumptions as those of consumers: (9) Z_g is closed, convex, and has a lower bound for $\geq {}^I_g$; (10) there is local nonsatiation in Z_g; (11) the set of all investment bundles weakly preferred to a given $z_g \in Z_g$ (i.e., $Z_g' = \{z_g' \mid z_g' \geq^I_g z_g\}$) is closed; (12) If z_g and z_g'' are two points in Z_g with $z_g'' >^I_g z_g$,[18] and r is a real number in $]0,1]$, then $(1-r)z_g + rz_g'' >^I_g z_g$; and (13) there exists a $z_g^0 \in Z_g$ such that $z_g^0 \ll t_g$. These assumptions allow investors' preferences to be represented by an investor's "utility function," $u^I_g(z_g)$. The ith investor then faces the following problem:

$$\text{Max } u^I_g(z_g) \quad \text{s.t. } f_g \geq p \cdot (z_g - t_g - d_g) + q \cdot d_g \quad \text{or } a_g s \geq p \cdot (z_g - t_g - d_g)$$

$$\text{and } z_g - t_g \geq d_g \text{ (or } z_g \in Z_g) \tag{4}$$

An investor is plan-constrained with respect to a particular good if he receives a positive plan allocation but does not purchase any of the good on the market (and this does not happen to be exactly the amount he would have purchased in the absence of the plan constraint). Investors not plan-constrained for any good are defined as unconstrained. If $s < q \cdot d$, all investors are completely plan-constrained (due to financial constraints), and there is no market demand for any investment good.

The Planning System

The planning system determines (1) plan targets for producers, consumers, and investors $((v_j),(c_i),(d_g))$; (2) plan prices q; (3) wages (w_{ij}); and (4) shares of profits going to investors above those required for purchase of plan-allocated investment goods (a_g). As was already mentioned, plan prices are fixed in relation to the price of the first commodity (p_1), and the same is true of wages w_{ij}. So the planning system actually fixes all q_k/p_1 and w_{ij}/p_1. Plan parameters (1) – (4) are all taken as given by the agents in the economy (producers, consumers, and investors). Certain other variables are treated as exogenous by both agents and the planning system (at least in the short run): (1) consumers' and investors' resources $((e_i),(t_g))$; (2) factor endowments of producers (which determine production sets Y_j); and (3) consumers' and investors' preferences and choice sets $(X_i),(Z_g)$. Most of these variables may be subject to manipulation by the planning system over the medium term, but they are taken as given for the purposes of this static model.

The behavior and decision processes of the planning system are not explicit in the model. Certain consistency requirements must be met, however, for agents to be able to act in conformity with plans and for market equilibrium to be possible. It is assumed that the planning system manipulates the variables under its control to achieve this minimal degree of consistency, rather than engaging in explicit optimization.

For the plan-consistent consumption, production, and investment sets (X_i, Y_j, Z_g) to be nonempty, the sets of possible plan targets C_i, D_g, and V_j must satisfy the following consistency conditions: (14) $C_i = \{c_i + e_i \in X_i\}$; (15) $D_g = \{d_g + t_g \in Z_g\}$;

and (16) $V_j = \{v_j$ such that there exists $y_j' \in Y_j$ for which $v_j^+ = y_j'$ and there exists $y_j'' \in Y_j$ for which $v_j^- = y_j''^-\}$. To meet these requirements, it would seem that the planning system needs to know the production, consumption, and investment sets of every agent, implying unrealistic centralization of information. It could rely on "planning from the achieved level," however, and assign targets based on past performance, or there could be a planning process during which assignment of inconsistent targets would stimulate a response to this effect by agents; the planning system would then adjust these targets until they become consistent.

At the aggregate level, a fundamental consistency requirement is that plans must be balanced: the sum total of all allocations of goods to users should be just equal to total enterprise output targets, less their input allocations: (17) $v - (c + d) = 0$. This condition in principle is not hard to meet since plan targets are all set by the planning system itself.

Consumers' and investors' financial resources must be sufficient to permit them to purchase goods allocated to them through the plan. This is automatically ensured for investors by the way financial flows to them are determined. For consumers, it is required that (18) $w_{ij} \geq q \cdot c_i$ for all i. This condition in principle can be met rather easily, since the variables concerned are controlled by the planning system. But it also implies that wages are adjusted in response to changes in plan prices q or allocations c_i, whenever these changes would result in the condition being violated.

Enterprise Behavior

Unconstrained firms behave exactly as they would in a pure market environment, providing that they do not become plan-constrained as a result of any changes that may occur. Enterprises respond only to market prices, and changes in plan parameters (output targets, input allocations, or plan prices) have no effect on total output or purchase of any good by unconstrained enterprises. Such changes can affect the level of enterprise profits, but profit-maximizing firms are not subject to any "income effects" from these changes.[19] In effect, changes in plan parameters have a "lump sum" impact on unconstrained enterprises.

These results can be demonstrated using the enterprise profit function. The jth producer's profit is $s_j = p \cdot y_j + (q - p) \cdot v_j$. Let the unconstrained profit-maximizing choice be y_j^*, so $y_j^* = y_j \in Y_j$ / max $s_j = p \cdot (y_j - v_j) + q \cdot v_j$, and by assumption $v_j^*(y_j^* - v_j) > 0$ for all $v_j \neq 0$. Consider a change in plan targets and allocations from v_j to v_j'. Then the profit function becomes $s_j' = p \cdot y_j + (q - p) \cdot v_j'$. From inspection it is clear that y_j^* remains a profit-maximizing choice of input and output levels, since only that part of the profit function that is unrelated to enterprise choice variables (in the unconstrained situation) has changed. The same is true of a change in plan prices from q to q'.

For a plan-constrained producer, changes in the output target(s) or input allocation(s) for which it is plan-constrained cause exactly corresponding changes in output or purchases of the good(s) concerned, as long as the producer remains plan-constrained with respect to them.[20] On the other hand, changes in plan prices q have no impact, as in the unconstrained case (this can be verified by inspection of the profit function). The very definition of plan constraints implies that production or purchases of goods with respect to which a producer is plan-constrained will be higher than in the absence of the constraint. The interaction between output and input plan constraints can be complex, however.

Consumers' and Investors' Choices

Investors are automatically compensated for the income effects of changes in plan prices q, under the adjustment mechanism specified above. Hence, their optimal investment choices will be unaffected, regardless of whether or not they are plan-constrained. The same is not true, however, of changes in plan allocations of investment goods d_g. These results can be demonstrated by looking at changes in a typical investor's budget constraint.

$$f_g = q \cdot d_g + a_g(s - q \cdot d) \geqslant p \cdot (z_g - t_g - d_g) + q \cdot d_g$$

or

$$a_g(s - q \cdot d) \geqslant p \cdot (z_g - t_g - d_g).$$

The assumption of nonsatiation means that the equality will always hold in the budget constraint. A change in q to q' causes equal changes of $(q'- q) \cdot d$ in s and $q \cdot d$. Hence, the left side of the budget constraint remains unchanged. Nothing on the right side of the budget constraint changes, either, so if z_g^* was the optimal choice of investment initially, it will remain the optimal choice after the change in plan prices. This automatic compensation for income effects of plan price changes occurs regardless of whether or not an investor is plan-constrained.

For investor b, a change in plan allocations from d_b to d_b' changes the left side of the budget constraint by $-a_b p \cdot (d_b' - d_b)$, whereas it changes the right side by $- p \cdot (d_b' - d_b)$. These changes will not be the same except in the special case when $a_b = 1$. Hence, the optimal choice of investment will in general change with the change in plan allocation, even in the unconstrained situation. It is possible to "compensate" investors for the income effects of changing plan allocations (their own or those of other investors), by adjusting a_b to a_b', as follows:

$$a_b' = \frac{[a_b(s - q \cdot d) - p \cdot (d_b' - d_b)]}{[s - q \cdot d - p \cdot \Sigma \ (d_g' - d_g)]} . \tag{5}$$

The denominator in the above formula is the change in total profits left over after financing payments for plan-allocated investment goods, while the numerator is the amount of these profits accruing to investor b previously, plus the impact on his cost of purchasing plan-allocated investment goods from the changes. Compensation needed for investors due to changes in plan allocations to other investors also can be calculated from this formula.

The formula applies only when a_b' as calculated lies between zero and one, which requires on the one hand that $a_g(s - q \cdot d) \geq p \cdot (d_g' - d_g)$ and on the other that $a_b' \leq 1$. If these conditions are not met, full compensation of the investor concerned is impossible. The compensation formula is also based on the assumption that no producers of investment goods whose plan allocations are being changed are plan-constrained with respect to these goods.

Consumers face income effects from changes in both plan allocations and plan prices because of their fixed nominal budget constraints. As in the case of investors, these can be offset by compensating adjustments in wages. The compensation formulae can be derived from consumers' budget constraints.

$$w_{ij} \geq p \cdot (x_i - e_i - c_i) + q \cdot c_i.$$

A change in plan prices from q to q' and in plan allocations from c_i to c_i' changes the right side of the budget constraint by

$$- p \cdot (c_i' - c_i) + q' \cdot c_i' - q \cdot c_i$$

Hence the adjusted wage is

$$w_{ij}' = w_{ij} - p \cdot (c_i' - c_i) + q' \cdot c_i' - q \cdot c_i \tag{6}$$

Though the idea that consumers and investors would be compensated for all the effects of changes in plan parameters on their "real" incomes superficially appears implausible, it is less unrealistic in China than might be expected. The government has a strong commitment to maintain and indeed raise the real standard of living of the urban population. On two separate occasions in the past, urban residents were compensated with additional cash payments for the impact of changes in plan prices on their real incomes. In early 1988, China's top leadership announced a policy of "compensation" of urban wage-earners for the impact of changes in ration prices and ration quantities for food on their real incomes. Though compensation is likely to be crude and imperfect, it is a significant phenomenon in China, which agents and authorities take into account.

General Equilibrium

The economy E is completely described by the production sets Y_j of the m producers; the consumption sets X_i, resources e_i, and preferences $\geq {}^c{}_i$ of the n consumers; and the investment sets Z_g, resources t_g, and preferences $\geq {}^l{}_g$ of the o

investors. A state of the economy E is an m-list (y_j) of the productions of the different producers; an n-list (x_i) of the consumptions of the consumers; an o-list (z_g) of the investment choices made by the investors; vectors (v_j) of producers' plan targets; vectors $(c_i$ and $d_g)$ of plan allocations to consumers and investors; the wage rates w_{ij} of consumers; the shares a_g of profits beyond those needed for within-plan purchases of investment goods going to investors; a plan price vector q; and a market price vector p.

Attainable states. Based on the concept of plan-consistent sets developed earlier, an attainable state of the economy E is defined as follows: (1) $x_i \in X_i$ for all i; (2) $y_j \in Y_j$ for all j; (3) $z_g \in Z_g$ for all g; and (4) $y + e + t - x - z \geq 0$ (or $y - x^P - z^P \geq 0$). Each agent's action is an element of its plan-consistent set, and moreover total net supply of every good is at least equal to demand. The attainable consumption, production, and investment sets X_i^A, Y_j^A, and Z_g^A consist of the elements of these plan-consistent sets which are also in an attainable state of the economy.

Definition of equilibrium. A state of the economy is an equilibrium (denoted by the superscript $*$) if:

(1) For every consumer i, x_i^* is a best element for $\geq^{C_i}$ of
$\{x_i \in X_i \,/\, w_i \geq p^* \cdot (x_i^P - c_i) + q \cdot c_i\}$.

(2) For every producer j, y_j^* maximizes
$s_j = p^* \cdot (y_j - v_j) + q \cdot v_j - w_j$, for $y_j \in Y_j$.

(3) For every investor g, d_g^* is a best element for $\geq^I_g$ of
$\{z_g \in Z_g \,/\, f_g \geq p^* \cdot (z_g^P - d_g) + q \cdot d_g$.

(4) $y^* + e + t - x^* - z^* \geq 0$, with $p^* \geq 0$, and $p^* \cdot (y^* + e + t - x^* - z^*) = 0$.

Nonstandard Assumptions

The model differs in several respects from the standard Arrow-Debreu framework, so certain additional assumptions are required to demonstrate existence of equilibrium.

Overall consistency of plan targets. Given the assumption that all consumers and investors have resources that put them in the interior of their respective consumption and investment sets to start with, zero production ($y_j = 0$ for all j) comprises an attainable state of the economy in the absence of all plan targets (i.e., $v_j = c_i = d_g = 0$, for all j, i, g). But this is of course a trivial and uninteresting equilibrium,[21] and moreover there is no guarantee that there will be any attainable states in the economy if some plan parameters are nonzero.

A number of consistency requirements for plan parameters were mentioned in the previous section, but these alone are not sufficient to ensure that there are attainable states for the economy as a whole. A stronger, global assumption is needed. The basic requirement is that the intersection between the sum of the plan-consistent sets for all producers and the sum of plan-consistent sets for consumers and investors be nonempty. Let $Y = \Sigma\, Y_j$, $X = \Sigma\, X_i$, and $Z = \Sigma\, Z_g$. Then the consistency requirement is simply (19) $Y \cap X + Z \neq \{\ \}$. The degree of realism and feasibility of such a condition can be questioned, but knowledge of production sets, planning from the achieved level, or sufficient reductions in plan targets and allocations in the face of inconsistencies would allow the condition to be met.

Transfers from consumers to investors. Given the formula for financial flows to investors outlined earlier, there is a possibility that total funds accruing to them will exceed total profits, i.e., $s < q \cdot d$, which would destroy aggregate financial balance in the economy. This problem can be dealt with by downward adjustments in nominal wages (imposed automatically) whenever necessary. Letting w_{ij} and w be the individual wage and total wage bill originally set by the planning system, the required adjustments in wages could be determined as follows:

$$w_{ij} = \mathbf{w}_{ij} \quad\text{and}\quad w = \mathbf{w}, \quad\text{if}\quad s \geqslant q \cdot d$$

$$w_{ij} = \mathbf{w}_{ij} - (q \cdot d - s)(\mathbf{w}_{ij}/\mathbf{w}) \tag{7}$$

$$\text{and}\quad w = \mathbf{w} - (q \cdot d - s), \quad\text{if}\quad s < q \cdot d$$

Under this adjustment mechanism, if total net profits of producers are insufficient to finance purchases of plan-allocated investment goods by investors, each consumer's wages are reduced proportionately to cover the shortfall. For the purposes of most of the analysis, we will assume that the general equilibrium solution point lies in the region where $s \geq q \cdot d$. This adjustment mechanism does allow existence of equilibrium even when $s < q \cdot d$, however. Wages of course are still taken as given by consumers, but they now may vary with market prices p, i.e., $w_{ij} = w_{ij}(p)$. Hence the budget constraints of consumers (given in [2] above) should be modified accordingly.

Given the assumption that there are some attainable states allowed by the plan parameters chosen by the planning system, it can be shown that total cash flow in the economy is sufficient for total purchases of consumption and investment goods through the plan. The aggregate financial balance for the economy is $p \cdot (y - v) + q \cdot v = s + w.$[22] Since $v = c + d$, $q \cdot v = q \cdot c + q \cdot d$. Substituting, we obtain: $p \cdot (y - c - d) + q \cdot c + q \cdot d = s + w$. In an attainable state of the economy, $y \geq c + d$ (in the case of intermediate goods $y \geq 0$, and for consumption and investment goods, $y \geq c$ and $y \geq d$ respectively), which means that $s + w \geq q \cdot c + q \cdot d$. Thus, in an attainable state of the economy, total cash flow will be sufficient to finance purchases of all consumption and investment goods allocated through the plan.[23]

The aggregate production set. Since labor and other factors of production are excluded from the production sets Y_j, some of the assumptions in the Arrow-Debreu framework are not appropriate. In particular, the assumption that $Y \cap \{-Y\} = \{0\}$ does not make sense.[24] An alternative assumption that is sufficient for the purposes of the existence proof is that the aggregate production function Y is strictly convex at one point: (20) for at least two points y', y'' on the boundary of Y, there exists a point $y \in Y$, such that $ay' + (1 - a)y'' \ll y$. Though this is a strong assumption, since it implies that each individual production set Y_j also is strictly convex at one or more points, it is not unreasonable in the context of fixed factors of production. In fact, even stronger assumptions, like strict convexity of production sets beyond a certain point, or even bounded production sets, are not implausible.

Demand for the first commodity. Since plan prices and wage rates are "anchored" to p_1, p_1 cannot be allowed to go to zero, unlike other prices. Since the first commodity provides utility to consumers and investors as a medium of exchange, it is logical to assume: (21) for at least some consumer or investor, there is always local nonsatiation for the first commodity. This means that total demand for the first commodity always exceeds supply as p_1 approaches zero, so p_1 never goes to zero at equilibrium.

Existence of Equilibrium

We can now state a proposition on existence of general equilibrium.

Proposition 1: Given assumptions (1) – (21), the economy E has an equilibrium.

Proof: The approach is to demonstrate a standard existence result based on the Arrow-Debreu framework (whose detailed steps are not repeated here). The agents in the economy are the m producers, the n consumers, the o investors, and the market.[25] Their choice sets are the plan-consistent sets (Y_j), (X_i), (Z_g), and P (the set of all possible market prices). The utility function of the ith consumer is u_i, that of the jth producer profit s_j, and that of the gth investor u_g. The utility function of the market agent is the value (at market prices) of excess demand:

$$p \cdot [\sum (y_j - v_j) - \sum (x_i - c_i - e_i) - \sum (z_g - d_g - t_g)] \tag{8}$$

Given market prices p, the choices of consumers and investors are restricted to those elements of their plan-consistent sets that can be purchased given their wages and shares of profits, respectively. The choice sets of producers are not affected by market prices. What must be shown is that the correspondence that consists of the Cartesian product of the optimizing choices by all agents, given their budgetary and technological constraints and the choices of other agents (including the market prices set by the market agent), has a fixed point. This requires verifying that the conditions required for the Kakutani fixed point theorem hold, namely, that the restricted choice set for the economy as a whole (the Cartesian product of the choice sets of all agents) is nonempty, compact, and convex, and that the optimizing correspondence is upper hemicontinuous and convex-valued (Debreu 1982, 699).

The set of possible market price vectors is normalized to sum to 1; as a result $P = \{p \mid p \in \{R_h+\}$ and $\Sigma\, p_k = 1\}$. P is a nonempty, compact, and convex set. Since plan prices q_k and wages w_{ij} are fixed in relation to p_1, optimal choices of all agents (consumers, investors, producers, and the market) are invariant with respect to equiproportional changes in all market prices.[26]

The choice sets (Y_j), (X_i), and (Z_g) are not necessarily compact, necessitating some modifications as in the traditional Arrow-Debreu approach. Consider the attainable production, consumption, and investment sets Y_f^A, X_i^A, and Z_i^A. Arrow and Debreu (1954, 276–77) demonstrate that the attainable production and consumption sets are bounded, but some of their assumptions on production sets have not been used in this model. Therefore, it is necessary to show that Y_f^A are bounded in this economy as well. This can be done easily, using assumption (20).

The aggregate production set Y is closed and convex (as the sum of closed, convex sets), includes the point 0 in its interior (since all the individual firms' production sets do), and is strictly convex in at least one place (by assumption). Given these conditions, the set of points $y \in Y$ for which $-y \in Y$ is bounded. If this were not true, then for some y, it would be the case that the sequences of points ry, $-ry \in Y$, for $r \to \infty$. But given the assumptions on Y, the distance between a straight line connecting two points on the surface of Y and the surface of y must eventually increase as the points are moved directly away from each other. This means that eventually such a line cannot pass through the origin (since the origin is at a fixed distance from the surface of the aggregate production set. In particular, the line containing the points ry, $-ry$ beyond a certain point must contain points that are not elements of Y. This contradiction shows that the set of points $y \in Y$ for which $-y \in Y$ is indeed bounded.

Since $Y_j \subset Y$, for $y_j \in Y_j$ and $y_j \in Y_f^A$ both to hold, it must be true that $-y_j \in Y$. Hence, all the sets Y_f^A are bounded, and it can be demonstrated that the sets X_i^A and Z_g^A also are bounded, as is shown in Arrow and Debreu (1954, 277). With the attainable production, consumption, and investment sets bounded, it is possible to construct a cube that contains in its interior all X_i^A, Y_j^A, and Z_g^A. A new economy is then created, where the choice sets are intersections of the respective plan-consistent sets with this cube. In this new economy, all the requirements for existence of general equilibrium are satisfied (in particular compactness of choice sets). It is straightforward, then, to show that the equilibrium of this new economy is equivalent to an equilibrium of the economy E (ibid., 279), which completes the proof.

The main purpose of proving existence of equilibrium is to set a solid foundation for the efficiency/welfare analysis that follows. Hence, technical refinements and possibilities for weakening the assumptions are ignored. Moreover, it is generally assumed in the subsequent analysis that financial constraints on consumers and investors with respect to their purchases of plan-allocated consumption and investment goods are not binding, or in other words, $w_{ij} > q \cdot c_i$ and $s > q \cdot d$.

Types of equilibria. An unconstrained equilibrium is one in which no agent is plan-constrained, so each agent is participating in the market at least at the margin for all goods that it actually purchases or produces. In a constrained equilibrium at least one agent is plan-constrained, but there are active markets for all goods with nonzero plan targets and allocations. If total demand and supply are plan-constrained for one or more goods, the outcome is a constrained equilibrium with nonfunctioning markets.

There are whole families of unconstrained equilibria that are "equivalent" to each other in having exactly the same production, consumption, and investment $((y_j^*),(x_i^*),(z_g^*))$ by all agents, and the same market prices p^*; they may differ in their plan parameters $((v_j),(c_i),(d_g))$, plan prices q, wages (w_i), and profit shares (a_g). In other words, the variables that are exogenous to agents but determined by the planning system can vary to a considerable degree, leaving total production, consumption, and investment by each agent unchanged. Moreover, every unconstrained equilibrium is "equivalent" to (and has the same properties as) some "pure" market equilibrium in which there are no plan targets and allocations.

Lemma 1: If $((y_j^*),(x_i^*),(z_g^*),(p^*))$ is an unconstrained equilibrium of the economy, with plan targets $((v_j^*),(c_i^*),(d_g^*))$, plan prices q^*, and wages (w_{ij}^*), there exists another equilibrium of the economy with $((y_j^*),(x_i^*),(z_g^*),(p^*))$ and $v_j = c_i = d_g = 0$ for all j, i, and g.

Proof: The equivalent equilibrium (indicated by **) can be obtained by making the following adjustments in wages and profit shares:

$$w_{ij}^{**} = w_{ij}^* + (p^* - q^*) \cdot c_i^*$$

$$a_g^{**} = \frac{[a_g^*(s^* - q^* \cdot d_g^*) + p^* \cdot d_g^*]}{[s^* - q \cdot d^* + p^* \cdot d^*]} \qquad (9)$$

These are simply the adjustment formulas (6) and (5), for the special case where plan parameters are all changed to zero. Of course, the second set of adjustments only are possible if they result in $0 \leq a_g^{**} \leq 1$.[27]

It is then easy to verify by looking at producers' profit functions and consumers' and investors' budget constraints that their optimal choices remain unchanged, given market prices p^*. This means that the state of the economy $((y_j^*),(x_i^*),(z_g^*),(p^*))$, with $v_j = c_i = d_g = 0$ for all j, i, and g and (w_{ij}^{**}) and (a_g^{**}) is an equilibrium, completing the proof.

Efficiency Properties of the Model

Unconstrained equilibrium has strong welfare/efficiency properties, which are demonstrated using the Pareto criterion. Planning in many respects is irrelevant to the unconstrained equilibrium outcome. Properties of constrained equilibrium and constrained equilibrium with nonfunctioning markets also are described.

Pareto Optimality

Among two attainable states, one is at least as desirable as the other if every consumer and investor is at least as well off in it as in the other. If $A^1 = (x_i^1, y_j^1, z_g^1, p^1)$ and $A^2 = (x_i^2, y_j^2, z_g^2, p^2)$ are two attainable states of the economy E, then $A^1 \geq A^2$ if and only if $x_i^1 \geq^{C_i} x_i^2$ for all i and $z_i^1 \geq {}^I_g z_i^2$ for all g. An attainable state is preferred to another if, in addition, at least one agent is better off, that is $x_i^1 \geq^{C_i} x_i^2$ for all i, $z_i^1 \geq {}^I_g z_i^2$ for all g *and* $x_i^1 >^{C_i} x_i^2$ or $z_g^1 > {}^I_g z_g^2$ for at least one i or g. $A^1 > A^2$ implies $A^1 \geq A^2$; $A^1 \geq A^2$ means it is not true that $A^2 > A^1$; and $A^1 \geq A^2$ and $A^2 \geq A^1$ imply $A^1 = A^2$.

A *constrained Pareto optimum* of the economy E is an attainable state to which no other attainable state is preferred (equivalently, it is at least as desirable as any other state), with given values of v_j, c_i, d_g, q, a_g, w_{ij}, for all h, g, i, j. An *unconstrained Pareto optimum* is an attainable state to which no other attainable state is preferred, regardless of the values of these plan parameters. Any unconstrained Pareto optimum is also a constrained Pareto optimum, but not vice versa.

Equivalence of Pareto Optima and Unconstrained Equilibria

Standard theorems of welfare economics can be applied to the model.

Proposition 2: If a certain state of the economy E is an equilibrium, it is also a constrained Pareto optimum.

Proof: Let $A^* = ((y_j^*), (x_i^*), (z_g^*), (p^*))$ be an equilibrium, with $((v_j^*), (c_i^*), (d_g^*), (q^*), (w_{ij}^*), (a_g^*))$. Suppose A^* is not constrained Pareto optimal, so there is some attainable state $A' > A^*$, which means $x_i' \geq^{C_i} x_i^*$ and $z_g' \geq {}^I_g z_g^*$ for all i, g and $x_i' >^{C_i} x_i^*$ for some i or $z_g' > {}^I_g z_g^*$ for some g. For a consumer who strictly prefers A' over A^*, $p^* \cdot (x_i' - e_i - c_i^*) + q^* \cdot c_i > w_{ij}^*$ must hold. Otherwise it would have been possible for him to purchase x_i' in the original equilibrium and he would have done so. Similarly, for $z_g' > {}^I_g z_g^*$, it must be the case that $p^* \cdot (z_g' - t_g - c_i^*) + q^* \cdot d_g^* > f_g$. Summing the budget constraints yields $p^* \cdot [(x' - e - c^*) + (z' - t - d^*)] + q^* \cdot (c^* + d^*) > w^* + s^*$.

Given that A' is an attainable state, $y' + e + t \geq x' + z'$. Using $v = c + d$ and substituting, we get $p^* \cdot (y' - v^*) + q^* \cdot v^* > w^* + s^* = p^* \cdot (y^* - v^*) + q^* \cdot v^*$. The right side is total profits in the original equilibrium. This implies that with the original equilibrium market prices p^*, aggregate profits in the preferred attainable state are higher than in the original equilibrium. But if this were true, producers would have chosen y' rather than y^* in the original equilibrium (otherwise they would not have been maximizing profits). Hence A^* is not an equilibrium, a contradiction that completes the proof.

Proposition 3: Any unconstrained Pareto optimum of the economy E can be recreated by an equilibrium of the model with zero plan parameters.

Proof (sketch): The standard argument can be applied that there exists a supporting hyperplane for the set of all levels of resources that permit preferred states of the economy to the unconstrained Pareto optimal state, which goes through the state (on the boundary of the set), and whose normal defines a price vector that is the equilibrium market price vector (with plan targets and allocations all set at zero) for that unconstrained Pareto optimal state (Debreu 1959, 95–96).

Before demonstrating that an equilibrium is an unconstrained Pareto optimum if and only if it is an unconstrained equilibrium, it is useful to establish the following:

Lemma 2: An equilibrium of the economy E with no plan targets (i.e., $v_j = c_i = z_g = 0$ for all j, i, g) is an unconstrained Pareto optimum.

Proof: Let A^* be an equilibrium, with $((y_j^*),(x_i^*),(z_g^*),(p^*))$ and $v_j = c_i = z_g = 0$. Suppose A'', with $((y''),(x''),(z''))$, is preferred to A^*. This means $p^* \cdot y'' > p^* \cdot y^*$. Given the first assumption, A'' must not be an attainable state when all plan parameters are zero. But the set of attainable states with arbitrary plan parameters is a subset of the set of attainable states with zero plan parameters. Suppose $((y_i''),(x_i''),(z_g''))$ is an attainable state, with $((v_j''), (c_i''),(d_g''),q'')$; hence $(y'' - v') + e + t - (x'' - c') - (z'' - d') \geq 0$. Since $v'' = c'' + d'', y'' + e + t - x'' - z'' \geq 0$. $y_j'' \in Y_j$, $x_i'' \in X_i$, and $z_g'' \in Z_g$ for all j, i, g. Moreover, the plan-constrained choice sets are subsets of the unconstrained sets, so $Y_j \subset Y_j, X_i \subset X_i$, and $Z_g \subset Z_g$ for all j, i, g. Thus, all the conditions for $((y_j''),(x_i''),(z_g''))$ to be an attainable state of the economy E with plan targets set at zero have been met. $((y_j''),(x_i''),(z_g''))$ is an attainable state of the "pure" market economy with zero plan targets and allocations, so $p^* \cdot y'' > p^* \cdot y^*$ contradicts the assumption that $((y_j^*),(x_i^*),(z_g^*), (p^*))$ is an equilibrium, completing the proof.

Proposition 4: An equilibrium of the economy E is an unconstrained Pareto optimum if and only if it is an unconstrained equilibrium.

Proof: The first ("if") part of the proposition follows from Lemmas 1 and 2. An unconstrained equilibrium is "equivalent" to one with zero plan targets (Lemma 1), which in turn is an unconstrained Pareto optimum (Lemma 2). The second ("only if") part of the proposition can be demonstrated as follows. From proposition 3, any unconstrained Pareto optimum of the economy E is also the equilibrium of a suitable price vector, with plan parameters set at zero and suitable values for wages and profit shares. Conversely, if an attainable state is not the equilibrium of a market price vector with zero plan parameters, it is not an unconstrained Pareto optimum. A constrained equilibrium is not equivalent to an equilibrium of a market price vector with zero plan parameters. This is because in constrained equilibrium, at least one agent's choice by definition is not what it would have been if he were maximizing utility (or profits) subject only to technological, factor endowment, and budget constraints. Therefore, a constrained equilibrium of the economy E is not an unconstrained Pareto optimum.

Proposition 4 means that not only is any unconstrained equilibrium of the model an unconstrained Pareto optimum, but moreover, Pareto optimality is lost as soon as plan constraints are imposed on any agents. This is a powerful result, whose main implication is that plan output targets and input allocations as well as plan allocations of final goods should be kept low enough that all agents can participate in the market, imbuing the economy with the efficiency properties associated with market systems.

Irrelevance of Planning

Many plan parameters have no impact on the unconstrained equlibrium solution of the model, whereas for others the effects of changes can be offset by appropriate "compensation." Some plan parameters are "irrelevant" in constrained equilibrium as well. These properties of the model follow directly from the results established earlier, so they are simply presented and discussed.

For intermediate goods, changes in output plan targets (v_j^+), input allocations (v_j^-), and plan prices q have no effect on the equilibrium solution. This is trivial in the case of changes in q, since there are offsetting changes in profits of different producers and no "income effects." For changes in plan targets and allocations for intermediate good k, we know $v_k = \sum v_{jk} = 0$. Since producer j is not plan-constrained, changes in v_{jk} have no effect on y_{jk}. Aggregating across producers, total production and demand at the equilibrium market price (y_k^+ and y_k^-) remain unchanged, with changes in market demand and supply exactly offsetting changes in plan targets and allocations. Total net profits remain unchanged (changes for different producers exactly offset each other), so there is no effect on investors, and the same is true of consumers. Hence, the original equilibrium market price vector will remain an equilibrium price vector for the economy.

In the case of investment goods, changes in plan prices q similarly have no effect on equilibrium outputs and market prices, regardless of whether or not some investors are plan-constrained. This can be verified from producers' profit functions, investors' budget constraints, and changes in total net profits. Changes in plan allocations (d_g) do have income effects on investors, but these can be offset by appropriate adjustments in a_g (if these are possible), leaving aggregate production of investment goods and use by each investor unchanged, at the same equilibrium market price vector. This latter result only applies in unconstrained equilibrium, however.

For consumer goods, changing plan targets, allocations, and/or prices can affect the equilibrium outcome, but with suitable adjustments in wages (according to (6)), the original equilibrium outcome is preserved. Producers' and consumers' optimal choices are the same, facing the original market equilibrium price vector, and total net profits, and hence the optimal choices of investors remain unchanged.

All in all, if there are no ''distributional'' effects within or between the two components of final demand (consumption and investment), then changes in plan parameters for any goods will not affect production or demand by any agent, and hence the equilibrium outcome in terms of production and use of every commodity will remain the same and market prices will be unchanged. This result holds as long as changes in plan parameters and any necessary compensating adjustments leave all agents unconstrained. Compensation for distributional effects is unnecessary for profit-maximizing producers and can be achieved through appropriate adjustments in wages and profit shares for consumers and investors. Thus in unconstrained equilibrium the planning system is irrelevant for the production and input purchase decisions of enterprises and, under certain conditions, for consumers and investors as well. Changes in plan parameters do cause changes in the shares of plan and market in total output of individual commodities, however. These shares can vary greatly, without any change in the equilibrium solution.

Impact of Plan Parameters in Constrained Equilibrium

If the equilibrium solution involves plan constraints on some agents, many properties of unconstrained equilibrium no longer hold. But changes in plan prices for intermediate goods and investment goods still have no impact, and the same is true of ''compensated'' plan price changes for consumption goods. This is obvious in the case of intermediate goods; producers' and users' profits are affected equally by a change in the plan price q, and there is no net effect on total profits or on investors' or consumers' demands. Production remains unchanged, since the price change has only income effects on producers. In the case of investment goods, investors are automatically compensated for changes in plan prices. Moreover, these compensating adjustments are just equal in their effect on total use of funds by investors to the induced change in total net profits of producers. Producers remain completely unaffected, so there is no change in equilibrium outputs or market prices. In the case of consumer goods, changing plan prices affects total net profits and also costs to consumers. These effects can be offset by the wage adjustments (6), leaving equilibrium production and demand by every agent unchanged.

It is always possible to move to a preferred outcome for the economy as a whole by releasing all agents from their plan constraints. For any constrained equilibrium of the economy, there exists a Pareto-superior unconstrained equilibrium that can be generated by releasing all plan-constrained agents from their plan constraints (through reductions in their plan output targets and input allocations) and making suitable adjustments in wages and/or profit-sharing formulae. This is easy to show. A constrained equilibrium is not an unconstrained Pareto optimum (proposition 4). Therefore, there exists an attainable state of the economy that is Pareto-superior to the constrained equilibrium and is an unconstrained Pareto optimal state. This latter Pareto optimum can be generated as an unconstrained equilibrium of the economy by setting wages and profit shares at appropriate levels (proposition 3). This result is important because it suggests an appropriate direction of reform for the economy.

It is more difficult to derive similar results for changes in plan parameters that move the economy from one constrained equilibrium to another. Additional work would be required to confirm any conjectures. It can be hypothesized, however, that judicious reductions in plan output targets and input allocations would move the economy to a Pareto-superior outcome. Since plan constraints can be viewed as enterprise-specific implicit subsidies for production or purchase of the goods concerned, it should be possible to apply the literature on general equilibrium with taxation to this problem.

Nonfunctioning Markets

The influence of planning is greatest in constrained equilibrium with nonfunctioning markets, since plans at both aggregate and individual levels are taut to the point where markets for some goods do not even exist. Only with nonfunctioning markets do plan parameters completely determine production and consumption, both in aggregate and for individual agents.

As the number of commodities with nonfunctioning markets increases, the price elasticity of demand and supply on the remaining, functioning markets tends to decline. Thus, the economy becomes more rigid and market price movements more volatile. Increasing the number of commodities for which there are nonfunctioning markets entails increasing plan constraints on individual agents and the imposition of plan constraints on additional agents who were previously not plan-constrained. Thus, the price responsiveness of agents' demand and supply on the remaining, functioning markets will be reduced (an application of the generalized Le Chatelier Principle; Samuelson 1947, 36–39), which means that aggregate demand and supply will become less price elastic. Conversely, reducing the number of nonfunctioning markets entails releasing some plan-constrained agents from plan constraints, which increases price elasticity of demand and supply on all markets.

With nonfunctioning markets for all investment goods due to financial constraints (if $s < q \cdot d$), the economy has some of the characteristics of a traditional centrally planned economic system. Investment goods are entirely subject to allocation through the plan. Moreover, plan controls are exactly consistent with and reinforced by the allocation of funds to investors—each investor gets no more than exactly the amount of money needed to finance purchases of plan-allocated investment goods. Actual wages are a residual—what is left over after the needs of financing investment are met. Thus, the planning system has direct control over both the aggregate level of investment in the economy and the detailed allocation of investment goods. On the other hand, the allocation of consumer goods may be left largely to the market (if most consumers are not plan-constrained).

Conclusions and Implications

This chapter has presented a simple static general equilibrium model of the Chinese economy, designed to illuminate patterns of resource allocation in the state-owned industrial sector. The model brings together a novel combination of elements, like the assumption that firms maximize profits, the modeling of plan targets as minimum constraints on enterprises' inflows and outflows of goods, and the twin assumptions of fixed factor endowments and fixed (or automatically adjusting) nominal wage rates.

It is straightforward to demonstrate existence of general equilibrium in the model, though this requires certain assumptions on plan parameters. Equilibria can be divided into two main types: (1) those in which no agent is plan-constrained and (2) those in which some agents are plan-constrained.

Two main types of welfare/efficiency results can be derived for the unconstrained equilibrium case. It is Pareto-optimal; moreover, it is "equivalent" to a "pure" market equilibrium without any planning (but with fixed enterprise factor endowments). The other main result concerns the irrelevance of planning— changes in plan parameters do not affect the equilibrium solution, under certain conditions.

Constrained equilibrium is not Pareto optimal, though it is "constrained Pareto optimal," given plan parameters, wage rates, and profit-sharing rates. In general, changes in plan targets and input allocations do affect the equilibrium outcome, but changes in plan prices have no effect for intermediate goods and investment goods. (In the case of consumer goods, income effects can be offset by compensating wage adjustments.) It is always possible to improve the efficiency of the economy by eliminating plan constraints and if necessary making adjustments in wage rates and profit shares, so as to ensure that all agents are at least as well off as before.

The model should be kept in perspective. The static context limits the significance of the results, as does the assumption of fixed factor endowments. Moreover, it is assumed that the agents follow the rules of the system, even though they have strong incentives to divert goods from plan to market channels. The assumption that enterprises maximize profits also is debatable. Finally, the relatively simple modeling of the planning process limits the degree of depth of analysis possible with the model alone. Overall, though these and other short-comings of the model do detract somewhat from the results obtained, they for the most part do not negate the model's main thrust. Some of the possible extensions of the model discussed in chapter 7 may ameliorate its weaknesses.

The model has some important implications for the evaluation of the present

Chinese economic system and for the choice of future reform policies. In the first place, production planning and administrative allocation of industrial goods have indeed to a large extent lost their direct role in resource allocation, as is implied by the model. Remaining influence is mainly through "income effects" or redistribution of rents among various claimants (see chapter 5). The model can be used to trace the movement of rents embodied in plan-allocated goods through the economy, but it is not well suited for analysis of "rent-seeking behavior" and its impact.

More generally, the model suggests that it is possible for an economic system to function efficiently in a narrow sense, despite the existence of the whole apparatus and activities of mandatory planning. The key requirements include slack production planning (in relation to capacity, not necessarily in relation to input requirements) and profit maximization on the part of firms. Needless to say, misallocation and rigidity of factors of production can be a more important source of inefficiency than poor functioning of goods markets.

Turning to the future, a major implication of the model is that the appropriate method for nurturing the further development of the market mechanism is judicious reductions in plan targets and allocations, releasing more and more agents from plan constraints and encouraging greater participation in markets. If necessary, compensation can be used to ensure that agents are not too severely affected by these changes.

Another important implication of the model is that changes in plan prices will be ineffective in either improving efficiency or expanding the role of markets. Plan prices can affect the allocation of resources only through their effect on rents and redistribution in the system. Thus, a great deal of effort should not be expended in trying to rationalize government-fixed prices for plan-allocated goods. Such administrative price reform is likely to degenerate into bargaining among those who stand to gain or lose from plan price changes.

At a more fundamental level, to the extent that the model accurately distills some key elements of Chinese reality, its results imply that the system in 1985–87 appeared to be moving in the right direction, at least with respect to short-term production and distribution of goods in the economy. The share of mandatory planning in demand and supply for industrial goods has been declining, while correspondingly the share of the market mechanism has been rising. Even though the model is static, not dynamic, its results appear to be broadly consistent with dynamic patterns and trends in Chinese industry (see chapter 9).

7. Assumptions, Limitations, and Extensions of the Model

GIVEN the strong results obtained from the general equilibrium model developed in chapter 6, it is necessary to reexamine its main assumptions and ascertain how closely they fit with Chinese reality. The limitations of the model also need to be reviewed to ascertain whether and to what extent they weaken its explanatory power. Certain fairly straightforward extensions of the model enhance its ability to simulate and interpret the evolving Chinese economy; hence they are worth outlining briefly. Finally, the earlier discussion of rents and rent-seeking behavior in chapter 5 can be at least to some extent formally incorporated in the model, enhancing its usefulness as an analytical tool. This chapter looks at each of these topics in turn.

Assumptions and Limitations

This section starts by looking at some of the technical assumptions, then at the question of restrictions on participation in markets. The main limitations of the model are then reviewed, including the static context; the exclusion of factor allocation; failure to model planning authorities' objectives and actions explicitly; failure explicitly to include the planning process; inadequate modeling of government and its investment; and the insufficient richness of distributional effects. Overall, though the obvious limitations of the model to some extent undermine the strong results obtained, they do not negate their main thrust.

Technical Assumptions

Some of the basic assumptions underlying the model, such as profit maximization, have already been discussed at length (see chapter 5). Certain other technical assumptions, like convexity of production sets, consumption sets, and preferences, have been examined extensively in the literature. The required assumption that the aggregate production set be strictly convex at least at one point is stronger than the assumptions normally used in general equilibrium theory. In the context of this model, however, convexity of production sets may not be unreasonable, since factors of production are fixed. Increasing returns to scale are much less likely with fixed factors than when factor inputs can be varied. Capacity and labor constraints may reasonably be expected to impose bounds on many production sets.

The exclusion of uncertainty is unrealistic but may be justified in the interest of simplicity. An extension of the model incorporating uncertainty is outlined in a later section of this chapter. As is shown there, if uncertainty does not affect plan parameters and plan target fulfillment, the basic results do not change with risk-neutral agents. But once positive probability of nonfulfillment of plan targets is allowed, serious problems arise for the model.

Another assumption discussed earlier is that plan parameters are set in a way that allows attainable states of the economy. Failure to achieve attainable states is not likely to be a problem in practice, given the slackness of plan targets in China and adjustment mechanisms that would come into play if targets are too high.

The assumption of balanced plans—that total output targets and total input allocations for each good are just equal to each other—seems innocuous on the surface but may be hard for the planning system to accomplish in practice, given chronic pressures to increase allocations to users and hold down output targets of producers. Assuming a fixed proportional shortfall of plan input allocations in relation to output targets for some or all products would not change the results of the model, but it would introduce a probably unnecessary degree of arbitrariness. The impact of unbalanced plans is similar to that of leakages, discussed later in the chapter.

Assumptions about Market Participation

Certain of the assumptions about participation in the market by the various agents in the model are crucial to the strong welfare/efficiency results obtained.

Plan constraints. The model duplicates a competitive market equilibrium only if no agent is plan-constrained on either the input or the output side. This would seem to be a very strong assumption, but given the way the Chinese system works in practice, it may be met for the bulk of agents. On the input side, the pressure of general excess demand at the plan price might ensure that few if any firms are in a position where they would voluntarily refuse to purchase inputs on the market. In fact, the need to rely on market purchases probably provides good evidence for enterprises to point to in bargaining with higher-level authorities to increase or maintain their plan-based input allocations. Similarly, given general excess demand at within-plan prices, it is hard to envisage that either component of final demand would voluntarily decline involvement in the market, so the share of plan-constrained allocations in total final demand is probably small.

The output side has been more problematic in the past, with binding plan constraints much more likely for large state enterprises. Nevertheless, the Chinese system has rapidly moved toward a situation where most firms are allowed to engage in "self-sales" at the margin, with flexible prices (see chapters 4 and 9). This means setting mandatory plan targets below capacity, so that there is room for market sales. Another, probably even more important, factor in this evolution is the increasing shortage of material inputs at the disposal of the government for allocation through mandatory plans. Since output plans at least in principle tend to be linked to provision of inputs at low prices, a shortage of the latter translates into lower mandatory output plan targets and hence greater likelihood that producers will not be plan-constrained on the output side. This process can be self-reinforcing, particularly if there are "leakages"—diversion of goods from plan allocation channels to the parallel market.

All in all, though the assumption of no plan constraints is not fully satisfied in detail, the pressures for "egalitarian" distribution of output targets and input quotas may be fairly strong and would tend to limit the quantitative importance of plan constraints. Thus, even where firms are subject to binding output constraints, the impact on equilibrium and on the efficiency and optimality properties of the system may be relatively small. The number of firms subject to binding output constraints and their share in total production may have become fairly small in the late 1980s.

Restrictions on participation. Prohibitions against market transactions and price controls can have a harmful impact and were common in the early 1980s, particularly for larger state-owned firms. Participation in the parallel market by large firms has been restricted by prohibitions against selling goods on the market; price controls affecting sales outside the plan; and high output targets and input allocations, which give firms no incentive to get involved in production for the market and in market transactions.

Before May 1984, many larger enterprises were supposed to sell all output at the state price, whether it was within the plan or outside the plan. Moreover, there were often restrictions on the amounts or shares of output that could be sold on the market, even at controlled prices. This forced firms to resort to barter-like tied transactions, selling their above-plan output only to entities willing to sell them something that was similarly underpriced and not easily available in return.

In May 1984 the right of enterprises to directly market above-plan output was reaffirmed, and most firms were permitted to sell this output at a price up to 20 percent above the state price (*China Economic Yearbook* Editorial Committee 1985, X/21–22). In the early stages this latter provision was not fully implemented. The Shenyang Smelter, for example, had still not been allowed to charge a higher price for production outside the plan as of October 1984 (interview information). Even when implemented, this new flexibility did not mean much in practice, since market prices for most goods exceeded plan prices by much more than 20 percent. The above-plan price stuck to the ceiling and still left a gap between demand and supply.

At the beginning of 1985, enterprises' right to engage in self-sales again was affirmed, but much more important, prices for above-plan sales of the bulk of industrial producer goods were completely decontrolled (Shen and Han 1986, 18). This represented a fundamental change from the past attitude that large firms should not fully participate in the parallel market. Administrative restrictions on participation in market transactions and price controls henceforth played only a minor if not insignificant role. A massive decontrol of prices of consumer durables in October 1986, as well as an earlier and continuing decontrol of prices of "minor" consumer goods, must also have increased market participation by producers.

All along, most enterprises have been much freer to participate in the parallel market on the purchasing side. Nonparticipation on the buying side has been much more the result of lack of profitability of such transactions, which could be caused by output price controls or prohibitions against market sales of output for larger firms potentially interested in making input purchases on the market. Restrictions on participation in the parallel market on the output side thus have had an impact on participation in markets for inputs, but this has been greatly reduced by liberalization of the former.

Dynamic Considerations

A great deal is lost by looking at the Chinese economy in a purely static framework. It is easy to envision a dynamic analogue of the model, but the conditions required for efficiency are much more stringent and unrealistic. The model would become one of long-run equilibrium, with agents making decisions on the basis of perfect foresight or expectations about the future. The conditions for dynamic optimality would be: (1) all the conditions for static optimality discussed earlier; (2) no ratchet effect or similar performance-based increases in plan targets; and (3) no "income effects" from plan targets and plan prices on investment.

This last condition is crucial and much more stringent than the conditions for static optimality. The system generates windfall profits for some firms and very low profits (or even losses) for others. If these profit differentials affect investment in different sectors and industries, the result is unlikely to be long-run Pareto optimal, even if market prices are otherwise giving appropriate signals. Enterprise profit retention makes firms' investments at least somewhat related to retained profits and overall profitability, which means that income effects would influence the direction of investment.

If there is free capital mobility, with capital costlessly seeking the highest-profit investments, then differential profits due to plan parameters would not affect investment decisions. Alternatively, if enterprises had complete freedom to enter new activities (also costlessly, and with the further assumption of no scale economies or diseconomies in investment), free diversification would substitute for perfect capital mobility. Neither of these assumptions is realistic in the Chinese context, however.

There is in any case some justification for the use of a static model. A focus on long-run equilibrium in the Chinese situation would be inappropriate. The economy is undergoing rapid economic development and major structural changes; reforms are transforming the institutional and policy environment; even the fundamental sources of enterprise motivation have been undergoing changes. Any tendencies toward long-run equilibrium are overwhelmed by the continuing "shocks" from reform and structural change. Hence, long-run equilibrium is much less meaningful as an object of attention than any short-run equilibrium the system may move toward.

Factor Allocation

Closely related to the static framework is the exclusion of factor allocation. One question is whether this is realistic in a static context, which depends on how easily and quickly factors can be reallocated. In China the bulk of the labor force of state enterprises cannot be moved in the short run, but there are certain sources of flexibility, related to the use of rural temporary workers, collective workers, and other nonregular employees (Byrd and Tidrick 1987, 70–72). The assumption of capital immobility also is reasonable, given system rigidities and the time required to make big changes in capital assets of sizable firms. This is even more true of land, whose transfer is subject to municipal administrative restrictions and red tape (see ibid., 76–78).

The failure to incorporate factor allocation into the model is thus not a major weakness in the static context, particularly if the focus is on large state enterprises. A dynamic approach would be necessary to look at factor allocation. From this perspective, the model has an essentially negative view: factors simply do not move, and factor allocation is completely rigid. This may not be unreasonable in the case of labor allocation even over the medium term. Medium-term rigidity of land allocation is also probably a reasonable assumption. In the case of capital assets, however, this assumption is clearly inappropriate.

Planners' Objectives and Actions

Failure to include planners' preferences, decision-making processes, and actions constitutes a big gap in the model. Plan parameters are all taken as given by firms, but there is nothing in the model to show how they are determined. Essentially, planning impinges on the system as an exogenous, arbitrary force. This negative role for planning is clearly not in line with Chinese reality, but going to the opposite extreme of assuming a single central planner who sets optimization-based targets is even more unrealistic. The planning system in China is highly fragmented and often works at cross-purposes. Targets may be based largely on the principle of "planning from the achieved level." Because of the large rents carried by plan allocations, planners are subject to great pressures, to which they can respond most easily by making "egalitarian" allocations. In sum, planning in China may generate certain regularities and patterns, but it is not appropriate to model it as centralized maximizing behavior.

Some of the objectives that may be important to Chinese planners are: (1) to increase aggregate production and improve efficiency; (2) to maintain or improve real standards of living; (3) to keep prices for investment goods low to maximize the "real" impact of given nominal budgetary resources; and (4) to maintain a certain degree of control over the economy in aggregate. Goal 1 is accomplished in the context of the model by ensuring that all agents are free of plan constraints. In a dynamic context, it would be furthered by a high investment rate, which would conflict in the short run with goal 2. Goals 2 and 3 are furthered by setting high wage rates and high plan targets for consumption and investment goods, but beyond a certain point this conflicts with goal 1. Finally, goal 4 is inconsistent with a system largely free from plan constraints, though control could be achieved by other means, for example, through the factor allocation system.

Planning Process

The above discussion has implicitly assumed that if they were included in the model, planners would set targets independently, without any involvement by firms. The model is consistent with this perspective because firms take plan targets and plan prices as exogenous. But Chinese enterprises participate extensively in planning, which is an iterative bargaining process with their supervisory agencies, who in turn bargain with *their* bureaucratic superiors. It is not so much the arbitrary nature of plan targets in the model that is unrealistic, but rather the implicit assumption that firms take these targets as exogenous and always give top priority to plan fulfillment.

The planning process could be modeled as a game between enterprise and supervisory agency, in which there are both divergent interests and gains to cooperation. Supervisory agencies must distribute the limited resources they obtain from higher levels among the firms under their jurisdiction, which means that from the individual enterprise point of view there is a conflict with the supervisory agency. These agencies are themselves evaluated on the basis of the performance of the enterprises under their jurisdiction, however, so there is also a confluence of interests.

Investment and the Government Budget

There is no separate government sector in the model; it is implicitly included as an undifferentiated part of the "investors" category. This is highly unrealistic: government investment behavior may differ from that of firms; profit distribution between enterprises and government is an important part of the system; and there is no room in the model for government consumption expenditures or transfers. It would be possible to include government saving and investment without much difficulty. This would require some form of taxes or profit sharing between enterprises and government. Government would spend its revenues on investment projects. Enterprise behavior would not be affected by a proportional profit tax.

Such an extension of the model would generate richer redistributional effects. If government and enterprises demand a different mix of investment goods, then changes in plan targets, plan prices, and profit-sharing rates could have an impact on equilibrium outputs and market prices. But this modeling of the government sector is fairly mechanical and would not capture the full range of interactions between government and enterprises, even less that between government and individuals, which is based to a large extent on government consumption expenditures and transfers.

A further extension of the model to include commodity taxation would be relatively straightforward. Taxes would cut into enterprise profits and serve as a source of funds for government investment. It would also be possible to include financial flows from government to individuals and government spending on consumer goods, but these would add greatly to the model's complexity and confuse many of the results.

Distributional Effects

Paradoxically, one weakness of the model is insufficient modeling of the rich redistributional flows that pervade the Chinese economy and planning system. Distributional effects among agents are largely nullified through various devices, especially in unconstrained equilibrium. Firms as profit maximizers are immune from income effects of changes in plan parameters. Distributional effects on the household and investor sectors can be negated through appropriate compensation. Investors are insulated from many distributional effects because their budget constraints are determined by total net profits. The lack of an independent government sector or banking system also reduces the scope for redistributional effects.

This excessive simplification is useful in that it allows the model to display fully its resource allocation properties. The ability of the model to mimic the properties of a market economy in unconstrained equilibrium depends on this lack of distributional effects. Thus, despite its lack of realism, the model is useful in demonstrating the unimportance of planning in resource allocation. With additional institutional detail and assumptions about the presence or absence of compensation for various agents, the model could be used to study distributional issues more explicitly.

Possible Extensions of the Model

The following extensions of the model and their implications are briefly reviewed in this section: "leakages"—diversion of goods from plan to market channels; resales of plan-allocated inputs on the market by their recipients; various types of uncertainty; enterprise maximization of gross value of output or sales, subject to a profit or "resource" constraint; and product variation within commodity categories used in planning. In some areas, such as uncertainty, possible extensions of the model highlight its strengths. In others, like product variation, extensions of the model cause it to lose some of its main results but allow it to come to grips with a different set of phenomena.

Leakages

The model assumes that all output procured from firms through the plan becomes available to user firms or to final demand in the form of plan-based input allocations. There are no "leakages" from the planned part of the economy to the market, even though these appear to be common in China. Furthermore, recipients of plan input allocations are required to fully use their allocations themselves. Neither refusal of allocations nor reselling allocated goods at the market price is permitted.

Leakages could easily be incorporated into the model. A certain percentage of output subject to compulsory procurement could be diverted to the market by commercial intermediaries, for example. The proportion of plan procurement diverted in this way could depend on the gap between the plan price and the market price, since the incentives for such diversion to occur would be greater, the larger the price differential. The profits from leakages would augment consumption and/or investment demand.

Leakages would have a number of effects. They would guarantee the existence of a market for every good. Hence, market activities would be established more widely, and the transition to a market system might be eased. On the other hand, the illegitimacy of leakages might make their impact on parallel markets more ambiguous, akin to that of black markets. Moreover, if leakages occur through commercial intermediaries, producers remain insulated from market demand, and associated improvements in efficiency and performance may be largely lost.

Leakages would have no effect on total supply of a good, since diversion only involves shifting part of total output from plan to market distribution channels. Provided there are no effects on the demand side, total demand at existing market prices would remain the same, and the main properties of unconstrained equilibrium in the model would still hold. The only change would be in the relative shares of plan and market. For consumer goods, leakages would have an income effect on demand by reducing the amount of goods available to consumers at plan prices, unless this is offset by compensating changes in nominal wages.

If the situation without leakages involves output plan constraints for some firms, leakages would effectively reduce plan allocations and make it less likely that enterprises would be demand-constrained. This would improve efficiency: lowering plan allocations in order to reduce the incidence of plan constraints is a way of improving the efficiency of the system, and this is what occurs unintendedly in the case of leakages.

Resales of Plan-Allocated Commodities

Relaxing the rule that agents are not allowed to resell plan-allocated commodities changes some of the properties of equilibrium and suggests another possible avenue of reform. It means that no producer will be plan-constrained on the input side, and no investor or consumer will be plan-constrained. Previously plan-constrained agents would resell some of their allocations, to the point where they are indifferent between keeping the goods and further resales and hence are no longer plan-constrained. Since output plan targets are assumed to remain obligatory, plan constraints on the output side are still a possibility for producers.[1]

If no producer is plan-constrained on the output side, then the economy can reach an unconstrained Pareto optimal equilibrium solution, regardless of the initial distribution of plan input allocations and plan allocations of consumption and investment goods. In principle, it should be easier to achieve a situation where no producer is plan-constrained on the output side than it is to ensure that no agent in the economy is constrained (including producers on both input and output sides), as is required for optimality in the absence of resales. Even if some producers are plan-constrained, release of consumers and investors from any plan constraints they may be subject to by allowing resales may allow the economy to reach a Pareto-superior equilibrium solution.

Permitting resales thus would appear to be a possible direction of reform, expanding the role of markets and improving efficiency. The monetization and appropriation of embodied rents, however, might provide some agents with large windfall gains, possibly leading to resentment and political problems. The value of such embodied rents can be quite substantial, as was shown in chapter 5 (see table 5.5). Hence, incentives for arbitrage between the plan and market spheres are great, and such activity must occur even in the face of prohibitions against it. Legalizing resales would facilitate appropriation of rents in this manner and would make the rents accruing to various agents through plan allocations even more visible. On the other hand, it might lead to declines in market prices and consequent reductions in the total value of embodied rents.

Uncertainty

The model could be recast into a framework of uncertainty, with risk-neutral agents maximizing expected utility or profits. Several kinds of uncertainty could be incorporated: (1) technical uncertainty concerning the amount of output produced with a given supply of inputs; (2) uncertainty affecting deliveries of plan-allocated materials to firms; (3) market uncertainty, which could affect market prices; and (4) "political" uncertainty, generated by unstable incentives and pervasive bargaining.

Under certain conditions, none of the results of the model would change. The Chinese system might well be much better able to deal with uncertainty than a traditional centrally planned economy, by virtue of the flexible cushion provided by markets. In theory, the planned part of the economy could be insulated from uncertainty altogether, letting the full impact of uncertainty be felt in the market sphere. The results of the model would still hold, and moreover an important new feature is incorporated.

The insulation of the planning system from uncertainty requires a number of preconditions, however: (1) firms give absolute priority to fulfilling mandatory output and compulsory delivery targets, as is assumed in the model; (2) agents are risk-neutral; (3) no agent is plan-constrained; and (4) there is enough slack in plans that firms are in no danger of becoming plan-constrained ex post as a result of particularly bad outcomes. Condition 3 has already been discussed at length (see chapter 5). Condition 4's degree of realism depends on the kind of uncertainty in the model. For instance, uncertainty in input-output coefficients may be limited and could be taken care of by sufficient slackness in targets. On the other hand, supply uncertainties could easily threaten plan fulfillment. Condition 2 may not be an unreasonable assumption.

Much stronger doubts can be raised about Condition 1, which is crucial. Enterprises are supposed to fulfill their mandatory output targets before engaging in any production for the market, but they have strong incentives to do otherwise. These are present even under certainty, but uncertainty and imperfect information give firms more scope to take advantage of the situation. If the planning system is weak and, as in China, pervaded by bargaining and ex post adjustments in targets, leakages and resales may be much easier to engage in without penalty and hence more common, possibly leading to a breakdown or to strong pressures for changes (see chapter 9).

A simple example will illustrate this point. Suppose that the only uncertainty is technical uncertainty about how much output a given amount of inputs will generate. The enterprise's choice of the amount of inputs to purchase and devote to within-plan production does not guarantee a particular level of output but instead generates a probability distribution over the set of possible production levels. It would also generate a probability or expectation that production would fulfill or exceed the plan target, which is simply one minus the probability density function generated by the input choice. If the firm can allocate inputs and facilities separately for within-plan and outside-of-plan production, it would generally not allocate so much to the plan portion that plan fulfillment is completely assured, and indeed this would generally not be optimal for the system as a whole, either. But once a probability of less than one that the enterprise will fulfill its output plan target is permitted, it becomes very hard to prevent firms from cheating—putting less inputs into production for the plan, and then if the output target is not fulfilled, blaming it on a particularly bad outcome of an uncertain situation.[2] Inability to fulfill output targets could be justified on a variety of grounds, ranging from bad weather to equipment failure, late delivery or nondelivery of plan-allocated supplies, or failure of transport departments to ship out goods on time.

Under these conditions, the impact of uncertainty in the system may well be felt disproportionately by the plan sphere, a pattern that could become self-reinforcing. Stability of the two-tier system might well be threatened once plan targets are no longer seen as binding constraints that have to be met. There is some indication that this was happening in 1988 (see table 9.3).

Output-Maximizing Enterprises

The reasons why profit maximization may be a better approximation of the enterprise objective function than output maximization subject to a profit constraint were discussed in chapter 5. But the question naturally arises as to whether output-maximizing firms would affect the main results of the model. One issue is the level of the profit constraint and whether it differs for different firms. A zero profit constraint would mean zero net profits overall and hence zero demand for investment goods. Some positive profit constraint therefore must be specified, but whether it is related to assets or sales or other enterprise characteristics is arbitrary.

Another, more difficult problem concerns constraint priorities. In the model, fulfillment of output plan targets is a binding requirement on enterprises. The natural analogue in the case of output-maximizing firms is to assume that firms have to fulfill output targets even if their profits dip below the constraint level, but this raises conceptual problems.[3] The opposite assumption, that the profit constraint has priority over meeting the plan target, means it is possible to underfulfill plan targets even in the absence of uncertainty. It could be assumed that ex post, plan targets are reduced to the level of actual output, but the resulting shortfall in allocations to purchasers must then be allocated among them.

Ignoring the issue of constraint priorities, which requires an ad hoc solution, it is clear that general equilibrium in a model with output-maximizing firms does exist. Supply behavior remains well defined given the market price, and all the other conditions required for existence of general equilibrium are met. Equilibrium with output-maximizing firms is not a Pareto optimum, however. Firms are making negative profits at the margin, so reducing output would result in improved efficiency and welfare. But the pure market version of the model (with all plan targets set at zero) also is no longer a Pareto optimum if enterprises maximize output.

A key question is whether and to what extent the propositions on the equivalence between unconstrained equilibria of the model and equilibria in the absence of plan targets still hold when enterprises maximize output. It is put forward as a conjecture that the equivalence still holds, provided that enterprise profit constraints can be adjusted to offset the "income effects" from changing plan parameters. In unconstrained equilibrium, changes in plan parameters affect resource flows to firms, which would have an impact on production. Adjustments in profit constraints would affect the amount an enterprise can produce with given resources. Thus, changes in the one could be used to offset changes in the other. These would have offsetting effects on total profits in the case of intermediate goods, while for investment goods the change in profits would be offset by the changed cost of purchasing the same bundle of investment goods by investors. Wages could be adjusted to preserve equivalence in the case of consumer goods.

Product Variation

The model assumes homogeneous products. This is not an obstacle to realism because multiproduct firms are possible and any degree of fineness in product specifications could be incorporated. But it is also implicitly assumed that output targets and input allocations for goods have the same degree of fineness in specifications as they have in actual production and market demand. This is impossible for any planning system to achieve. Thus, with a realistic specification of products in the model, the planning system must aggregate across commodities that are "close to" each other in setting plan targets and plan prices.

One example is time of delivery. It makes an important difference whether a good is available for planned distribution near the beginning of the year or near the end. Another example is precise quality or grade, which is often not specified in Chinese plans. The Shenyang Smelter, for instance, had a compulsory delivery target for zinc specified only as grade 1 or grade 2 quality. Since grade 1 carried a higher price and production costs for the two were virtually the same, Shenyang came to make only grade 1 zinc, even though grade 2 was sufficient for most customers (see Byrd 1985b, 48).

Allowing for product differentiation within plan commodity categories requires some modifications in the model and affects its results. The simplest approach is to keep the product definitions as established by the planning system but assume that these products can vary in a number of "characteristics."[4] These might include exact time of production and delivery within the plan period, precise specifications, purity (if relevant), quality, finishing, packaging, durability, and so on. Depending on choices made concerning these characteristics, goods would be more or less desirable to customers and to the economy as a whole. Making a good more desirable to the demand side in terms of its characteristics often entails substantial costs to the producer. Thus, firms would have an incentive to make improved products only if this makes it easier to sell the product; it permits the producer to charge a higher price to recover the extra costs; or a combination of both. Presuming each enterprise still acts as a price taker, under the market mechanism the "optimal" product characteristics would be chosen, in terms of their desirability and costs.[5]

In the model, plan prices are artificially low and there is excess demand at those prices. Moreover, the scope for price flexibility for goods produced within the plan is minimal—firms are not allowed openly to charge a higher price because they deliver a product early, match it closely with customer requirements, or in other ways improve it. Therefore, the financial incentives for producers to improve product characteristics are extremely weak; on the contrary, they would try to produce the "cheapest" possible products, to the detriment of customers.

On the demand side, due to chronic shortages government authorities and users may be forced to accept "poor" products delivered as part of the plan. Within-plan production hence would be characterized by low quality, mismatch with user requirements, late delivery, poor finishing and packaging, and other similar problems. The difficulties associated with chronic shortage in centrally planned economies emerge naturally in this extended version of the model.

Tendencies for goods produced as part of the plan to deteriorate in terms of their desirable characteristics can be partly offset by special incentives for high-quality products, nonmonetary rewards, exhortations and directives, and even engineering pride on the part of enterprise managers. But there will always be tendencies to "cheapen" products in dimensions not covered by directives or special incentive schemes. The greater autonomy enjoyed by firms as part of reforms also may help them resist demands by users or government agencies to improve products they deliver within the plan. Supply contracts for within-plan output, concluded between producers and material supply units or major users, are much more disaggregated than plan output targets and hence conceivably could serve as a means of forcing improvements in products allocated through the plan.[6] But contract details are difficult to enforce in a shortage situation and hence may be largely meaningless. The fact that in 1988 there was a marked deterioration in performance in filling state plan contracts purely in quantitative terms (see chapter 9) would suggest that deterioration in terms of quality and other product characteristics also has become a severe problem.

In production for the market, firms have an incentive to improve products if on the demand side there is willingness to pay more for better goods. On the supply side, there are at least three different possibilities:

1. Product characteristics can be altered for part of total output at little or no extra cost. (The cost of altering characteristics of a certain proportion of total output is not much more than that proportion of the cost of altering characteristics for total output.)

2. Due to cost or technical considerations, product characteristics must be the same for total output of the good concerned.

3. Certain characteristics by their nature must vary, and the choice made for one part of total output effectively determines that characteristic for the rest of total output.

For characteristics of type 1, the firm's optimal strategy is to produce the "cheapest" possible product to meet its output plan target. In production for the market, choices on product characteristics will be made so as to maximize profits, so the producer will be responsive to concerns of customers. In the case of type 3 characteristics, enterprises will hold back the goods with the "better" characteristics for market sale, leaving the "worse" products for plan delivery. For example, they may guarantee timely delivery of goods they sell on the market while leaving plan deliveries to the last possible moment. For characteristics of type 2, the producer's decision depends on whether the extra cost of producing a "better" product can be recouped from the higher profits earned on the portion of output sold on the parallel market. If plan prices cannot be raised to recover any extra costs, the relative shares of within-plan production and production for the market can have a substantial impact on choices concerning product characteristics. A high plan share and small market share would bias the decision toward "cheaper" products, whereas a high share of market transactions might induce enterprises to produce a better commodity.

Competition may well affect the extent to which improvements in product characteristics of type 3 occur. If some firms are entirely free from plan targets and therefore reap the full benefits of an improved product, while others with identical technology are forced to deliver part of their output through the plan, competition among the former may bid down the price differential between "better" and "worse" varieties to the point where it is profitable to produce the better products only if all or nearly all output is sold on the open market. In this case firms with substantial compulsory within-plan delivery quotas will make only the worse product.

For type 1 characteristics, the larger the share of the market in total supply, the "better" will be the average level of the product. For type 2 products, small changes in the share of output subject to plan allocation may have no impact, but at a certain point a major shift may occur, with all output of a given producer switching from a worse to a better product. Changing the relative shares of plan and market will have no impact on the average quality of a good in terms of type 3 characteristics.

An extended version of the model along the lines outlined above can incorporate many of the harmful features of chronic shortage, as compellingly described by Kornai (1980). The plan portion of supply faces severe, persistent excess demand. Producers have no incentive to improve or even to maintain the characteristics of their products. Product quality will suffer; deliveries within the plan will tend to be on the late side; producers will make little effort to meet user requirements; and there will be little or no genuine development of new and better products, though bogus new product development may occur as a means of raising prices in a disguised manner.

In one respect this approach departs significantly from the Kornai model: Since equilibrium prevails in the parallel market, sufficient increases in plan prices would eventually clear the market. This contradicts Kornai's assertion that no feasible increases in prices would clear the market. The only way in which Kornai's argument can be made compatible with equilibrium prices on the parallel market is if firms with soft budget constraints are prohibited from participation in the market. But in practice, restrictions on buying goods on the market have been extremely lax if not altogether abandoned. A "political" version of Kornai's argument may still apply, however. Even though sufficient price increases would eventually clear the market if they were implemented and resulted in changes in relative prices, such increases might not occur because they would hurt the interests of purchasers of the goods concerned, or their impact might be so diluted by resulting inflation in the prices of other goods that excess demand would remain in the system.

In this extended version of the model, changes in plan targets can have a substantial impact on product characteristics and hence on overall efficiency. Changes in plan prices could also influence the economic situation by affecting the intensity of shortage. Finally, the equivalence between unconstrained equilibrium of the model and a corresponding "pure" market equilibrium would no longer hold. In the context of product variation, the Chinese stress on differentiating price according to product quality may make some sense. What affects firm decision making on product characteristics is not so much the absolute level of the price of the good concerned, but rather the extent to which it can vary with product characteristics. Allowing more of this flexibility for goods produced for within-plan distribution might help generate improved products.

Rents and Rent-Seeking Behavior

Rents and rent-seeking behavior were discussed in the analysis of the Chinese planning system in chapter 5. Here the concept of rents is incorporated into the model, and the implications of rent-seeking behavior for the model's results are assessed. The model can be used to trace the generation of rents and their flow through the economy, but it is not well suited for rigorous analysis of rent-seeking behavior and its consequences. It should also be kept in mind that the formal concept of rents developed in this section by no means encompasses all of the different types of administratively generated rents or rent-seeking behavior in the Chinese economy.

Generation and Flows of Rents in the Economy

Plan-allocated goods can be viewed as carrying rents because they are traded at controlled prices which in general differ from market prices. Let $r_k = p_k - q_k$ be the per-unit rent carried by good k. Rents are positive when $p_k > q_k$, negative when $p_k < q_k$. The vector of rents is $r = p - q$. The net value of rents for producer j is $r \cdot v_j$, for all producers $r \cdot v$. If $p \geq q$, the net value of rents for the enterprise sector as a whole cannot be greater than zero, and if there are any plan allocations to final demand, net rents for the enterprise sector are negative. Rents accruing to consumer i are $r \cdot c_i$, to investor g $r \cdot d_g$. These will be nonnegative if $p \geq q$. The total value of rents for consumers and investors are $r \cdot d$ and $r \cdot c$, respectively.

From the perspective of the demand side, the assumption $p \geq q$ is a reasonable one. Producers, consumers, and investors would refuse to purchase their plan-allocated goods if $p < q$, because they could do better by buying them on the market. Thus, it is reasonable to assume that there would be a breakdown of planned allocation of the goods concerned and consequently a move toward market allocation. In China's own experience, when the market price moved below the controlled price such breakdowns frequently occurred, though some inertia and slowness of downward price adjustments were evident (see chapter 4).

The concept of rents used here is a marginal one, since it is based on the existing market price, which is not necessarily the market price that would prevail in an equilibrium with rents eliminated or monetized. If all agents tried to appropriate the rents embodied in their plan-allocated goods by reselling them, the market price might well change. But it is the marginal rents that individual agents may try to appropriate, and that determine the strength of incentives for "cheating."

Compensation of investors and consumers for changes in plan parameters can now be equated with changes in the value of embodied rents they receive. For example, the wage adjustment mechanism (6) in chapter 6 can be rewritten as $w_{ij}' = w_{ij} - r \cdot (c_i' - c_i) - (r' - r) \cdot c_i$. The change in the value of embodied rents accruing to consumer i is subtracted from his wages. For investor g, based on (5) in chapter 6, changes in plan allocations from d to d' (including from d_g to d_g') and in plan prices from q to q' lead to the following change in total funds f_g accruing to him, provided there is full compensation:

$$f_g' = f_g - p \cdot (d_g' - d_g) + q' \cdot d_g' - q \cdot d_g, \quad \text{or}$$
$$f_g' = f_g - (r' - r) \cdot d_b - r' \cdot (d_g' - d_g).$$

Again, the change in the value of embodied rents accruing to investor g is subtracted from his total funds to compensate him for the change.

Given the prohibition against resales of plan-allocated goods, embodied rents cannot be converted directly into monetary form. The net value of rents accruing to a producer depends on the vector of input and output plan allocations and targets and on the vector of plan prices. For each investor and consumer, rents are always nonnegative as long as $p \geq q$, but they must be consumed or invested and cannot be converted to monetary form.

Finally, the system of profit remittance and taxation, which has not been incorporated into the model, also is an important determinant of rent flows. If substantial rents accrue to final demand, however, the net value of rents to the enterprise sector is negative. If these negative rents are distributed fairly evenly (particular producers rarely if ever get large positive net rents), then profit distribution cannot play an important role in directing rent flows.[7] Also, since rents accruing to final demand are embodied in goods and cannot be monetized, it is hard to tax them away directly, though wage policy and plan parameters for investors can be used to influence the amount of funds available to them.

Rent-Seeking Behavior

The large embodied rents generated by the Chinese planning system could naturally be expected to elicit various forms of rent-seeking behavior by different agents.[8] The most obvious is bargaining over output targets, input allocations, and profit distribution. This occurs between different levels of government as well as between government supervisory agencies and firms. The supervisory agency has conflicting objectives, since it is evaluated largely on the basis of the performance of subordinate firms. It must try both to limit the requests of enterprises and to bargain with higher levels for more rents. Government at different levels can engage in rent-seeking, with respect to "their" firms and vis-à-vis higher levels of government.

Under certain conditions, bargaining over plan parameters might not carry any significant efficiency costs. If there are no resource costs to such activity (which may not be entirely unrealistic given that it is not a competitive rent-seeking situation); if there is no ratchet effect—that is, enterprises do not distort their performance to affect future targets and allocations; and if there are no plan constraints, it should be possible to reach a Pareto optimal equilibrium solution.

Though the direct costs involved in rent seeking may be low, there are other costs and distortions. Large investments to gain access to future plan allocations of inputs required by the new facilities and investments in processing facilities for low-priced local materials to reap the profits from lucrative "downstream" processing are just two examples. The ratchet effect may not be operative if the share of the market is relatively large, but there may be withholding or distortion of information by enterprises.

In any case, the diversion of managerial time and attention from making profits through efficient operations to seeking rents from the planning system may be the most serious problem. The planning system as well may become increasingly oriented toward distributional infighting rather than effective management of the economy. Rents and rent seeking also distort information flows in the economy. In addition to hiding of capacities and reserves by lower levels of government and firms that is likely to occur, measurement and comparison of efficiency at the enterprise level become very difficult. Profits due to X-efficiency or efficient resource allocation are hard to distinguish from profits earned through access to embodied rents.

Overall Assessment of the Model

This chapter has looked at some of the more questionable assumptions of the general equilibrium model of plan and market in the Chinese economy, its weaknesses and limitations, and a few possible extensions. In addition, the concept of "embodied rents" discussed in chapter 5 has been formalized in the context of the model. Though the obvious limitations of the model to some extent undermine the strong results obtained in chapter 6, they by no means negate their general thrust.

The model clearly is only of limited usefulness in addressing certain very important topics like the dynamic tendencies and trends of the Chinese industrial sector. These are examined, without the aid of a formal model, in chapter 9. The long-term analogue of the model is not a satisfactory tool for analysis of Chinese industry, for reasons that have already been discussed.

Among the weaknesses of the model in its own domain of static analysis, the failure to model the planning process explicitly may be the greatest. It is not the arbitrary nature of plan targets that is unrealistic, but rather the implicit assumption that enterprises take these targets as exogenous and unchangeable and place top priority on output plan fulfillment. More generally, the broad assumption that firms obey the rules of the system, even though it is in their interest to break them—by not fulfilling plan targets, diverting output from plan to market channels, reselling plan-allocated inputs on the market for a profit, and so on—is the most problematic feature of the model.

Several extensions of the model have been sketched out and their likely implications assessed. In some areas, such as uncertainty, possible extensions of the model highlight its strengths or at least do not weaken it. The model can incorporate leakages and resales fairly easily, which broaden the marketized sphere and if anything increase the likelihood that conditions required for efficient resource allocation are met. Inclusion of product variation within plan commodity categories causes the model to lose some of its main results but allows it to come to grips with a new phenomenon, chronic shortage. The strength of the model is also shown by the ability to formally incorporate the concept of rents embodied in plan-allocated goods.

All in all, the model seems to have survived the scrutiny it received in this chapter rather well. Knowledge of its limitations helps in evaluating the results presented in chapter 6, and also in narrowing the model's scope of coverage to areas where it does provide some valuable insights. Finally, the extensions outlined in this chapter both strengthen the model and provide testimony to its analytical value.

8. Market Price Trends and Market Integration

HOW WELL are markets for Chinese industrial producer goods functioning? Are they promoting efficient resource allocation, or are they obstructed to such an extent that they do not play the roles attributed to well-functioning markets? This question was looked at from a qualitative perspective in chapter 3. Here it is addressed by examining the quality of the price signals emanating from markets, or in other words, the "performance" of markets as indicated by the market prices they generate. There is an extensive literature on this subject, which emerged as part of the analysis of markets for agricultural products in developing countries (see Harriss 1979). This literature looks at relationships between market prices for the same commodity in different localities, to assess the degree of market "integration." Similar work on developed countries has focused on how to define a single market for antitrust and related purposes (see, for example, Stigler and Sherwin 1985).

Until the mid-1980s, correlation coefficients between levels and first differences of prices in different localities were almost universally used as the primary indicator of market integration. High correlation coefficients were taken as a sign of well-integrated markets, low correlation coefficients as showing fragmented, poorly functioning markets. This approach has serious problems, however (see Blyn 1973; Timmer 1974; and Harriss 1979, among others). Subsequently, a new method based on regression analysis of current and lagged prices at local markets and a central "reference market" was developed by Ravallion (1985; 1986),[1] which in principle can be applied to the analysis of markets for industrial products in China.

Market Price Patterns and Trends

Market prices for Chinese industrial producer goods have diverged sharply from state plan prices and moreover have fluctuated over time. Data for the city of Shanghai can be used to gauge trends through most of the 1980s. Table 8.1 gives state plan and Shanghai market price data for some different steel products; table 8.2, for a range of other industrial producer goods. One striking feature is that by the late 1980s, market prices for all of the products listed exceeded state plan

Table 8.1

State Plan and Shanghai Market Prices for Steel Products, 1979–89
(yuan/ton)

	Steel wire rod	Threaded steel rod	Angular steel rod	Medium thick plate	Cold-rolled thin plate	Casting-quality pig iron
State ex-factory price						
1979–81	560	—	460[a]	—	720	240
1985	—	—	—	570	870	293
1988	610	592	—	570	870	293
Shanghai trade fairs[b]						
1979 (3d fair)	750	—	510	—	800	210
1980 (3d fair)	750	—	660	—	1,430[c]	288[c]
1981 (1st fair)	650	—	—	—	—	—
Shanghai market						
1984 (August)	1,400	1,000	1,300	—	—	—
1984 (December)	1,500	1,450	1,420	1,250[d]	1,450[d]	—
1985 (December)	1,600	1,600	1,605[e]	1,460[e]	1,740	—
1986 (December)	1,497	1,602	1,451	1,483	1,904	550[f]
1987 (December)	1,410	1,501	1,323	1,470	2,200	525
1988 (December)	1,526	1,566	1,419	1,580	4,642	760
1989 (February)	1,990	1,900	—	1,615	5,500	—

Sources: Byrd (1985a, 16); *Wuzi shangqing,* various issues; Ji (1988, 56–57); *Zhongguo wuzi bao,* various issues.

a. State wholesale price, which is normally slightly above the state ex-factory price.

b. Reported "high" transaction prices.

c. Prices for the second trade fair of 1980, in the absence of comparable data for the third trade fair.

d. February 1985 prices.

e. January 1986 prices.

f. November 1986 prices.

prices by wide margins, ranging from 65 percent (trucks) to 532 percent (cold-rolled thin steel plate). Only for two of the products was the gap less than 200 percent. For most goods a large gap between plan and market prices was evident from 1984 onward. There were some increases in state plan prices in the 1980s, but these were far short of what would have been needed to equilibrate markets and did not even maintain the dollar value of these goods, given a substantial decrease in the value of China's domestic currency over this period (from 1.50 yuan per U.S. dollar in 1980 to 3.72 yuan in 1987). Gaps between plan and market prices in 1979–81 were much smaller than subsequently, and cases of market prices below state plan prices were sometimes observed.

Market price trends for most industrial producer goods have been broadly similar: an initial sharp run-up in late 1984 and early 1985, as prices found

Table 8.2

State Plan and Shanghai Market Prices for Other Industrial Producer Goods, 1979–89
(yuan/ton unless otherwise indicated)

	Aluminum	Copper	Soda ash	Cement[a]	Dongfeng trucks[b]
State ex-factory price					
1979–81	2,760	5,500	200	47	19,500[c]
1985	4,000	5,500	–	90	–
1988	4,000	5,500	390	90	25,800
Shanghai trade fairs[d]					
1979 (3d fair)	3,023	7,000	330	78	–
1980 (3d fair)	3,650[e]	6,000[e]	270	80	–
1981 (1st fair)	2,900	5,650	–	–	–
Shanghai market					
1984 (August)	4,700	6,900	–	–	37,500
1984 (December)	4,600	6,700	550[f]	105[f]	39,500
1985 (December)	6,500	6,900	625[g]	162	42,000
1986 (December)	6,421	6,900	650	151	36,487
1987 (December)	7,340	7,180[h]	710	153	34,897
1988 (December)	11,000	18,890[i]	1,030[j]	279	37,800
1989 (February)	17,940	22,740	1,550[k]	–	42,500

Sources: Byrd (1985a, 16–17); *Wuzi shangqing*, various issues; Ji (1988, 56–57); *Zhongguo wuzi bao*, various issues.

a. For 1979–81 the commodity is grade 400 ordinary cement; from 1984 onward it is grade 425 ordinary cement.

b. Price in Y/truck.

c. State ex-factory price for 1982.

d. Reported "high" transaction prices.

e. Prices for the second trade fair of 1980, in the absence of comparable data for the third trade fair.

f. January 1985 price.

g. January 1986 price.

h. September 1987 price.

i. January 1989 price.

j. September 1988 price.

k. Price for Yantai City, Shandong Province.

something approaching their equilibrium levels, perhaps even overshooting for a time; subsequently relatively level prices for most goods, lasting until 1987 or 1988, with some significant declines especially in 1986; and a further sharp jump in market prices in late 1988 and early 1989. Aluminum, cold-rolled thin steel plate, and soda ash exhibited more steady price increases in the mid- and late 1980s, yet even for them there were periods of stagnation or gradual rises.

Data on average market prices at a number of large cities around China for the period 1987–89, shown in table 8.3, confirm this general picture. The recent sharp increases in market prices for the most part occurred in the second half of 1988. For a few goods like cold-rolled thin plate, caustic soda, and aluminum, prices took off in the first half of the year. An austerity policy may have begun to take hold in early 1989 and dampened demand somewhat, which may be reflected in the new plateau reached by many prices at that time. But there were continuing increases for some products.

Price Stability in 1985–87: Some Possible Explanations

Given the strong and increasing inflationary pressures in the Chinese economy from 1984 onward, generally stable market prices from late 1985 through 1987 (and into 1988 for some products) need to be explained. There are several possible reasons, not necessarily mutually exclusive:

1. To some degree, price stability may reflect the overshooting that occurred initially, which must have resulted in weakened pressures for price rises subsequently. But this could only have been a temporary factor, particularly since for some products price declines were observed after the initial run-up, eliminating any subsequent moderating influence.

2. There was a clampdown on state investment imposed in response to the "overheating" of the economy in late 1984 and early 1985, which may have had a dampening effect on market prices. But in 1987 the investment boom resumed, so this factor cannot explain price stability in that year.

3. There was a supply response to the sharp price increases of 1984–85, especially evident in the coal industry, which may have lowered equilibrium price levels somewhat or at least restrained increases.

4. Improved market functioning, despite high demand, may have permitted declining transaction costs and margins and allowed lower market prices than otherwise would have been possible. With better market management, price swings became smaller.

5. The rise in the share of many investment goods and intermediate products traded at high market prices as opposed to low state-set prices may have had a strong "income effect" on demand, reducing the purchasing power available to many investors and hence their ability to buy large amounts at market prices. This is particularly true because many investment budgets were denominated in nominal terms—so higher prices meant lower real investment or a lower real value of investment goods purchased. Moreover, changing official plan and market shares were only part of the story. The tremendous gaps between plan and market prices stimulated a host of different efforts and measures to capture the "rents" embodied in plan-allocated goods, which over time must have raised the effective price paid for goods allocated through the plan to users (see chapter 9). This also may have had a

Table 8.3

Market Price Trends, Average, 1987–89[a]

	State plan price[b]	1987			1988			1989	
		January	June	December	June	September	December	January	February
Steel wire rod	610	1,452	1,423	1,402	1,443	1,776	1,889	2,030	2,087
Threaded steel	520	1,513	1,513	1,495	1,477	1,671	1,708	1,895	1,866
Cold-rolled thin plate	870	1,780	1,907	2,031	2,986	3,986	5,606	5,271	5,260
Medium thick plate	570	1,491	1,493	1,480	1,541	1,975	2,282	2,621	3,101
Aluminum	4,000	6,301	6,403	7,123	8,420	12,689	16,572	16,200	16,860
Casting pig iron	293	502	473	484	505	563	639	706	810
Cement	90	129	133	136	152	169	197	236	–
Soda ash	390	670	706	708	831	1,094	1,231	1,382	1,514
Caustic soda	640	1,285	1,453	1,463	2,438	2,956	3,308	3,368	3,446
Dongfeng brand trucks[c]	25,800	35,161	34,725	37,428	40,306	42,573	48,614	46,893	47,106

Sources: Ji (1988, 32–33); *Jiage lilun yu shijian* (August 1988, 60); *Wuzi shangqing*, October 11, 1988, 2; *Zhongguo wuzi bao*, various issues.
   a. Arithmetic mean of market prices at all cities for which prices were given for the date concerned.
   b. As of late 1988.
   c. Yuan/unit.

significant income effect, dampening investment demand and weakening pressures on market prices.

6. The nature of the price data themselves and the transactions they purport to represent could generate distortions. It is clear from abundant evidence that outside-of-plan transactions can occur at numerous different prices, ranging from the state plan price or slightly above it to reported "high" market prices. Moreover, transactions at almost any price can be voluntary if exchange for other goods or resources is involved. In this situation, there could be major changes in average prices even though reported "high" transaction prices are stable. Changes in the approach to reporting market prices, for instance from reporting the highest price to reporting something closer to the average price, also could result in reported price series understating the extent of price inflation.

7. Finally, stable prices may not reflect market equilibria at all but rather local price controls or at least informal ceilings. It was noted in chapter 3 that reported market prices in the mid- and late 1980s seem to have been "posted prices" rather than prices at which actual transactions occurred. They may even represent "ceiling prices" set by provincial and municipal governments to "guide" local markets. But there is enough monthly and even shorter-term variation that even if this last statement is true, local authorities must have been revising prices fairly frequently in response to market conditions.

Assessing the relative importance of different explanatory factors is difficult. Hypothesis 5 may well be quite important, though it requires that extra profits earned by producers from higher market prices be partly dissipated in some way, so that they are not fully reflected in additional demand for the same goods. Such dissipation could occur if larger financial returns for producers led to higher wages for their employees or other forms of personal consumption. Concerning 7, informal local price controls may have been present, but it is not clear that they were much stronger in 1986–87 than in 1985, when slightly higher market prices were generally observed. Hence, 7 alone does not provide a convincing explanation. Hypothesis 6 may have played an important role, but additional fieldwork and research would be necessary to confirm this. Hypotheses 1–4 may have had some influence for certain products and over certain periods of time, but they appear to be insufficient to explain three years of relative price stability.

To the extent that hypothesis 5 largely explains the period of near-stability in market prices, it can also provide some insight into the subsequent resumed inflationary trend. What it suggests is that by 1988, several years of changing plan and market shares and rising effective prices for goods allocated through the state plan had brought the share of output transacted at relatively high effective prices close to one, or at least high enough that there was little room for further "absorption" of inflationary pressures. As a result, continued high investment demand and accommodating monetary policy translated directly into sharp price increases in late 1988, unlike in the earlier period. If this is true, it suggests that market prices for industrial producer goods in China are now much more closely reflecting economywide trends in investment demand and general inflationary pressures, as long as effective price controls are not reimposed.

Regional Patterns and Differentials

Regional market price patterns and trends can be reviewed using the main data base for this chapter, which consists of market transaction prices for a number of industrial goods in some large cities, covering the period from August 1984 to November 1987. Generally percentage gaps in market prices across cities are relatively low, for the most part not statistically significant. For most goods at most points in time, reported market prices in different cities fall within a 10 percent or at most 20 percent ''band.'' The only exceptions occurred when there were sharp price movements, in which case some cities lagged, opening up larger though temporary differentials.

Given relatively small regional price differences, correlations between price levels in different cities are fairly high, though not uniformly so. Table 8.4 gives correlations between prices in Shanghai and in various other cities for eight products. Observed correlations for the three steel goods are all above 0.58 and mostly above 0.7. For aluminum they are even higher except for two cities. In the case of cement they are much lower, sometimes even negative, which is not surprising considering the high weight-to-value ratio for cement and resulting ''natural'' market segmentation. Correlations generally are not as high as one would find in the case of homogeneous industrial commodities in market economies, where equilibrating adjustments are almost instantaneous; they are in the same range as what is found in many markets for agricultural goods in developing countries.

The lack of correlation between price movements in different markets is striking, however. Correlation coefficients between first differences of prices on a monthly basis were computed for the same products and cities. As can be seen from table 8.5, in a large number of cases correlations are actually negative, and only rarely are they significantly positive. This suggests that market prices in different cities do not move together most of the time, at least on a month-to-month basis. But the high correlations between price levels and the relatively small percentage changes in prices in most months mean that the lack of a close relationship between price movements does not have much effect on price differentials. Contrary or unrelated short-run price movements occur within an overall environment of small intercity price differentials.

A Method of Testing for Market Integration

For about two decades, simple correlation coefficients on price levels and price movements were the accepted analytical tool for assessment of market integration. But aside from their value in providing a crude idea of spatial patterns,

Table 8.4

Correlations between Levels of Market Prices in Shanghai and Various Other Cities, 1984–87

	Angular steel rod	Steel rod	Threaded steel rod	Medium thick plate	Aluminum	Cement	Dongfeng trucks	Jiefang trucks
Beijing	0.717	0.669	0.735	—	0.958	—	—	0.412
Changsha	0.833	0.856	0.630	0.270	0.413	—	0.750	—
Chengdu	0.861	0.842	0.708	0.601	0.919	0.635	—	—
Fuzhou	0.782	0.740	0.727	—	—	-0.129	—	—
Hangzhou	0.905	0.733	0.783	0.441	—	—	—	—
Hefei	0.682	0.781	0.687	—	0.553	0.156	—	—
Jinan	0.741	0.785	0.703	0.278	0.965	0.835	0.867	0.914
Nanchang	0.860	0.900	0.643	—	0.661	—	0.879	0.909
Nanjing	0.744	—	0.747	0.619	0.955	—	—	—
Shijiazhuang	0.806	0.831	0.788	0.478	0.900	0.665	0.840	0.890
Taiyuan	0.588	0.641	0.747	-0.076	0.908	0.786	0.846	0.793
Wuhan	0.767	0.766	0.728	0.320	0.896	-0.255	0.839	0.788
Xian	0.584	0.850	0.651	—	0.889	—	—	—
Zhengzhou	0.815	0.718	0.748	—	0.964	—	—	—

Source: Wuzi shangqing, various issues.

Note: Cities for which the total number of nonmissing observations was less than thirty were left out of the analysis.

Table 8.5

Correlations between Monthly Changes in Market Prices in Shanghai and Other Cities, 1984–87

	Angular steel rod	Steel rod	Threaded steel rod	Medium thick plate	Aluminum	Cement	Dongfeng trucks	Jiefang trucks
Beijing	-0.232	0.162	0.102	—	-0.200	—	—	-0.263
Changsha	0.006	0.309	0.548	-0.024	0.349	—	-0.130	—
Chengdu	-0.036	0.186	0.387	0.374	-0.478	0.088	—	—
Fuzhou	-0.087	0.081	0.320	—	—	-0.062	—	—
Hangzhou	-0.172	-0.351	0.371	-0.115	—	—	—	—
Hefei	-0.183	-0.372	0.010	—	0.389	-0.027	-0.161	-0.101
Jinan	0.008	-0.038	-0.010	-0.143	0.426	0.024	0.226	0.135
Nanchang	-0.162	0.088	0.616	0.209	-0.204	0.541	—	—
Nanjing	-0.370	0.344	-0.009	0.763	-0.284	—	—	—
Shijiazhuang	-0.343	-0.148	0.283	0.633	-0.115	-0.698	0.271	0.295
Taiyuan	-0.060	0.293	-0.180	-0.287	-0.117	-0.006	-0.747	0.171
Wuhan	-0.082	-0.436	-0.049	0.353	-0.493	-0.111	0.180	0.001
Xian	0.324	0.296	-0.415	—	-0.075	—	—	—
Zhengzhou	0.401	-0.338	-0.333	—	0.410	—	—	—

Sources: Wuzi shangqing, various issues.
Note: Cities for which the total number of nonmissing observations was less than thirty were left out of the analysis.

there are serious conceptual problems with the use of correlation coefficients (Harriss 1979). High correlations particularly in levels can mask severe market segmentation; when a certain variable has a strong influence on market prices in different localities, high correlation coefficients will typically result. In a period of secularly rising prices due to general inflation in the economy, correlation coefficients are likely to be high even in the absence of market integration. Price controls or monopoly procurement also can generate high correlation coefficients. On the other hand, under some circumstances like reversals of trade flows on a seasonal or other basis, integrated markets can generate low correlation coefficients in price movements (Timmer 1974). There is also no clear yardstick on what degree of correlation constitutes adequate evidence of market integration.

A new and more sophisticated methodology for the analysis of market integration, still based on observed price data for different local markets, was developed by Ravallion (1985; 1986). The new method incorporates an articulated, dynamic theory of price adjustments (see also Heytens 1986). The basic approach is to select one market as the "reference market," based on independent information, and then separately regress prices in each local market against current and lagged values of the reference market price, lagged values of the local market price, and other variables affecting local market conditions. Factors that influence all markets together are presumed to be taken into account by including the reference market price in the regression. Explaining price trends in the reference market is a separate task, on which the analysis of market integration does not depend.

In the simplest case, only one-period lags are used. Letting P_{it} be the market price in locality i at time t, R_t the reference market price at time t, V_{it} a vector of factors influencing local market conditions, and e_{it} the error term, the following equation is estimated:

$$P_{it} = a_0 + a_1 P_{it-1} + b_0 R_t + b_1 R_{t-1} + c V_{it} + e_{it}. \tag{1}$$

The coefficient c is a vector, whereas the others are scalars.[2] The generalized version of the above equation simply adds more lagged terms for the local market price and reference market price.

Alternative hypotheses about market structure can be tested by imposing restrictions on the coefficients and evaluating the appropriate F-statistics. The hypothesis of complete market segmentation would require that current and lagged values of the reference market price have no influence on the local market price, or:

$$b_0 = b_1 = 0. \tag{2}$$

Under market segmentation, the local market price is completely determined by its own lagged values and by local influences particular to that market.

At the opposite extreme, short-run market integration would imply that the local price depends only on the reference market price and that equilibrating adjustments are complete within one period:

$$b_0 = 1; a_1 = b_1 = 0. \tag{3}$$

Weaker forms of market integration also can be investigated. Long-run market integration would require that in long-term equilibrium, the local market price is determined only by the equilibrium level of the reference market price. The appropriate restriction on the coefficients is then that they sum to 1 (see Ravallion 1986, 105, for the derivation):

$$a_1 + b_0 + b_1 = 1. \tag{4}$$

Short-run market integration implies long-run integration but not vice versa; more problematic, market segmentation and long-run market integration may be simultaneously accepted in a statistical sense (if $a_1 = 1$, $b_0 = b_1 = 0$ is accepted). Hence, acceptance of the market segmentation hypothesis means that long-run market integration must be ruled out even though it also may be statistically accepted by the standard criteria. The mere fact, however, that market segmentation is not rejected of course does not mean that it should be automatically accepted, particularly if the F-value is high and close to the 5 percent critical level.

The speed of adjustment to shocks in the reference market price under long-run integration varies depending on the respective coefficients of a_1, b_0, and b_1. For example, if $a_1 = 0.5$, $b_0 = 0.2$, and $b_1 = 0.3$, about 90 percent of a given one-time change in the reference market price will be reflected in the local price after three periods. The higher the coefficient of a_1, the slower the speed of adjustment. If $a_1 = 0.7$, $b_0 = 0.1$, and $b_1 = 0.2$, only 69 percent of a reference market price shock will be reflected in the local price after three periods, and it takes six periods before this figure reaches close to 90 percent.

Other hypotheses can be tested within the general distributed lag model. Overall, the approach is a flexible one that allows rich hypothesis testing. Here a three-period lag structure also will be used for some products with a sufficiently large number of observations. The base equation becomes:

$$P_{it} = a_0 + a_1 P_{it-1} + a_2 P_{it-2} + a_3 P_{it-3} + b_0 R_t + b_1 R_{t-1} + b_2 R_{t-2}$$
$$+ b_3 R_{t-3} + c V_{it} + e_{it}. \tag{5}$$

And the different hypothesis tests are:

$$b_0 = b_1 = b_2 = b_3 = 0 \text{ (market segmentation)} \tag{6}$$

$$b_0 = 1; a_1 = a_2 = a_3 = b_1 = b_2 = b_3 = 0 \text{ (short-run integration)} \tag{7}$$

$$a_1 + a_2 + a_3 + b_0 + b_1 + b_2 + b_3 = 1 \quad \text{(long-run integration)}. \qquad (8)$$

One obvious problem with the Ravallion method is the likely strong serial correlation in time series of market prices, which could lead to multicollinearity. For example, in testing for market integration, a high standard error on b_0 may be due to its close correlation with lagged prices rather than to weak market integration (Ravallion 1986, 105). One means of ameliorating this problem is first to test for long-run market integration and then, if that is accepted, impose the restriction of long-run market integration on the model and engage in hypothesis testing.

Another possible problem is simultaneous equations bias (Heytens 1986, 39). This can be dealt with by the usual methods, or simply by hoping that the distortion is not too great. Choice of the reference market and the implicit "radial" assumption about market interactions also may be problematic. Finally, the reliability of price data, particularly in the case of agricultural products markets, is a major concern.

Application to Chinese Industrial Market Prices

The rationale for applying this method to market prices for industrial producer goods in China is that in the Chinese context serious questions arise about the basic functioning of goods markets, similar in some ways to the research issues concerning developing-country markets for agricultural products. In addition to the usual concerns about market segmentation, which could arise from bureaucratic as well as geographical or infrastructural constraints, the possibility that market price flexibility is severely restricted by central and/or local price controls of an informal nature cannot be ignored. The basic model and econometric tests discussed above can be applied to Chinese data without change, though there are a number of conceptual, methodological, and data-related issues that must be addressed. But first a brief digression on the nature of the available price data and the adjustments made to facilitate quantitative analysis.

Chinese Market Price Data and Adjustments

The data are in the form of reports, usually appearing every ten days, of transactions prices for a set of industrial producer goods in a number of major cities, which appeared in the newspaper *Wuzi shangqing* (Materials market situation), published by the State Material Supply Bureau (now the Ministry of Material Supply). They are at present available for the period from August 1984 to November 1987. Each report has a list of products and cities, with market prices by product and city at a particular point in time. The reports appear a maximum of three times a month, though in numerous months only one or two reports were put out and in some months none. Out of 118 possible observations (over a period of forty months), there are actually 74 reports. For particular products and cities the number of observations is invariably considerably smaller than this due to the variation in products and cities in different reports. The data base is usable despite these gaps because of the large total number of observations available. The magnitude of the missing data problem as well as other considerations dictated use of monthly rather than ten-day intervals in data analysis.

Simply taking all available observations for prices and one-month lagged prices from the raw data, the method used in calculating the correlation coefficients in tables 8.4 and 8.5, avoids any adjustment of the data. But it results in an insufficient number of observations for the regression analysis and hypothesis testing with a multiperiod lag structure and, for many goods, even with a one-period lag structure. Moreover, bunching of data may lead to certain biases. Some months may contain three price observations, others none. Finally, much valuable information from the data set is lost, because observations falling in consecutive months but not exactly one month apart are not being used.

The following adjustments were made in the database to maximize the number of monthly observations. For each of eleven products for which numerous observations from a number of cities are available, data were first taken for the ten-day interval within each month for which the maximum number of reports existed. Then the data were augmented by judiciously adding observations from the other ten-day intervals where available. Efforts were made to ensure that the intervals between observations drawn for use in the regression analysis were no less than twenty days and no more than forty days, but in a few cases data fifty or, rarely, ten days apart had to be used for lack of alternatives. These adjustments generated data series with large numbers of observations and with relatively few gaps, which are suitable for analysis.

Data Problems

A more fundamental question about the data concerns the nature of the prices reported. Though supposedly average prices in actual local market transactions, the data much more exhibit the character of "posted prices," which do not instantaneously clear the market but rather are adjusted frequently or irregularly over time in response to local quantity signals or information emanating from other markets (see also chapter 3). This means that though still responsive to supply and demand conditions, market prices may not adjust instantaneously or even very quickly, and price adjustments when they occur may be discrete, sometimes fairly large. Posted prices also are more vulnerable to local government controls or pressures.

It is clear that local authorities promulgated informal "ceilings" for market prices of key industrial producer goods in some large cities. Reported "market" prices may often just reflect these ceilings, or transaction prices heavily influenced by the ceilings. In any case, many market transactions occurred at prices well below the reported market price because they involved exchange arrangements of various kinds. On the other hand, to the extent that the reported prices were indeed local government-set ceilings, some transactions may have occurred at prices above the ceilings. But the fact that reported market prices hardly ever stayed constant for months on end means that even if they were affected by local government ceilings, these were changed fairly often, presumably in response to local market conditions.

Other problems with the price data relate to the degree of homogeneity of products across cities and over time, and to precisely how reported prices were selected. The former problem is minimized by the choice of products with clear, narrow specifications. The severity of the second problem is hard to gauge, but sometimes there are substantial differences between prices ten days apart, larger than differences over monthly intervals. This suggests that different posted or transaction prices may sometimes be used in reporting. From other data sources, it is clear that "highest," "lowest," and "average" transaction prices can be reported for the same product in the same locality at the same time.[3] As a result, different sources commonly reported different prices for the same narrowly specified good in the same city, on or about the same date. Hence there are severe, probably intractable problems in trying to combine price data from different sources for analysis.

Since all the data used for quantitative analysis in this chapter are from a single source, multiple values for the same observation do not exist, and inconsistencies between prices at different points in time also should be minimized. Nevertheless, they may have crept in, if for some reports, products, and localities different prices were used than for others. The reliance on local authorities for reporting and lack of clearly specified criteria on which prices to report permit such problems to arise. One can only hope that the inconsistencies are not too severe, and that any "noise" introduced through occasional use of different types of transaction prices does not distort the results.

Conceptual and Methodological Issues

One issue concerns the extent of market-clearing interlocality trade. For most of the goods under consideration this was minimal, especially since the distances involved are often large. The goods generally have relatively high weight/value ratios, so transport costs could create a substantial band within which local price changes would not induce equilibrating trade. Severe bottlenecks in China's railway system, common in the 1980s, may have widened this band considerably. Thus interlocality trade was most probably not an effective equilibrating mechanism, except in the face of large price gaps.

A different mechanism that was at work was flows of information rather than of goods. These are extremely important in worldwide commodity markets. Prices in different markets respond to prices in other markets very quickly, due to the informational content of the price signals rather than as a result of equilibrating flows of goods, which would be impossible in the very short periods, measured in minutes, during which prices adjust. Active agents adjust their demand and supply in response to changing price signals from other markets, causing changes in the local equilibrium price. In China, local market price adjustments also seem to have been based on information flows, but these involved local authorities and market supervisors adjusting prices in response to signals from other markets as well as agents adjusting desired supplies and demands. The requirement in the original price decontrol directive of early 1985 that local authorities report market prices to the center, which then disseminated price information through circulars and newspapers, facilitated flows of market price information.[4] Hence, market integration, albeit with relatively long adjustment lags, may still be a meaningful concept worth testing for.

A more mundane question relates to the choice of the reference market. This is relatively easy in a "radial" spatial pattern with one market center (perhaps the capital of a small country) connected directly with numerous local markets, particularly if each locality has substantial trade with the central market. Even if some local markets are separated from the reference market by other, intervening markets, as long as the reference market is clearly dominant in size, visibility, and trade with a large number of local markets, the choice is clear.

Selection of the reference market for analysis of Chinese industrial producer goods markets is by no means so clear-cut. The cities reporting price data are scattered across the country and for the most part are large regional centers, which may serve as reference markets for smaller local markets in their hinterlands but among which the choice of a national reference market is not easy. With the wide publicity given to market prices for industrial producer goods in local and national newspapers, as well as, presumably, through faster communications media, price-setters may well take price trends in other cities into account in setting their own posted prices. Thus, the kind of informational equilibrium discussed above could be relevant. The question is whether most markets adjust largely in response to changes in a single market, which could be considered the reference market.

The Shanghai market is the obvious candidate for reference market status based on this criterion. Its established market for the means of production was by far the most important in China in the late 1970s and early 1980s. Though its relative importance has declined since then, it is still the most highly visible market center. Moreover, prices at the Shanghai market are still probably the most widely used for reference in setting prices elsewhere. A practical consideration is that Shanghai by and large has the most complete data, allowing the maximum possible number of pairwise comparisons. Thus, Shanghai was chosen as the reference market for the econometric analysis.[5]

The determination of the reference market price and the vector of factors influencing local market prices is another matter of concern. Though in principle the former can be analyzed independently of the issue of market integration, it would be desirable for the sake of completeness to have a satisfactory econometric explanation of movements in the reference market price, based on its own lagged values and other factors but not on price movements in other markets.[6] This has not been done. The earlier discussion of overall market price trends does provide a qualitative account, however. One problem is gathering and processing the monthly or quarterly quantitative data needed for such analysis, which for the most part are not available in most Chinese statistical publications.

It is even more difficult to obtain monthly or quarterly series of variables that could affect local market conditions, such as municipal or provincial industrial production, investment, and so forth. Hence, no such variables are included in the equations. This omission probably could be rectified only through extensive data gathering in various cities.

Interpretation of Hypothesis Tests

A final issue relates to interpretation of the results from hypothesis testing. The problem is that well-coordinated price controls could generate market price data consistent with the hypothesis of market integration, since prices would all move together and "adjustment" would be instantaneous (within one period). On the other hand, a finding of market segmentation would not rule out fragmented, uncoordinated local price controls. These problems of interpretation have been noted by others, but they are potentially more severe in China given possible local government influence over market prices.

One way to deal with this difficulty is to treat the various hypothesis tests as joint tests, for example, of market integration and/or centrally coordinated price controls, or market segmentation and/or fragmented price controls. This is not very satisfactory, however, since the hypotheses being jointly tested are contradictory with respect to their implications for the progress of economic reforms and the development of markets. Even a cursory examination of the data strongly suggests that coordinated, centralized administrative price setting has not been occurring. There are too many local price fluctuations, often in opposite directions, and the gaps across cities are not constant over time. At most, central government authorities may provide a certain amount of general "guidance" on directions of price movements and local price ceilings, but this does not translate into effective central control over short periods of time. Hence, a finding of short-run market integration most probably reflects effective market functioning rather than centralized price controls.

On the other hand, market segmentation may also be consistent with effective local price controls in some cities. A few examples where prices remained constant over periods of several months are suggestive of such controls, but these are exceptions, not the norm. The extent of monthly and even shorter-term fluctuations in most cities, most of the time, is such that rigid local price controls could not have been very important overall. Market-oriented, flexible adjustment of local price ceilings by municipal authorities is another matter, but this is not necessarily inconsistent with primarily market-based price determination and long-run market integration. Hence, a finding of long-run market integration is more suggestive of market influences making themselves felt over time than of meaningful price controls.

Test Results and Analysis

Tests of market segmentation and of short-run and long-run market integration were conducted for six steel products, aluminum, copper, cement, and two brands of trucks, using the single-period lag structure. A summary of the results is presented in table 8.6. The same tests were conducted with a three-period lag structure for two of the steel products and aluminum, also summarized in table 8.6. (Detailed coefficient estimates, summary statistics, and test results for each of the 166 equations estimated and 498 tests conducted are not reproduced here for space reasons.)

The explanatory power of the equations is satisfactory for the most part. Adjusted R-squared was above 0.5 in over 90 percent of all the equations and was relatively high (above 0.8) in many of them. Though such high R-squared values are common in time series analysis, given the small number of observations and degrees of freedom in many cases, the explanatory power of these equations should be considered adequate. The only products for which R-squared is generally on the low side are medium-thick steel plate and copper. Coefficient estimates occasionally have the wrong (negative) sign, but when this happens they are often not statistically significant, or, in the case of coefficients on the current and lagged reference market price, their sum is still positive.

A general pattern that emerges from the hypothesis tests is that short-run market integration is rejected in a large majority of cases (104 out of 128), mostly at the 1 percent significance level (in 89 cases). This result holds broadly for almost all products, the only exception being copper. Results from tests of short-run market segmentation were mixed, with that hypothesis being rejected in just over a third of all cases (48 out of 128, but 42 out of 89 for steel products). High F-values were common even where the market segmentation hypothesis could not be rejected at the 5 percent significance level. Moreover, in 21 of the 80 cases in which market segmentation was accepted, none of the three hypotheses can be rejected. (Table 8.7 shows the different possible combinations of test results.)

Long-run market integration was accepted in a large majority of tests (105 out of 128). This is an invalid result when the market segmentation hypothesis also is accepted, however, since in that case market integration can be accepted if $a_0 = 1$ and $b_0 = b_1 = 0$. If an F-value below the 5 percent critical level for rejection is taken to mean acceptance of market segmentation, then 71 of the

Table 8.6

Tests of Market Integration

	Number of cities	Short-run integration			Market segmentation			Long-run integration		
		Reject (1%)	Reject (5%)	Accept	Reject (1%)	Reject (5%)	Accept	Reject (1%)	Reject (5%)	Accept
One-period lag structure										
Steel wire rod	20	16	2	2	6	8	6	0	3	17
Steel rod	19	17	1	1	3	4	12	1	2	16
Threaded steel rod	18	16	1	1	10	3	5	3	3	12
Angular steel rod	15	9	0	6	3	2	10	0	0	15
Medium thick plate	9	5	3	1	0	1	8	1	2	6
Cold-rolled thin plate	8	2	3	3	1	1	6	0	2	6
Aluminum	12	5	3	4	1	1	10	0	0	12
Copper	6	2	0	4	0	0	6	0	1	6
Cement	9	7	0	2	0	1	8	2	1	6
Jiefang trucks	6	5	1	0	0	2	4	0	1	5
Dongfeng trucks	6	5	1	0	1	0	5	1	1	4
Totals	128	89	15	24	25	23	80	8	15	105
Three-period lag structure										
Steel wire rod	17	9	3	5	3	3	11	0	2	15
Threaded steel rod	14	8	1	5	0	3	11	0	2	12
Aluminum	7	1	1	5	0	1	6	0	0	7
Totals	38	18	5	15	3	7	28	0	4	34

Table 8.7

Productwise Configurations of Test Results[a]

	Number of cities	Reject SRI and LRI; accept MS	Reject SRI; accept MS and LRI	Accept SRI and LRI; reject MS	Reject SRI and LRI; reject MS	Reject SRI and MS; accept LRI	Reject all hypotheses
One-period lag structure							
Steel wire rod	20	0	5	1	10	3	1
Steel rod	19	1	11	1	4	2	0
Threaded steel rod	18	0	4	0	7	6	1
Angular steel rod	15	0	4	0	5	0	6
Medium thick plate	9	3	5	1	0	0	0
Cold-rolled thin plate	8	2	1	0	2	0	3
Aluminum	12	0	6	0	2	0	4
Copper	6	0	2	0	0	0	4
Cement	9	2	4	0	0	1	2
Dongfeng trucks	6	1	4	0	0	1	0
Jiefang trucks	6	0	4	0	1	1	0
Totals	128	9	50	3	31	14	21
Three-period lag structure							
Steel wire rod[b]	17	0	7	1	4	1	3
Threaded steel rod	14	1	5	0	2	1	5
Aluminum	7	0	1	0	1	0	5
Totals	38	1	13	1	7	2	13

a. Based on rejection or acceptance of the various hypotheses at the 5 percent significance level.

b. There was an anomalous case (Hangzhou), where short-run market integration was not rejected but long-run market integration was rejected.
SRI = short-run integration; LRI = long-run integration; MS = market segmentation.

long-run market integration results are invalidated. Only in the 34 cases where market segmentation is rejected at least at the 5 percent level can long-run market integration comfortably be accepted. In about 30 cases, however, F-values for the market segmentation test were much higher than for long-run integration (above 2 versus below 1, or above 1 versus below 0.5). The latter were often below 0.1. This suggests that in about half of all cases, long-run market integration should not be rejected outright.

As can be seen from table 8.7, the relative frequency of unambiguous acceptance of long-run integration (that is, where market segmentation is simultaneously rejected) varies across products. In the case of steel wire rod, long-run integration is accepted for 11 out of 20 cities, market segmentation for only 5, and the other 4 test results are ambiguous. Moreover, among the 5, 4 have high F-values for market segmentation of over 2 along with very low (0.00–0.19) F-values for market integration. Hence three-quarters of the cities show at least some indication of long-run market integration. At the other extreme among steel products, in the case of medium-thick plate market segmentation is at least weakly accepted for 8 out of 9 cities, with only one of them showing a very high F-value for segmentation and low value for long-run integration. In the case of steel rod, market segmentation cannot be rejected for 12 out of 19 cities, and long-run integration is accepted in only 5. Among the 12, only a few have high F-values for segmentation and low ones for integration. Trucks also show poor long-run market integration, with segmentation accepted in 9 out of 12 cases. Cement shows signs of market segmentation as well.

There is considerable variation in the degree of long-run market integration across cities (table 8.8). At one extreme, for Fuzhou City, long-run market integration is accepted for 4 out of 5 products, including all 4 steel products. In the case of other cities, such as Changsha, Shijiazhuang, Xian, and Zhengzhou, long-run integration is accepted for a plurality of the products tested. At the opposite extreme, in Beijing market segmentation is accepted for 5 out of 6 products, in Nanchang for 7 out of 10, and in Taiyuan for 7 out of 11. It would appear that geographical proximity to Shanghai plays no role in determining the degree of market integration. The closest city to Shanghai on the list is Hangzhou, where market segmentation is accepted for 3 out of 5 products. Another city relatively close to Shanghai is Nanjing, where market segmentation is accepted for 5 out of 8 commodities. This suggests that the modest degree of long-run market integration observed in the sample is the result of the kind of informational equilibrium discussed earlier and is not based on substantial inter-locality flows of goods. Moreover, the information on which local market price adjustments is based apparently circulates nationwide, with little or no geographical concentration. The observed differences in degree of market integration across cities may in part reflect differing degrees to which price-setters take into account prices in other markets, most notably Shanghai, in fixing or influencing local market prices.[7]

Table 8.8

Citywise Configurations of Test Results, One-Period Lag Structure

City	Number of products	Reject SRI and LRI; accept MS	Reject SRI; accept MS and LRI	Accept SRI and LRI; reject MS	Reject SRI and MS; accept LRI	Reject all hypotheses	Accept all hypotheses
Beijing	6	0	5	0	0	1	0
Changsha	8	1	1	2	1	1	2
Chengdu	8	0	6	0	1	0	1
Fuzhou	5	0	1	0	4	0	0
Guangzhou	5	0	2	0	2	0	1
Haerbin	3	0	2	0	0	0	1
Hangzhou	5	1	2	0	1	0	1
Hefei	7	2	1	0	2	1	1
Jinan	11	1	4	1	5	0	0
Kunming	1	0	0	0	0	0	1
Nanchang	10	2	5	0	0	2	1
Nanjing	8	0	5	0	0	1	2
Shenyang	3	0	1	0	0	2	0
Shijiazhuang	11	0	3	0	4	2	2
Taiyuan	11	1	6	0	4	0	0
Tianjin	3	0	0	0	1	1	1
Wuhan	10	1	5	0	1	1	2
Xiamen	3	0	0	0	1	2	0
Xian	5	0	1	0	2	0	2
Zhengzhou	5	0	0	0	2	0	3
Totals	128	9	50	3	31	14	21

Notes: Based on rejection or acceptance of the various hypotheses at the 5 percent significance level. SRI = short-run integration; LRI = long-run integration; MS = market segmentation.

Overall, there is strong evidence against short-run market integration, and market segmentation seems to hold in a plurality of cases where tests differentiated among the various hypotheses (i.e., did not accept or reject all of them simultaneously). But long-run market integration is unambiguously accepted in about a quarter of all cases, and in many others rejection is just barely avoided for the market segmentation hypothesis at the 5 percent level, while F-values for the long-run integration hypothesis are very low. Hence, the picture is decidedly a mixed one. Use of the 5 percent criterion and rejection of long-run market integration when both it and market segmentation are accepted bias the results against the former. Nevertheless, it is clear that Chinese markets for industrial producer goods on the whole are much less integrated than corresponding markets in industrialized market economies. Adjustment is slow, occurring over periods of months rather than weeks or days, and in a fair number of cases the link between local and reference market prices is statistically insignificant. The lack of market integration stands out especially in the case of pure nonferrous metals like copper and aluminum, for which international markets are closely linked.

Hypothesis testing with a three-period lag structure suffered from drastically reduced degrees of freedom, which rendered estimation impossible for many products. In nearly a third of the tests, data were insufficient to reject any of the hypotheses, compared with only a sixth in the tests with one-period lag structure. Nevertheless, results are broadly consistent with those of the one-period lag model, as can be seen from tables 8.6 and 8.7. Only in 8 out of 38 cases is long-run market integration unambiguously accepted. On the other hand, in 14 cases market segmentation is accepted, though in 5 of them there are high F-values for segmentation in combination with low ones for long-run integration.

Conclusions: Market Functioning in Chinese Industry

Despite the conceptual and data-related problems discussed earlier in this chapter, as well as the ambiguous nature of some of the test results, a few tentative observations can be made.

First, in terms of price determination, markets for industrial producer goods in China, particularly for homogeneous commodities like graded nonferrous metals and narrowly specified steel products, are functioning differently from markets for similar commodities in the industrialized capitalist countries. Local prices do not respond quickly to changes in prices on the reference market, despite the relatively small percentage differences in price levels across markets. There is evidence of long-run market integration in many cases, which implies gradual adjustment of prices over periods of three to six months. This reflects information flows linking markets in different cities rather than commodity flows.

Rejection of the short-run market integration hypothesis also means that effective, coordinated central price controls are not influencing price movements in local markets. In the context of long-run market integration, price "guidance" by local authorities may not mean much in practice, since by all indications it is responsive to market conditions and reasonably flexible. This all suggests that the role of central government fiat in market price determination is limited.

For a considerable period of time the expansion of markets for industrial producer goods seems to have had a stabilizing rather than an inflationary impact on market prices. Market prices for the most part were relatively stable between their initial surge in 1984–85 and the subsequent resurgence of high open price inflation in 1988. The "income effect" on demand from increasing shares of transactions at higher prices as well as other factors helped preserve price stability in the midst of rapid industrial growth and high demand. But as a result of sharp increases in the share of output of most commodities sold at higher market prices and increases in effective prices of plan-allocated goods, the ability of markets to continue to act as buffers against severe price inflation has been eroded. Hence the sharp price rises observed in 1988–89. Further increases can reasonably be expected, given the strong inflationary pressures manifest in the Chinese economy of the late 1980s.

It appears that the degree of market integration is not closely related to distances between cities, though the issue has not been rigorously analyzed. There is no indication of a strong positive relationship between degree of market integration and geographical proximity. This in turn supports the assertion that interlocality goods flows are not an important factor in influencing local market prices.

There are some interesting findings related to particular products. The lack of evidence in favor of integration among secondary markets for the two brands of trucks is puzzling; it is possible that this reflects nonhomogeneity of the product, if both used and new truck prices were haphazardly reported. Generally the degree of long-run market integration is greater for most of the steel products than for other commodities. The lack of strong evidence in favor of market integration for nonferrous metals, especially copper, is unexpected, since they are homogeneous, high value/weight ratio commodities. (The paucity of observations for copper means that test results are not very satisfactory, with no hypothesis being rejected in the majority of cases.)

The data and analysis present a general picture of markets that are still in the process of formation, with a fairly weak institutional base; subject to shocks and, to some extent, local government pressures; and lacking a dense network of agents and information channels that smooth market fluctuations and enhance market functioning. This should not be surprising given the short timespan of reform implementation so far. Development of markets for industrial producer goods up to early 1989 should not be considered unsatisfactory merely because of the lack of strong confirmation for short-run market integration from econometric tests.

A number of caveats and qualifications need to be kept in mind. In the first place, the estimation procedures and hypothesis tests do not directly attack issues related to market competition and efficiency. What they say about relationships between market prices in different cities does have some implications for these broader questions, however. Segmented markets are likely to be less competitive, since there are fewer competing actors and local authorities will be tempted to intervene to limit competition among local firms (see chapter 4). Segmentation also means price signals are not appropriately directing resource allocation from a national perspective. So the fact that the econometric tests do not indicate a dominant pattern of market segmentation does provide some limited evidence in favor of the effectiveness of markets.

Other caveats relate to the nature of the data, its quality, and the limited number of observations for many cities and products, discussed earlier. They do not negate the value of the exercise, though caution is needed in interpretation of the results. Finally, there are some questions about the Ravallion methodology, which has been recently developed, applied exclusively to markets for agricultural goods, and not yet modified in the light of experience with applications. There is probably room for further development and refinement of both the theory and the hypothesis tests.

9. The Atrophy of Central Planning in Chinese Industry

IN CHAPTER 5 it was argued that mandatory planning and administrative controls have largely lost their direct impact on the short-run allocation of Chinese industrial goods. Chapter 3 showed that the share of the market mechanism in Chinese industry has been rising and that markets have become very important in quantitative terms. Moreover, despite numerous problems and obstacles, the actual functioning of markets is already far removed from administrative allocation. (Evidence on the extent of market integration, analyzed in chapter 8, is mixed, but there is no sign of effective central price controls, and local government price controls seem not to have played an important role.) Chapter 4 asserted that market forces have had a strong impact on enterprise behavior and performance and supported this contention with evidence from case studies. This chapter sketches out an analysis of how the transition from plan to market is occurring, with primary focus on the two-tier plan/market system for industrial producer goods.

The Demise of the "Command System" in Chinese Industry

There are at least three levels on which the argument for the demise of the command system in Chinese industry can be advanced, and they are progressively stronger and more forceful in their implications. The first relates to the slackness and looseness of production planning for firms. The second is based on the growing importance of the market mechanism at the margin. The third and strongest argument, which unlike the other two was not advanced in chapter 5, asserts that the share of mandatory planning is being drastically reduced, to the point where it is dominated even in an absolute sense by market forces and hence is becoming irrelevant and vestigial.

The evidence for slack and loose production planning in Chinese industry was presented in chapter 5. If enterprises chronically exceed their production plans, then plan targets, or plan-based incentives focused on achievement of plan targets, do not determine their output. Similarly, if plan targets are easy to revise in the light of actual performance to ensure that they are achieved ex post, they will not be taken seriously and their influence over resource allocation will be weakened.

A second, different argument was also formulated in chapter 5 and subjected to rigorous analysis in chapter 6. It relates to the impact of markets on enterprise production decisions at the margin. If firms maximize profits, and if all of them engage in at least some market transactions for all of their inputs and outputs, then plan targets and plan prices have no impact on the level of industrial production, supply, and demand.

The strongest and most unassailable argument for the irrelevance of command planning in China is that the actual share of the market mechanism in total production, supply, and demand for at least some commodities and for many enterprises has become so large that the market now dominates planning even in an absolute sense. If this is true, then the issues that arise in the case of the first two arguments can be dispensed with.

A high, even dominant share of the market mechanism could arise as a result of conscious policy to reduce the share of output subject to mandatory planning, or more gradually if incremental growth consists entirely or largely of production for the market while the absolute amount of plan-allocated output stagnates or rises only slowly. Planning can also become irrelevant if plan prices are raised to the point where purchasers no longer place a high value on getting allocations, as opposed to relying on market purchases. This can happen either through sharp hikes in official state-set prices or through various kinds of disguised measures that raise effective prices of within-plan output to producers and users. Finally, the system can break down if producers stop taking their state plan production and compulsory delivery targets seriously, for whatever reason. These different modes of transition are explored later in this chapter.

To the extent that this third and strongest argument for the demise of command planning in Chinese industry holds, at least as an indication of trends, it means quite simply that in terms of short-term nonfactor resource allocation, China is essentially becoming a market economy. Questions can be raised about how well Chinese markets function, since they are still weak, fragmented, and subject to administrative intervention. But this does not detract from the major transition that has been occurring from a system where short-term resource allocation was largely determined by government administrative directives to one where it is increasingly determined by voluntary transactions between economic agents.

Obviously, this conclusion depends on the quality of the evidence presented in chapters 3, 4, and 7 as well as in this chapter. It is possible to envision a situation where the ''command system'' indeed has been dismantled and where enterprise production activities are no longer directly determined by mandatory plans, but where government control over short-run resource allocation is exercised in other ways, for example, through control over financial flows to firms. However, the existence of functioning markets at which industrial goods are traded on a voluntary basis with a considerable degree of price flexibility (chapters 3 and 7) strongly suggests that in China the demise of the command system has indeed been accompanied by the emergence of goods markets. The evidence of market-oriented behavior on the part of industrial firms (chapter 4) provides further support for this contention.

In any case, the narrow scope of the argument in this chapter should be stressed. It relates to the allocation of industrial goods, not factors of production like land, labor, and capital. The efficiency benefits from a dominant market mechanism in the allocation of industrial goods are limited if the factor allocation system remains rigid, as has been the case in China. Furthermore, rigidities in the system of enterprise finance and capital allocation can hinder the smooth functioning of goods markets.

The Two-Tier System: Origins and Development

The evolution from a plan-dominated to a market-dominated goods allocation system in Chinese industry has been inextricably linked with the phenomenon of multiple allocation channels and multiple pricing, including markets with flexible prices at one extreme, which will henceforth be termed the two-tier plan/market system. The two-tier system had some roots in the prereform period but reached fruition in the mid-1980s.

Basic Definition

There are a number of ways in which plan and market can be combined in an economy, depending on the dimension along which the demarcation between the two occurs. Some goods could be subject to plan allocation, others could be allocated by the market. Alternatively, the bifurcation could be along enterprise lines, with some firms having their inputs and outputs regulated by plan, others by market. Still another possibility is for the demarcation to cut across individual inputs and outputs of particular firms. In this situation, many firms would have part of their total supply or demand for each input and output subject to plan allocation, part transacted on the market. This last alternative, modeled in chapter 6, is the most general one and also the one that corresponds most closely to Chinese reality.

Formally, the two-tier system involves each enterprise facing a vector of output plan targets, targets for compulsory procurement of output, and input allocations, with input purchases, production, and output sales above these target levels occurring through the market at flexible prices (see chapter 6). All types of mandatory production planning, compulsory procurement of output, and administrative allocation of supplies are included in the "plan" part, while the market portion is only that part of production, supply, and demand that is subject to market allocation on a voluntary basis, at market-determined prices. Market prices normally are presumed to be higher than plan prices. Many variations and complications are possible, for instance, splitting above-quota production between plan allocation and market allocation at specified ratios, or explicit linkage of input quotas and output targets. It is also possible to simplify, for instance, by assuming that compulsory procurement targets are identical to output targets.

Prereform Roots of the Two-Tier System

The prereform roots of the two-tier system were the practices of cost-based multiple pricing for different firms and localities (see chapter 5); the related phenomenon of multiple planning and supply channels; and a fringe of market and market-like resource allocation activities which, however, remained relatively undeveloped (see chapter 3). These were all closely tied in with the tendency toward decentralized, autarchic industrialization of the Cultural Revolution period.

The limitations of the prereform roots of the two-tier system are readily apparent. In the first place, prices remained administratively controlled, even though such control was exercised at a lower level of government. There is no reason to believe that local governments were more flexible in their pricing practices than the central government. Second, goods flows remained subject to local government direction, with little scope for enterprise autonomy. Even the transactors were often government agencies rather than firms. Finally, the share of the more market-like of the prereform allocation channels in total economic activity remained relatively small. Thus, prereform practices served to create potential for subsequent development of the two-tier system, but they should not be confused with the two-tier system itself.

Patterns of Adjustment to Buyers' and Sellers' Markets

Starting in the late 1970s, Chinese policies of reform and adjustment were superimposed on this system of multiple administrative allocation channels and pricing. A key aspect has been the expansion of the role of the market in resource allocation. Patterns of adjustment by firms and government agencies in response to market forces were discussed in chapter 4. It was argued that a critical determinant of enterprise behavior and performance in the early 1980s was whether reform and liberalization occurred in the context of a chronic sellers' market (excess demand) or a buyers' market (equilibrium or excess supply) for output. The response of the system also depended on this dichotomy.

There has been a basic asymmetry in price pressures and adjustments as between a buyers' market and a sellers' market. In a situation of excess supply, downward pressure is exerted on the price of the entire supply of the good concerned. Buyers are almost always able to refuse to purchase high-priced goods allocated to them through the plan, and they have no incentive to accept such goods if the price can be bargained down in the open market. There may be resistance against sharp downward price movements by the beneficiaries of high prices, like budgetary authorities who may derive substantial revenues from the taxes and profits generated, which may delay price reductions. But whether or not prices are actually forced down, the pressures of the buyers' market affect the entire supply of a good. In this situation, the tendency is for directive planning eventually to break down and for market allocation and pricing to take over.

The chronic sellers' market was more typical in prereform China. Reforms strengthening the influence of market forces exacerbated the strong economic pressures for price increases already present. These interacted with the existing multiple channel allocation and multiple pricing system to create the full-blown two-tier system, with genuine market allocation at the margin. In a sellers' market, users with access to plan allocations are not willing to give them up and oppose any price increase. But would-be purchasers without allocations as well as those who need more than they are allocated would be willing to pay market-determined prices for what they cannot get through the plan. Thus there is a strong tendency for some part of output, particularly incremental output, to be sold at a higher price, as a "safety valve" and response to the strong pressures of the sellers' market.

The multiple pricing/allocation system already in place for many industrial producer goods lent itself to this, since markets could simply be added as another commodity distribution channel among many. The transition to the two-tier system was also helped along by innovations like setting up "markets for the means of production," "materials trade centers," and specialized markets for particular producer goods like steel and trucks in a number of large cities. More recently, wholesale markets for consumer goods have proliferated as well.

A key element of contrast between adjustment to a sellers' market and to a buyers' market is that in the case of the former, the existing multiple allocation and pricing system remained in place and tended to evolve into the two-tier system. A strong, sustained buyers' market, on the other hand, tended to erode the system of multiple allocation channels and prices (if it was present in the first place[1]), by putting downward pressure on prices of the entire supply.

In sum, the two-tier system emerged in China in the early 1980s as a result of the implementation of market-oriented reforms in a chronic sellers' market for many industrial producer goods. The response of the system to market forces was to provide a "safety valve" at the margin, which could absorb some of the pressure of excess demand, while maintaining low plan prices for the benefit of purchasers with plan allocations.

Government Pricing Policies

A number of pricing reforms encouraged the emergence and development of the two-tier system.[2] At first selective but then progressively greater relaxation of price controls and introduction of several new or transformed price categories were the most important reform measures. Floating prices, negotiated prices, and market prices are discussed briefly below. There have also been some major adjustments in state prices. Finally, the rapid growth of the nonstate sector in industry, which has much greater flexibility in pricing than the state sector, has been a very important development.

Floating prices were introduced relatively early, though initially primarily in a downward direction. In 1979 prices of electronics goods and in 1980 those of sixteen types of machinery and electrical equipment were allowed to float downward, by as much as 20 percent compared with ministry-set prices.[3] Sometimes upward flotation was permitted for better-quality products or those that had won national awards for quality. A State Council circular of May 1984 allowed industrial firms making key producer goods to market directly their output above the state plan, at prices that could float upward or downward by as much as 20 percent (*China Economic Yearbook* Editorial Committee 1985, X–21).

Negotiated prices were not unknown in the prereform period, but they have proliferated since the late 1970s, especially for consumer goods. At one extreme, negotiated prices may be little different from prices set and controlled by local governments. Though nominally determined by negotiations between buyer and seller, they are vulnerable to administrative pressure and intervention. At the opposite extreme, negotiated prices may be no different from market prices, voluntarily agreed to by agents and sensitive to supply and demand conditions. There may have been some movement from the former extreme toward the latter end of the spectrum in 1984–85.

"Market" prices are less ambiguous than negotiated prices, but they also are vulnerable to administrative intervention (see chapter 3). The checkered history of pricing at the Shanghai market for producer goods in the early 1980s (see Byrd 1985a) provides an indication of how market pricing can be subverted. But prices of many goods had considerable flexibility in some periods. Moreover, as Naughton (1986c, 15) notes, local government intervention and price pegging is done in the interest of smoothing fluctuations rather than maintaining prices at nonequilibrium levels.

The most important yet largely unheralded reform in late 1984 and early 1985 was the general decontrol of prices of industrial producer goods produced and sold outside the plan (Shen and Han 1986, 18), which in effect consummated the two-tier system by completely freeing the market portion from price restrictions. In October 1986, prices of the entire supply of bicycles, black and white television sets, cassette tape recorders, washing machines, sewing machines, refrigerators, electric fans, and some textile products were officially decontrolled (*China Daily*, October 1, 1986). These and other related measures in the mid-1980s went a long way toward allowing uninhibited market pricing at least for the portion of industrial output not subject to state plan allocation.

Thus, despite problems, market pricing has become well established and appears to be at least reasonably reflective of market equilibrium conditions. Certainly the considerable decline in the market price of coal in 1985 suggests that market prices are strongly affected by supply and demand.[4] Moreover, the growth of the nonstate (collective and private) sector has helped generate and nourish the "market" side of the two-tier system; state enterprises increasingly can participate in the markets created by the nonstate sector, on the supply and particularly on the demand sides. Nonstate enterprises account for the bulk of industrial firms in China—over 95 percent in 1984—and over 30 percent of China's gross value of industrial output in the same year (State Statistical Bureau 1985a, 239, 291–306).

Dynamic Impact of the Two-Tier System

As the two-tier system became established and began to affect a significant proportion of industrial output, its own internal tendencies and dynamics started to have an influence on patterns of resource allocation and on the behavior of industrial decision makers. This in turn affected the environment in which the two-tier system operated and its subsequent evolution. Thus, it is important to understand what, in theory, the impact of the two-tier system should be on resource allocation, and especially its influence on plan and market shares in the total output of a commodity.

Based on the analysis of chapter 6, this section starts with a brief review of the static impact of the two-tier system, assuming that agents follow the "rules" of the system. Though static results are of interest, dynamic effects determine evolution over time. Incentives and opportunities to undermine the rules by diverting goods from plan to market channels in order to earn windfall profits; the degree to which the two-tier system is self-enforcing and possibilities for monitoring and policing it; and the role of central government policy receive attention.

Static Impact

The static resource allocation effects of an "ideal model" of the two-tier system have already been derived, along with the assumptions required for them to hold (see chapter 6). If all firms participate in the market for at least part of the supply of each of their inputs and part of the sales of each of their outputs, and further-more if firms maximize profits in short-run production decisions, then not only will there be a meaningful equilibrium solution, but that equilibrium will be Pareto optimal, given fixed enterprise endowments of factors of production. While these assumptions do not hold in their entirety, they may not be too far off as "approximate" stylized facts.

These static results are limited even if the required assumptions hold, how-ever. In particular, the optimality result is narrow because it takes factor endow-ments as given. Inappropriate factor endowments and the lack of a mechanism to reallocate them over time can be a much greater source of inefficiency than

distortions in goods markets (see Byrd and Tidrick 1987). Similarly, static effi-
ciency results or their absence mean less in a situation of rapid changes in the
economic and institutional structure of the economy. Nevertheless, they do say
something about the lack of importance of planning in short-term resource allo-
cation.

The Constellation of Economic Forces

The incentives and relative strengths of the different actors involved can affect
the dynamics of the two-tier system. The system emerged from a persistent
sellers' market, so the economic position of producers and sellers is inherently
much stronger than that of the demand side. Purchasers are in a fundamentally
weak position economically and cannot be very assertive in making demands on
the supply side. Thus, overall, the economic forces in the two-tier system
strongly favor sellers.

The introduction of the two-tier system with market allocation at the fringe
changes the constellation of economic forces in one important way: whereas in
the traditional sellers' market availability of goods is in question, in the two-tier
system the benefits of access to plan-allocated inputs have essentially been mon-
etized—the goods can be obtained one way or another, and the only difference is
the price paid. Thus, goods subject to within-plan allocation at low fixed prices
carry implicit, embodied rents (discussed in chapter 5 and formalized in chapter
7). This change makes the benefits accruing to users as well as the losses to
producers due to low plan prices quite obvious. Indeed, monetization strengthens
the hand of the latter, who now at least in principle have an alternative channel
for sales through which they can gain profits that would otherwise go to purchas-
ers with plan-based input allocations.

In this way as well as by allowing producers to sell some output at higher
market prices, the two-tier system enhances the economic position of producers
and sellers as compared with their position under a comprehensively planned
system. Thus, to some extent the strong underlying economic pressures in a
chronic sellers' market become openly manifested in the two-tier system. Since
enterprises function as both buyers and sellers, the effect on any individual firm
is not unequivocal, however.

The Constellation of Political Forces

There are two main beneficiaries of the two-tier system: purchasers of goods
with access to plan allocations and the allocators themselves. The benefits to
users with plan allocations are obvious: a cheaper price for the goods they need
than would otherwise be possible. Whether or not users actually appropriate
these rents depends on whether they can resell plan-allocated goods at the market
price or use them as inputs in the production of a good that can be sold at a high

price, which in turn depends on the degree to which their output targets are tightly linked to input quotas. The benefits to allocators are associated with their ability to determine which agents get plan allocations and associated benefits. Allocators may individually gain financial benefits from this authority, but if they use it to appropriate rents by diverting goods from plan to market channels, they will undermine the two-tier system over the long run.[5]

The beneficiaries of the two-tier system obviously will fight to maintain or increase the plan-allocated portion of output of key goods. Firms with access to large amounts of inputs through the plan may be quite willing to continue to sell their output through the plan, providing that this enables them to keep their input allocations. Neither users nor plan allocators, however, are likely to be unanimously in favor of the status quo. Users without access to plan-based input quotas and those with inadequate plan allocations have an incentive to bid supplies away from others. Some allocators may individually gain from undermining the system, but the burden of fending off competing users fighting for shares of plan quotas may be greater than any benefits conferred by this authority. Lack of unanimity among users and probably planners as well, exacerbated by the fact that the bulk of users are also producers and sellers, may greatly weaken the forces opposing the economic tendencies that favor the production/supply side.

"Growing Out of the Plan"

In looking at the dynamic properties of the two-tier system, it is first assumed that agents behave as they are supposed to: producers always meet their targets for output and compulsory delivery at the state price, while commercial intermediaries and allocators resist the temptation to earn easy profits by diverting goods from plan to market channels. Even with these idealistic assumptions, there are strong tendencies for the market share of output to expand over time.

One question is whether there is a "ratchet effect" or similar mechanism by which plan targets automatically increase over time. If they increase in proportion with total output of the good concerned, then "growing out of the plan"[6] cannot occur. Tidrick (1987) argues that the ratchet effect to a large extent does not operate in China.[7] If the ratchet effect is weak or nonexistent, and if plan targets and allocations do not fall in absolute terms, the share of the economy governed by plan would fall over time as total output grows. This is precisely the meaning of growing out of the plan: there is no frontal attack on the planning system or attempt to abolish mandatory planning outright, but its share in economic activity declines because the portion subject to planning does not grow with the economy as a whole.

Another reason for a rise in the share of the market is that incentives for investment in expansion are much greater for the market portion than for the plan portion, since the former usually earns higher returns than the latter. The different actors involved in investment decision making have become more profit-oriented in recent years. Enterprises might simply refuse to put their funds into projects for which output would have to be sold through the plan at a low price (unless they thereby get entitlements to low-priced plan-allocated inputs). Banks and even planners also may be increasingly responsive to profitability considerations in deciding on which projects to finance.

This tendency to grow out of the plan through profit-oriented investment decisions could be offset by massive use of state investment funds for expansion of the planned sector. But this is not as potent a force as might appear at first sight. State budget investment funds now account for a much lower share of total investment, so their ability to reverse the natural tendencies of the system is more limited. Moreover, many large projects are now jointly financed by the central government, local governments, and other sources of funds; pressures from the more profit-oriented investors would require that market pricing be allowed for at least a considerable part of output generated by these projects. Investments that do get made to increase production at plan prices most likely involve special arrangements like compensation trade deals, which typically pre-assign output to users.

Finally, producers may well exert political pressure for increases in state prices and other legal changes in the two-tier system through government directives. This is conceptually distinct from undermining the system by not following its rules, but the two are closely related, and the threat or reality of the latter may be a potent force promoting the former.

Incentives to Undermine the System

Producers subject to mandatory planning are "losing" potential profits by being forced to sell part or most of their output at the low plan price. On the other hand, because of chronic excess demand at the state price, they are in a strong position economically. Thus, they have an obvious incentive to divert output from plan to market channels, or to impose side payments or other costs on purchasers.

Such diversion can be accomplished in a number of ways, even in the face of a system that frowns on this kind of activity. One is simply inflation of input-output coefficients in bargaining over plan targets. While this creates reserves or above-plan production in traditional centrally planned economies, in the Chinese two-tier system it also creates the opportunity to convert low-priced inputs into high-priced output for sale on the market. Another means of diversion is to produce first for the market and then for the plan only late in the year, with the possibility that due to "circumstances beyond the enterprise's control," the plan target in the end cannot be achieved. In a relatively weak planning system like China's such behavior is hard to police or penalize, particularly if there is uncertainty. Even passive behavior by producers, like refusing to produce for plan delivery until state-allocated inputs have arrived and can be used, will undermine the system, particularly if many producers do this.

Commercial intermediaries trading in plan-allocated goods have the same incentives as producers to divert goods from plan to market channels. Since the goods are merely passing through the hands of commercial units, there is no room for diversion through inflated input-output ratios, timing of production, and so forth. But there are opportunities to force customers to give side payments in one form or another to get low-priced goods. Plan-allocated goods handled by commercial units are often in small amounts, allocated as "blocks" without specifying users—large, regular supplies go directly from producer to user. This leaves much room for abuse. Small, scattered buyers without unit-specific allocations vying for these goods would be in a poor position to complain about price gouging.

Another way in which the commercial system can raise the effective price of plan-allocated goods is through levying fees and service charges. Stipulated commercial margins on most goods are low, but these can be padded by extra charges for storage, loading and unloading, and so on. Even if no individual commercial unit profits excessively in this way, the price of a good can be jacked up greatly by passing through a number of intermediaries. An egregious example involved some steel plate in Northeast China in 1982, which reportedly changed hands eight times and rose in price from 473 yuan per ton to 773 yuan per ton, an increase of over 63 percent.[8]

Precarious Forces in Favor of Stability

What pressures, forces, and incentives keep the unstable compromise represented by the two-tier system from quickly breaking down? The most powerful force restraining producers from taking advantage of their strong economic position is the linkage between planned input allocations and output/delivery targets. If a producer (who is, after all, also a purchaser of inputs) knows that diverting goods from plan to market channels will jeopardize his low-priced input allocations, he may find it in his best interest not to do so.

This linkage has numerous problematic aspects in the Chinese context, however. Incentives to undermine the system are still present, if this can be done without loss of future input allocations. Second, the linkage may be destabilizing at a broader level, if it works symmetrically in both upward and downward directions. Diversion of goods from plan to market channels means that "downstream" purchasers do not get the input allocations provided for in their plans. These in turn could legitimately refuse to fulfill their output plans, and so on. The linkage between input allocations and output/delivery targets can be a two-edged sword.

The linkage itself may be weak and highly imperfect. Since provision of inputs must precede production, for it to work there must be some kind of a downward ratchet: a failure to fulfill the output/delivery target in one year must mean a reduction in input allocations for the following year, since inputs for current-year production have already been provided. With pervasive bargaining over plan targets and input allocations, this kind of ratchet probably does not work very well in a downward direction, just as there does not appear to be a strong upward ratchet effect. Moreover, initial input allocations for the following year are made before current-year production is known, further attenuating any possible linkage. Planning authorities would be harming themselves as much as the firms concerned if a reduction in input allocations in the following year were accompanied by a reduction in the compulsory procurement plan. On the other hand, they would find it difficult to cut input allocations punitively for delinquent enterprises while maintaining their compulsory procurement targets at the same level.

Some examples illustrate the difficulties authorities would run into in trying to impose and enforce punitive sanctions against firms that fail to fulfill their output/delivery targets. The Mindong Electrical Machinery Corporation chronically "borrowed" against plan-based input allocations of rolled steel and silicon steel for subsequent years, but it is not clear whether and in what way these borrowings would be "repaid." In 1984, 500 tons of rolled steel were borrowed in this manner (interview information, November 1984). The No. 2 Auto Plant was involved in a lengthy conflict with material supply authorities over plan-allocated inputs that the factory had used to produce trucks for market sales in 1981, when orders through the plan were insufficient to fill production capacity. The enterprise's "debt" of trucks "owed" to the planning system was carried over for several years, but in the end it was "settled" without anything near full "repayment" by No. 2 (interview information, October–November 1984).

The "stick" of lower plan allocations in the next period carries even less weight for commercial units. Since the goods simply pass through their hands and legal commercial margins are fixed, cutting plan allocations in a subsequent period can hurt only the users and would have little effect on the commercial intermediary involved. Though such cutbacks may adversely affect a commercial enterprise's turnover, this could be made up by increasing market transactions.

Timing problems also can weaken the linkage between output targets and input allocations. A rational profit-oriented firm would try to shift production for the market forward within the year and production for the plan backward. This would mean late output deliveries, and any risk of lower-than-expected output would be borne by the plan rather than by production for the market, in contrast to the way the "ideal version" of the system is supposed to work. Late deliveries of producer goods through the plan mean late arrivals of input allocations for other firms, exacerbating the danger of underfulfillment of targets at downstream stages of production. A good example is the Anshan Iron and Steel Plant's underfulfillment of its state pig iron delivery plan in the first half of 1985, reportedly because it was more profitable to sell pig iron at negotiated prices on the market.[9]

The other main force buttressing the two-tier system, with an interest in preventing an immediate switch to complete market allocation, is users with plan allocations. Many of these are also producers, as has already been mentioned, but others are final users, most prominently the government investment budget and urban consumers. These elements have a strong interest in the maintenance of the two-tier system. But they are at least somewhat schizophrenic in that they are willing to bid supplies away from other users if their quotas are insufficient for their needs.

Monitoring and Enforcement Problems

A key determining factor, given the mix of incentives described above, is the extent to which monitoring and enforcement of the two-tier system are feasible. It appears that the possibilities for effective monitoring and enforcement are severely limited; hence, not only the incentives but also the opportunities available undermine the system. Only a strong enforcement effort, perhaps largely political in nature, would have a chance of success, and in the proreform atmosphere of 1984–85 this would have clashed with overall government policy.

Enforceability is especially difficult to achieve because buyers in market transactions involving diversion of goods from plan channels gain benefits and have little or no incentive to avoid them, let alone report the seller to authorities. The buyer may get a price at least slightly lower than the market price, in which case it shares in the benefits from diversion. Even if this does not occur, the buyer gets the benefit of buying the goods concerned at the market price and at worst treats the transaction as a straightforward market transaction. In many cases the buyer may not even know that the goods originally were allocated within the plan, at state prices.

Other problems with monitoring and enforcement include most prominently the "softness" of the planning system and, as has already been mentioned, the great difficulty of making any ex post penalties for diversion stick. There is also the almost intractable issue of time used in the production process and the ability of firms to shift uncertainty from the market portion to the planned portion of production.

All in all, the incentives inherent in the two-tier system, combined with internal contradictions in the forces trying to uphold it and the difficulties of monitoring and enforcement, render the system precarious. This section has emphasized the economic incentives and tendencies. Obviously, some features of the two-tier system and the behavior it engenders, combined with the economic interests of users in getting low-priced supplies, could provoke a political reaction, which might lead to a return to more comprehensive command planning. But in China up to 1989 the inherent economic tendencies of the system have dominated.[10]

Evolution of the Two-Tier System in the 1980s

It remains to explain how the two-tier system evolved in practice during the 1980s, once it emerged and became entrenched for certain commodities. This is done mainly with the use of case studies for a few representative industrial products of major importance in the economy. Some major policy changes that affected large numbers of goods will also be highlighted, as well as certain recent developments that may indicate an accelerated transformation of the two-tier system.

"Growing Out of the Plan": The Case of Coal

Coal is a good example of the tendencies inherent in the two-tier system for expansion of the share of output subject to market allocation, even if absolute amounts flowing through the plan are not cut back significantly. Table 9.1 shows the share of coal output produced by different types of coal mines over the period 1978–85. These figures do not correspond directly to plan and market shares; much coal produced by local mines is subject to allocation through local or provincial plans, while on the other hand some output of mines producing for the state plan undoubtedly was directly marketed. Nevertheless, the decline in the share of total national output of mines producing for the state plan (so-called *tongpei* or unified-allocation coal mines), from 55 percent in 1978 to 48 percent in 1984 and even less in 1985, strongly suggests that the share of market allocation has gone up by at least a similar margin. Indeed, the bulk of incremental coal output has been accounted for by small coal mines run by townships and villages, a large share of whose production is subject to market allocation at flexible prices. Thus, the share of the market may have risen by an even greater margin than the decline in the share of unified-allocation coal mines.

Coal pricing policy has increasingly moved toward decontrol of prices and allowing mines to market a larger portion of their output directly. A 1984 directive by the Ministry of Coal Industry (1985, 64) allowed local coal mines to sell all above-plan output themselves, at flexible prices. The market price of coal has fluctuated widely and reached very high levels before declining substantially in 1985, due to a strong supply response by small coal mines producing mainly for the market.

The pattern of coal has been broadly duplicated by other basic raw materials, for which deliveries through state plan contracts have tended to remain nearly constant in absolute terms even though production has increased by a considerable margin in many cases. As a result, the share of central plan allocations has declined moderately for many of them. Again, it is not possible to ascertain with any precision the share of the market, but for most of these goods the declining proportion of the state plan certainly was not fully offset by an increase in the share of output allocated through local administrative channels.

Sharp Decline in Plan Allocations: The Case of Trucks

Plan allocation of trucks provides a good example of the strong tendencies toward an increase in the share of the market in the two-tier system, as well as an

Table 9.1

Share of Coal Output by Different Types of Mines, 1978–85

	Share in total raw coal output (percent)		
Year	Unified allocation mines	Local state-owned mines	Nonstate mines
1978	55.3	29.1	15.6[a]
1979	56.3	26.7	17.0[a]
1980	55.5	26.2	18.3
1981	53.9	25.7	20.4
1982	52.5	25.6	21.9
1983	50.8 (52.5)[b]	25.4 (23.7)[b]	23.8
1984	47.9 (50.0)[b]	24.6 (22.5)[b]	27.5
1985	— (46.6)	— (20.9)	32.5
Share of incremental output, 1978–84	21.2	8.4	70.4

Sources: Ministry of Coal Industry (1982, 9, 16; 1983, 61; 1985, 12; 1986, 12); and Ministry of Agriculture (1981, 125; 1982, 50).

a. Based on the assumption that the ratio of total collective mine output to output by commune and brigade coal mines was the same in 1978 and 1979 as in 1980.

b. Sichuan Province's provincially run state coal mines were put in the unified-allocation category in 1984, which results in overstatement of the share of unified-allocation mines in the official statistics for 1984 and 1985. An adjustment was made for both 1983 and 1984, using actual output of the Sichuan provincial mines in 1983, and based on the assumption that their output grew at the same rate as that of national coal output subsequently. Thus, the figures in parentheses for 1983–85 include the Sichuan mines in the unified-allocation category, whereas the 1983 and 1984 figures outside of parentheses do not.

interesting case study of what happens when market conditions revert from excess supply to excess demand. Direct marketing of trucks by producers like the No. 2 Auto Plant started only in 1981, when the sharp cutback in state investment left many units that had been allocated trucks through the state plan with insufficient funds to consummate their purchases. What happened subsequently when market conditions reverted to excess demand was influenced by the strength of the largest truck producers, general proreform policies, and a major shift in the ownership composition of trucks toward rural individuals. Producers were able to hold onto substantial direct marketing rights, and the linkage between compulsory procurement of trucks through the state plan and plan-based input allocations at state prices was made explicit. But producers were still forced to sell all output at the state price or increase prices only to compensate for cost increases.

A secondary market in trucks arose quickly, with the plan entitlement for a truck (not including the truck itself) being worth up to 50,000 yuan at one point, compared with a state price of 20,000 yuan plus (interview information, August 1985). This led to complaints by producers about the "middleman" profits being reaped. The response of the system was to legalize the market for trucks, setting up trading centers at which trucks could be bought and sold and allowing producers to participate in them, getting at least part of the benefit of the higher market price. This generated a full-blown two-tier system. Market prices for trucks declined somewhat in 1986, due mainly to investment cutbacks, tighter monetary policy, and high imports in 1984–85.

There has been a sharp reduction in the share of trucks allocated through the central plan and an increase in the share of trucks sold by producers directly, many of them going to rural individuals in the newly permitted private truck transport business. The share of total national motor vehicle output allocated through the central plan was down to only 42 percent in 1985 (Xia 1985, 4).[11] The rest was subject to allocation by both local governments and enterprises, but by 1987 direct marketing by the latter accounted for 58 percent of total national truck output.

The experience of the No. 2 Auto Plant, China's largest truck producer, has been in line with national trends. As is shown in table 9.2, its direct marketing of trucks started in 1981, when purchasers were lacking for trucks allocated through the plan. In both 1981 and 1982 No. 2's share of "self-sales" in total output was over 50 percent. In late 1982 the market shifted back to strong excess demand, and as a result self-sales fell sharply in 1983. In 1984 general reforms and rapid growth of truck sales to individuals led to a resurgence in self-sales to over one-fifth of total output. In 1985–87 self-sales further increased their share in fast-growing output, reaching 52 percent by the latter year. Contrary to the comments of some Chinese sources,[12] exchanges of trucks for needed material inputs have not accounted for the bulk of enterprise direct marketing. At No. 2, only 29 percent of self-sales in both 1983 and 1984 consisted of such exchanges.

A Sharp Rise in Plan Price to Near-Market Levels: The Case of Cement

The two-tier system for cement evolved from an established multiple pricing system in the prereform period, based on substantial differences in unit costs between large and small cement plants. Relatively high "local" prices were common in the 1970s, but by 1984–85 even higher, market-determined prices had emerged. At the end of 1985 the state price of cement was raised sharply (by over 60 percent for most varieties); local fixed prices were kept roughly the same; and packaging fees (which may have been a means of disguised price increases) were standardized. In principle there were to be no further increases in the state price after that (see *Jingji cankao*, January 16, 1986, 4).

It is too early to ascertain the long-term results of this major price adjustment,

Table 9.2

Direct Marketing by the No. 2 Auto Plant, 1980–87

Year	Total production (units)	Share of national pro- duction (percent)	Directly marketed pro- duction (units)	Share of direct marketing in total (percent)
1980	31,500	14	0	0
1981	37,503	21	20,000	53
1982	51,171	26	30,000	59
1983	60,106	25	10,000	17
1984	70,173	22	15,000	21
1985	83,431	19	28,500	34
1986	87,592	24	32,500	37
1987 (est.)	107,000	23	56,000	52

Sources: Interview information (October 1984 and August 1985); State Statistical Bureau (1985b, 56, 141; 1985c, 307; 1987b, 151; 1989a, III; 1989b, 350); Hubei Statistical Bureau (1988, 357); and author's estimates.

and questions remain about the degree of price flexibility and relative roles of plan and market.[13] But what appears to have happened at least temporarily is the near-demise of the two-tier system through raising of plan prices to the point where embodied rents were drastically reduced if not eliminated. Any remaining price differential may have been largely offset by the inconvenience of obtaining goods through plan allocations as compared with the market. Planning thus would seem to have lost its redistributional as well as its resource allocation role.

In any case, the share of cement allocated by the central state plan in total output fell from 35 percent in 1980 to 19 percent in 1985, 16 percent in 1987, and an estimated 14 percent in 1988 (table 3.1), implying that growing out of the plan has occurred. Once the share of the state plan reached such a low level, a sharp increase in plan prices may have been relatively painless. Severe underfulfillment of state plan supply contracts for cement in 1988 (table 9.3) suggests, however, that a substantial differential between plan and market prices has reemerged with continuing inflation in the economy at large.

Where the Two-Tier System Survives: The Case of Steel

The two-tier system is still firmly entrenched in the case of rolled steel, though growing out of the plan has been occurring, and there have been problems with diversion of steel from plan to market channels. A large share of total supply is still allocated through the state plan at relatively low prices, while at the same time there is an active market for rolled steel in most major cities. Large steel plants can directly market 2 percent of within-plan output and all above-plan output, at increasingly flexible prices. The share of state plan allocation in total national output of rolled steel fell from 74 percent in 1980 to 57 percent in 1985, 47 percent in 1987, and an estimated 42 percent in 1988 (table 3.1).

An investigation of ten machinery plants in Shandong Province (State Price Bureau 1986) indicates that the share of rolled steel reaching typical users through the plan was already relatively low in the mid-1980s. State and local plan allocations together accounted for only 41 percent of these ten firms' total supply of rolled steel in 1985. The main ways in which the enterprises obtained steel outside of plans included (1) exchanging their products for rolled steel (22 percent); (2) directly buying above-plan output of steel producers (16 percent); (3) purchases from various kinds of commercial intermediaries (14 percent); and (4) exchanges of inputs with other machinery producers (2 percent).

The two-tier system seems more durable for rolled steel than for cement, timber, or trucks, perhaps in part because the importance of rolled steel as an input into production of other goods may have generated fears of the inflationary consequences of large inframarginal price increases. Also, steel output is more concentrated in a handful of large producers than is cement (but less so than in the case of trucks). Moreover, the scope for a supply response by small producers outside the plan is much less than in the case of coal, though by no means nonexistent.

There were some adjustments in the state price of rolled steel in 1984 and again in 1986, mainly based on input price increases. Certain kinds of high-quality steels have had their prices increased as well. But there were no plan price rises of the magnitude of those instituted for cement, and the two-tier system has survived. Nevertheless, the situation of rolled steel may not be so different from that of trucks; the two goods were singled out for priority development of markets in 1985 (Xia 1985, 4). The share of the state plan in total production has been gradually declining, a process that appears to have become difficult if not impossible to reverse.

Monetization and "Disembodiment" of Embodied Rents

This case study concerns a local material supply organ, not a specific product.[14] The Shijiazhuang Municipal Material Supply Bureau in Hebei Province instituted experimental reforms in late 1984 and 1985. For rolled steel, timber, pig iron, and soda ash, it made sales within the plan and outside the plan on the same basis, both at the same "market" prices. Holders of state plan input quotas were then separately given a sum of money to offset the difference between state and market prices for their plan allocations.

Under this system, the rents involved in state plan allocations have been "disembodied" from the goods concerned and turned over directly to users in the form of money. Thus, plan-based input allocations have been transformed into pure rents, separate from resource allocation. It is not clear how widespread practices such as this one have become, but the Shijiazhuang experiment has received considerable publicity, and other localities have begun to imitate it.[15] The number of products covered in Shijiazhuang was expanded to include copper, aluminum, lead, zinc, copper products, and aluminum products (for a total of ten), and part of the rents associated with state plan allocations were held back by the municipality for investment in raw materials production.

Key General Policy Changes

Overall government policies have been supportive of the trends for specific goods mentioned above. Perhaps most important was the relaxation of controls over prices for transactions outside the plan. In part this merely legalized behavior that was already pervasive. But it provided a needed stamp of approval for the two-tier system and allowed it to operate freely, permitting its dynamic tendencies to work themselves out. Another important facet of government policy was the general refusal to pull back from the two-tier system in the direction of more comprehensive planning and controls, even when problems arose. Rather than trying to restrict market sales and pricing of cement, the government instituted a sharp increase in state prices. In other cases this did not occur, but nevertheless there was little backsliding. Finally, in some areas the government made a conscious push for market-oriented reforms, independently from other considerations. The reduction of truck allocations through the central plan in the strong sellers' market of 1984 is an example.

Increases in Effective Plan Prices

Another trend that was increasingly apparent by the late 1980s was increases in the effective prices of goods allocated through the state plan, even in the absence of adjustments in official prices. This was happening in a number of ways, which can only be incompletely documented.

For a number of industrial producer goods, the government allowed enterprises to charge higher "temporary" prices for output produced within the plan, usually on the grounds that their costs had increased. A good example is copper. Effective in June 1988, the central government instituted higher temporary prices for pure copper produced by the handful of large smelters (*Jiage lilun yu shijian*, July 1988, 53–54). The new prices varied across firms and ranged between 6,600 and 7,000 yuan per metric ton—20–27 percent higher than the state ex-factory price of 5,500 yuan per ton. Another example is coal: in 1988, large coal mines subject to the state plan were allowed to charge an unspecified (apparently locally determined) surcharge on the coal they sold within the plan, along with a 100 percent surcharge on coal sold as part of the "guidance plan" (ibid., April 1988, 53). In other cases certain factories were allowed to shift from pricing in accordance with the state price to using higher provincial temporary prices already in place. Cost-based higher temporary prices requested by firms apparently were often granted almost on a routine basis in 1988.

Price differentiation by quality also has occurred and probably served as a means of raising effective prices. In July 1986, for example, it was stipulated that certain steel products previously designated as high-quality would carry prices 4–25 percent higher than state plan prices (ibid., February 1987, 41). In January 1987 the central government permitted producers of high-quality products in the nonferrous metals and chemical industries to charge higher prices for their output within the state plan (ibid., March 1987, 53). The Shenyang Smelter was allowed to price its within-plan output of copper 10 percent above the state ex-factory price. It is not clear precisely what standards were used in determining which firms' products could be considered of high quality, but they may have become increasingly lax.

Other means of raising effective prices of goods sold within the plan were less overt yet perhaps even more widespread. Quality deterioration was common in the coal industry from the early 1980s but may have become even more widespread subsequently. Padding the bill with various service charges and other fees was resorted to especially by intermediaries in the material supply system, but producers may also have gotten into the act. Side payments required to ensure delivery of goods subject to plan allocation may have become accepted practice, though reliable information is not available. Finally, implicit exchange arrangements, whereby delivery of goods nominally subject to state plan allocation required some other needed goods in return, may have emerged. It is impossible to document or quantify this last set of practices due to their hidden nature and dubious legality, but they may have contributed greatly to rising effective prices of plan-allocated goods.

Decline in Plan Fulfillment in 1988

More immediately threatening to the two-tier system than the price rises discussed above has been an increasing tendency to underfulfill state plan-based supply contracts, especially noticeable in 1988. In the early to mid-1980s the rate of fulfillment of state plan supply contracts—the ratio of goods actually delivered under contract to the amount for which state plan contracts were signed—was near 100 percent for most industrial producer goods. For example, in 1984 these figures were higher than 97 percent for all key industrial producer goods, above 98 percent for most of them (*China Encyclopedia* Editorial Committee 1985, 304). Most producers seem to have considered these contracts as overriding constraints that had to be met.

By the late 1980s this pattern had changed considerably. Table 9.3 shows state plan contract fulfillment rates for a number of goods in 1987–88. In contrast with the earlier period, most figures were significantly below 100 percent—

Table 9.3

Fulfillment of State Plan Contracts, 1987–88 (percent)

Item	1987	1988
Coal	93.1	92.9
Coke	92.7	88.9
Pig iron	95.6	86.1
Cement	99.2	90.4
Rolled steel	98.2	96.2
Copper	98.9	92.9
Aluminum	99.9	99.6
Lead	99.9	98.3
Zinc	93.6	92.8
Copper products	98.2	95.3
Aluminum products	99.5	100.0
Sulphuric acid	93.5	94.4
Nitric acid	95.1	91.2
Sodium bicarbonate	98.3	97.7
Soda ash	100.0	99.5
Rubber	96.5	89.0
Tires	95.9	97.5
Timber	95.3	85.6

Source: Zhongguo wuzi bao, March 14, 1989, 2.

more than half below 95 percent. Moreover, some sharp declines were observed between 1987 and 1988, including certain highly important producer goods, for example, cement (from 99 percent to 90 percent), timber (from 95 percent to 86 percent), rubber (from 97 percent to 89 percent), pig iron (from 96 percent to 86 percent), and copper (from 99 percent to 93 percent). These declines were unprecedented and indicate that a major change has occurred in the attitudes of producers toward fulfilling state plan delivery contracts. This is especially obvious because the directly marketed sales of firms producing for the state plan increased, sometimes sharply, in 1988. This was true of rolled steel, coal, cement, and timber, for example (*Zhongguo wuzi bao*, March 14, 1989, 2).

The reasons behind the sharp decline in plan fulfillment reportedly included shortfalls in plan-allocated supplies, probably representing a chain reaction of underfulfillment; inadequacy of transport, due in part to the fact that railway tariffs for goods transported outside the plan are much higher than those for goods transported within the plan; and enhanced managerial incentives resulting from various contractual "responsibility systems" introduced in 1986–87, which may have encouraged managers to become more oriented toward profits than toward plan fulfillment. But behind these lies a major change in attitudes, with firms no longer taking state plan contracts as binding (let alone sacred) commitments that had to be fulfilled. This incipient breakdown of mandatory planning due to failure of producers to treat it as a prior constraint is of the utmost importance. Once gone, respect for state plan delivery targets on the part of producers may be extremely difficult if not impossible to restore.

Conclusions

The two-tier system appears to have worked, in the Chinese context, as an effective mechanism for the transition from a "command system" (albeit territorially and administratively decentralized) to a system where the market is coming to play a dominant role in goods allocation. This transition has not been completed for all products and indeed may still be at a relatively early stage in the case of many goods. But the general pattern and direction is clear, and there are examples of how the transition is already occurring for a number of key products.

The question naturally arises as to whether there is any remaining place for the two-tier system over the medium term, or whether it will simply disappear when its transitional role is completed. The two-tier system appears to be on the way out for some of the main industrial producer goods. More abruptly, market pricing has been instituted for the entire supply of a number of consumer durable goods. The two-tier system of producer prices in agriculture has been drastically modified.

The two-tier system appears most entrenched for urban consumer prices of basic agricultural commodities, where it serves as a rent-transfer mechanism to the urban population. Since the bulk of the urban population has access to low-price grain and edible oil, their interests are relatively unified on this issue, unlike firms, which generally have a much more uneven pattern of access to state plan allocations. Finally, the state as commercial intermediary can insulate the producer and consumer price systems, preventing or at least reducing the destabilizing incentives of the two-tier system for producers.

More generally, the two-tier system tends to break down much more easily and quickly on the supply side than on the demand side. The places where it is most likely to survive are those where the system is operating on the demand side but not on the supply side, and where the interests of the beneficiaries are strong and relatively free from internal contradictions. The system of urban consumer prices of agricultural products fits both criteria. But even where the two-tier system remains, planning plays a primarily redistributional rather than resource allocation role.

Thus, in an only partly conscious and largely undesigned manner, China has been groping its way out of the system of directive planning and administrative allocation of industrial goods, after roughly a decade of reforms. Superficially this would put China on the same footing that Hungary achieved with one stroke in 1968, which might lead to questions as to whether China took the long way about. But there are probably some major, possibly even essential, benefits from China's tortuous, prolonged, and in the short run wasteful path of transition.

China has established and gained experience with functioning markets, where firms faced periods of severe competition and major price fluctuations. This would not have been possible if the abolition of the command system had occurred with one stroke of the pen. Even more important, the development of the two-tier system has been closely related to a great increase in commercial channels and a wider range of choice for selling output by most firms. This kind of commercial development appears not to have occurred to any great extent in a country like Hungary, perhaps partly because the formal abolition of the command system was so "easy."

It is probably impossible to sort out the precise relative importance of the inherent dynamics of the two-tier system, the changing constellation of political forces, and central government policy in contributing to the articulation, evolution, and prospective demise of the two-tier system. The economic forces inherent in the two-tier system and strongly proreform central government policy reinforced each other. Both may have been essential for the transition to work.[16]

A key feature of the two-tier system may be that it provides substantial and progressively increasing expression of the economic power inherently held by the seller in a sellers' market situation. This is manifested in higher prices and more money for producers (if only at the margin initially). Perhaps more important, it renders clearly visible the rents embodied in goods that flow through plan allocation channels and creates potential opportunities for their appropriation by sellers.

If the observations and arguments of this chapter are correct, what are the implications for the future? At the most fundamental level, for industrial products the issues of market allocation and to a lesser extent price reform are becoming passé and no longer need to be the prime focus of concern for reformers. Obviously, there is still a lot of "cleaning up" to be done with specific products and product categories, but the general direction is already clear, provided that the inherent dynamics of the two-tier system are judiciously reinforced by central government policy. Hence, the focus of attention can probably shift to the next "level" of resource allocation—the factor allocation system. China's factor allocation system is full of rigidities and problems (see Byrd and Tidrick 1987), but there are also some signs of movement. Forces from goods markets are already exerting increasing pressure on factor allocation, but this "push" alone may be insufficient to force major changes in the factor allocation system. Moreover, as was suggested in chapter 2, an unreformed factor allocation system can adversely affect the efficient functioning of goods markets.

10. Conclusions

THIS STUDY has analyzed the attempt to establish a functioning market system in Chinese state-owned industry during the decade of economic reforms from the late 1970s to the late 1980s. It has approached this crucial topic from a number of viewpoints and methodological perspectives, using both theoretical and empirical analysis. This chapter summarizes the main conclusions and brings together themes from different chapters.

The Chinese Planning System

In the prereform period and also to a considerable extent since the late 1970s as well, administrative directives by government agencies governed Chinese state-owned industry. In this fundamental sense, China resembled the Soviet Union and other centrally planned economies. Chinese industrial planning and administration departed from the Soviet model in significant ways even before the late 1970s, however, and since then reforms have wrought such important changes that the evolving Chinese planning system has a quite different impact on the economy from the traditional model of central planning.

Chapter 5, looking at directive production planning and compulsory administrative allocation of outputs and nonfactor inputs, argued that industrial planning in China has already largely lost the ability to affect directly the production and distribution of industrial goods in the short run. By the same token, planning no longer facilitates government control over the economy. Planning in Chinese industry also has lost any major role in mobilizing enterprise or individual effort and in drawing out hidden enterprise resources through plan-based incentive schemes.

Given the loss of its other functions, planning plays a primarily redistributional role, transferring from sellers to buyers rents embodied in goods subject to allocation at low prices fixed by government authorities. Thus, planning has an impact not through decisions that affect the allocation of resources directly—since the goods are available, albeit at higher prices, on "parallel" markets—but rather through its effects on financial flows and enterprise profits. Planning as redistribution has some obvious advantages, the most important of which is enhanced flexibility and a much reduced impact of planning "mistakes" on system performance, since these can be offset by market transactions. It also has some problematic aspects, most notably the diversion of attention of agents toward rent seeking and the distortions induced in profitability and other measures of efficiency.

Existence and Impact of Markets

Functioning markets have come into being in Chinese industry and have become increasingly important in resource allocation. This phenomenon was documented with available evidence in chapter 3. The share of markets in total output of many commodities and in total industrial output value became quite substantial by the mid-1980s and continued to rise in the late 1980s. The growing importance of the market has been intimately linked with the decline of the resource allocation role of planning.

Not surprisingly in view of their short history and the remaining scope for intervention by central, provincial, and local governments, markets in Chinese industry do not yet function as well as in the industrialized capitalist economies. Some obstacles to well-functioning markets in China were discussed in chapter 3. Nevertheless, Chinese markets for industrial goods have been characterized by widespread participation, voluntary interactions, and flexible prices. Moreover, they have had an impact on the decisions and behavior of state-owned industrial enterprises.

The impact of market forces on firms was analyzed in chapter 4, which found that enterprise response to market forces differs sharply as between a sellers' market (excess demand) and a buyers' market (excess supply). Firms facing a buyers' market have strong incentives to improve the desirability of their products to the demand side in order to be able to sell more, in a situation in which not all goods produced or for which production capacity exists can be sold. In a firmly entrenched sellers' market, on the other hand, producers have no incentive to respond to nonquantitative aspects of demand, since they can always sell whatever they produce immediately.

The dynamic evolution of enterprise response to buyers' and sellers' markets also differs sharply: firms facing a buyers' market tend at least eventually to move toward highly beneficial response patterns, but no such dynamic is at work in response to a sellers' market. This suggests that developing and maintaining buyers' markets for industrial products is important because it provides firms with strong incentives to be responsive to the demand side and to improve efficiency.

Market forces, enterprise response, and government response interact to generate certain dynamic tendencies and trends. Government response may dampen or exacerbate market conditions, but it generally appears not to be able to reverse them. (The major exception is a change in overall government investment policy, which if it generates a sharp increase in investment demand can very quickly

cause a buyers' market for investment goods and intermediate inputs into invest-
ment goods to revert to a sellers' market.) An important observation made in
chapter 4 was that in a buyers' market, downward pressure is exerted on the
price of the entire supply of the good concerned, whereas for goods in excess
demand, there has been a tendency in China for two-tier systems to emerge, with
the price of a large part of total supply continuing to be controlled at a low level
and the rest being allocated through the market at market-determined prices.

One of the main conclusions of chapter 4 was that buyers' markets for con-
sumer goods tend to be robust, whereas for investment goods and intermediate
inputs into investment goods they are much more fragile and easily revert back
to sellers' markets if government-sanctioned investment demand spurts. Thus,
the effectiveness of Chinese industrial reforms to a large extent hinges on the
impact and evolution of the two-tier systems that have emerged in chronic
sellers' market situations.

Market Prices and Market Functioning

Market price trends for the most important industrial producer goods, reviewed
in chapter 8, have been broadly similar: There was a sharp run-up of prices in
late 1984 and early 1985, mainly reflecting price decontrol for goods produced
and sold outside the state plan. Subsequently, in 1985–87 prices of most indus-
trial producer goods fluctuated but without a strong upward or downward trend,
remarkable in view of the generally strong investment demand and prevalent
inflationary pressures during that period. It appears that the "income effect" of
the increasing share of output transacted at high market prices as well as rises in
effective prices of within-plan output absorbed inflationary pressures for a time.
Resumed rapid open price inflation was evident in 1988–89, which suggests that
once the share of market transactions became very high or prices for goods
allocated within the plan rose sharply, inflationary pressures came to be reflected
more directly in market prices.

Given the existence of markets at which industrial producer goods are freely
traded at flexible prices, the question naturally arises as to how well these mar-
kets are functioning. In chapter 8, the econometric analysis of market prices of a
number of industrial producer goods in different cities over the 1984–87 period
found that prices by and large adjusted only slowly in response to price changes
in other markets, and hence that markets were not integrated in the short run.
There was some evidence, however, of responsive adjustments over periods of
three to six months, suggesting that something like long-term market integration
may hold in many if not most cases.

While the results of hypothesis tests give rise to doubts about how efficiently
markets for industrial producer goods are functioning in the Chinese context, at
the same time they demonstrate rather conclusively that nothing like effective
centrally imposed price controls of a formal or informal nature are at work. This

in turn means that the overall stability in market prices observed in 1985–87 was not to any significant extent due to price controls.

The Two-Tier Plan/Market System

The two-tier plan/market system that has emerged for most industrial producer goods is one of the most important innovations of Chinese economic reforms. It developed not through conscious design but naturally over time as a response to pressures on the system in situations where plan prices were well below market equilibrium levels. The two-tier system has some important implications for resource allocation.

The static aspects of the two-tier system were explored in chapter 6, with the aid of a simple general equilibrium model. Commodities flow through plan and market channels, with plan targets modeled as minimum constraints on the flow of goods to and from the various agents (firms, households, and "investors"). Enterprises are assumed to maximize profits, factor endowments (including labor) are fixed exogenously, workers are paid fixed nominal wages, and certain other, more technical assumptions are made that simplify the model's financial flows and highlight its resource allocation properties.

The model generates some strong results relating to the impact of planning and the efficiency of a two-tier plan/market system, particularly in the case where plan targets and allocations are not binding constraints on agents' choices. In this situation, given certain assumptions an equilibrium solution to the model exists, and moreover it is Pareto-optimal. In fact, such an "unconstrained" equilibrium duplicates the properties of a pure market economy (but with fixed enterprise factor endowments). One assumption required for this result is that enterprises maximize profits subject to meeting their plan output targets. (The merits of different possible enterprise "objective functions" were discussed in chapter 5.)

Plan parameters under certain conditions have no effect on the unconstrained equilibrium outcome. Changing plan targets and plan prices has no effect on the equilibrium solution for investment goods and intermediate goods. The impact of such changes in the case of consumer goods can be offset by appropriate adjustments in the wage bill. The model thus reflects the irrelevance of planning in terms of short-run resource allocation, in line with the verbal assertions in chapter 5.

Even when some agents are constrained by their plan targets—that is, for at least some inputs and/or outputs, plan targets force them to purchase or sell more than they otherwise would have at the market price—the model generates some important results. Equilibrium exists and is Pareto-optimal given the vector of plan targets. Changes in plan prices do not change the real outcome in the case of intermediate goods or, assuming no distributional effects among investors, for investment goods. The impact of plan price changes in the case of consumer goods can be offset by wage adjustments.

Relaxing plan constraints on constrained agents and transforming the outcome into unconstrained equilibrium always results in a Pareto-superior state of the economy, if appropriate adjustments are made in wages and profit shares. On the other hand, changes in plan prices are unlikely to result in improved efficiency. It is conjectured that judicious reductions in plan constraints also can generate a Pareto-superior outcome, even if the final situation still involves plan constraints on some agents.

The value of the model depends on the assumptions used. It was argued in chapter 7 that despite numerous caveats and qualifications, the model's assumptions are by and large defensible. In any case, relaxing some of the more problematic assumptions does not fundamentally alter the result that planning has largely lost its direct role in short-run resource allocation. The static nature of the model and the exclusion of factor movements limit the strength of the results obtained, but in any case the model was not designed to look at dynamic aspects, and Chinese state-owned industry is characterized by considerable rigidity in enterprise factor endowments.

Among possible extensions of the model to make it better conform with Chinese reality, one has a major impact on its results. The introduction of "product variation" within product categories used for planning and administrative allocation allows the model to incorporate many of the features commonly associated with chronic shortage phenomena in centrally planned economies. In particular, firms will produce "worse" products for planned distribution and "better" ones for market sales in many situations. Plan targets then could have a major effect on real outcomes in the model.

Chapter 7 also formalized the concept of rents embodied in plan-allocated goods, initially described in chapter 5. The model can be used to trace the generation of such rents and their movement through the economy, but it is not useful for analysis of rent-seeking behavior. Both chapters 5 and 7 argued that rent-seeking behavior engendered by rents in the system may have high costs in terms of diversion of attention and resources by firms and the planning apparatus.

Dynamics of the Two-Tier System

Dynamic patterns and trends in the two-tier system to a considerable extent determine its evolution over time and more generally the direction of market-oriented reforms in Chinese industry. The static general equilibrium model is not well-equipped for study of dynamic issues, however. Moreover, the model's dynamic analogue, with intertemporal general equilibrium, is highly unrealistic in the Chinese context of major ongoing reforms and structural changes.

Chapter 9 suggested that the economic incentives and tendencies inherent in the two-tier system generate strong pressures for expansion in the share of market allocation and reduction in the share of planning. Profit-oriented investment decisions would skew expansion toward the market portion. Producers would tend to press for output price increases or reductions in output plan targets. Moreover, agents have a powerful incentive to divert goods from plan to market channels in order to appropriate the rents "embodied" in these goods. There is no self-policing mechanism to prevent this, and monitoring and punishment of these kinds of violations would be difficult in the Chinese context. Overt or hidden increases in plan prices, if they go beyond a certain point, also may tend to undermine the two-tier system. Perhaps even more important, there were signs in 1988 that many producers no longer had an overriding commitment to fulfilling plan-based delivery quotas, which could accelerate the demise of the two-tier system.

Case studies indicate that the two-tier system may be unstable over the medium term; a secular tendency for the share of the state plan to decline and that of the market to increase has been observed for many key industrial goods. In cases such as coal and basic industrial materials, "growing out of the plan" has occurred, with the absolute amount of the good concerned subject to planned allocation remaining roughly constant, but most or all of incremental production being sold through markets. Sometimes, as in the case of trucks, the absolute amount of state plan allocation has been cut back deeply in response to pressures. Another possibility is for the price of plan-allocated production to be raised sharply to reduce the incentives for diversion, which occurred in the case of cement. Regardless of the precise mechanism, the general trend has been a continuing increase in the share of the market.

It might be expected that diversion from plan to market channels, rent-seeking behavior, and related corruption would lead to a political reaction against the two-tier system and to pressures for an increase in the share of plan allocations by the users benefiting from them. But this did not occur at least until early 1989. The inherent dynamics of the two-tier system, combined with a pragmatic, proreform stance by government leaders, predominated until then. After the political events of April–June 1989, the commitment of the central government to continue aggressive expansion of the role of the market mechanism evaporated, but whether any likely reaction can fully offset the strong internal dynamic tendencies of the two-tier system is questionable.

Prerequisites for Effectively Functioning Markets

This study included an attempt to grapple with the wider issue of prerequisites for well-functioning markets that promote dynamic growth and development. This first involved a search for the appropriate definition of the market mechanism and an understanding of its essence. Chapter 2 reviewed contrasting views of the market mechanism, including the neoclassical perspective and the Austrian approach. Particularly in the context of Chinese economic reforms, where dynamic markets must be created from a very weak foundation, the latter school's conception of the market mechanism as a dynamic process was found to be more relevant than neoclassical theory's emphasis on equilibrium states.

Chapter 2 avoided establishing any fixed criteria for "dynamic" markets. Yet it identified a small number of what would appear to be essential requirements for such markets, including the following: enterprise autonomy, at least in decisions on market transactions and related production aspects; financial discipline and an adequate degree of profit orientation on the part of firms; price flexibility, at least over the medium term; freedom of entry and exit; and effective competition among producers, which in turn requires a buyers' market or "buffered equilibrium."

The absence of some of these conditions results in poorly functioning markets, though certain prerequisites may be more essential than others. For example, there could be a buyers' market with effective competition of a sort even in the absence of strong enterprise financial discipline, but in this case competition will not focus on cost reductions. The Chinese buyers' markets discussed in chapter 4 seem to have this characteristic. Price rigidities similarly can result in poorly functioning markets, even if enterprise motivation is otherwise conducive to competition and efficiency.

Chinese Progress in Achieving Prerequisites

To what extent has China succeeded in establishing dynamic markets? This is a fundamental question addressed by this study, but as was mentioned in chapter 1 it is hard to answer, in the first place because of the difficulty of gauging the exact situation in China, and second due to problems in ascertaining what the required conditions really are for dynamic markets. Nevertheless, it is possible to make some tentative observations.

A considerable degree of enterprise autonomy in production decisions and market transactions has already been achieved by the reforms in Chinese industry. Particularly with the two-tier system, price flexibility also has been enhanced. Chinese state-owned industrial enterprises exhibit a strong profit orientation in their activities. On the other hand, they still are subject to relatively weak financial discipline, which has resulted in neglect of cost controls even in weak market situations and in excessively high demand for producer goods.

Competition has been heated in some industries when producers faced a buyers' market and has had obvious benefits to customers, though such competition typically has not focused on cost reductions. Also, competition has been restricted by the near impossibility of exit for state enterprises. Finally, as was mentioned in chapter 4, competition in Chinese industry may resemble competition in international trade more than it does competition within well-integrated national markets, due to locally oriented industrial policies and barriers to entry and interregional trade.

In industries characterized by the two-tier system, competition may have become increasingly important in the growing "market" portion of total production and supply. This is certainly evident in price competition, which sometimes has even driven down market prices of certain commodities like coal. However, the extent to which strong nonprice competition occurs under the two-tier system is harder to ascertain. Enterprises that still sell the bulk of their output through the plan may not develop competitive strategies geared toward doing well on the market, even though they may optimize production to maximize profit at the market price in the short run. Of course, firms facing a persistent sellers' market and those that are "plan-constrained" on the output side in a two-tier situation face no pressure at all to engage in effective competition.

To some extent, further evolution of China's system in the process of economic reforms will naturally create better conditions for effective competition. But major progress is needed in areas like weak enterprise financial discipline and in breaking down barriers to interregional competition. Thus, there is still a considerable way to go (as of the late 1980s) in achieving the prerequisites needed for dynamic markets, despite the great progress already made. Moreover, progress will be hard to achieve on difficult issues like financial discipline and exit in the absence of a strong political will to push ahead further with market-oriented reforms.

Overview and Policy Implications

A central conclusion of this study is that markets have already developed to the point that directive production planning and administrative allocation of inputs and outputs have lost any major role in directly determining the allocation of industrial goods in the short run. Moreover, dynamic tendencies and trends have been moving the Chinese industrial system ever farther away from mandatory planning. This does not necessarily mean, however, that the efficiency gains from well-functioning markets have been reaped. There is still a long way to go before markets in Chinese industry can play the highly beneficial role that is attributed to well-functioning markets in capitalist economies.

The policy implications of the analysis conducted in this study are fairly obvious. Markets can function and improve the allocation of resources even in a situation where part of total supply is still allocated by plan. In the two-tier system, relaxing plan constraints on agents by reducing plan targets and input allocations is likely to be much more efficacious in improving efficiency and welfare than adjustments in administratively-set prices. (The latter may be called for as a means of reducing incentives to divert goods from plan to market channels, however.) The strong tendencies toward expansion of the share of the market mechanism that are inherent in the two-tier system need only to be judiciously supported by government policy. Measures to promote effective competition, especially interregional competition, improve enterprise financial discipline, and facilitate exit of unviable firms are crucial further steps that need to be taken.

Notes

Chapter 1

1. There are other ways of organizing a study on reforms in Chinese industry. One alternative would be financial incentives, since a great deal of experimentation and change has gone on in this area.

2. It is beyond the scope of this study to discuss the prereform system in any detail. The prereform Chinese planning system is looked at in chapter 5, and the limited role played by product markets in Chinese industry before the late 1970s is discussed in chapter 3.

3. Some of these plants were a legacy of industrialization in the pre-1949 period, while others were the result of massive construction of plants with Soviet aid in the 1950s, which involved 1930s' technology that the Soviet Union had acquired from the United States and other countries earlier. Still other factories had backward technology and small scales of operation, though built in the 1970s.

4. A good example of multiheaded leadership and the more general problem of control by different government agencies over different enterprise activities is the Shenyang Smelter. See Byrd (1985b, 30–35).

5. Existing bonus schemes were commuted into fixed payments during the Cultural Revolution period.

6. The example of the Liaoning provincial construction system, which had a profit retention scheme starting as early as 1975, is cited in Byrd (1987b). But this did not extend down to the enterprise level until considerably later, when industrial reforms were already underway.

7. This assumes that Chen et al. (1988) were calculating average annual growth rates by the least squares method, which is the accepted procedure.

8. For example, the discontinuance of Third Front investment in the interior and large increases in imports of machinery and equipment as well as advanced technology since the late 1970s would have raised total factor productivity even in the absence of reforms.

9. Dynamic trends in a chronic sellers' market and the evolution of the two-tier plan/market system in the mid- and late 1980s are analyzed in chapter 9.

Chapter 2

1. China's Communist Party Central Committee has stated: "The essential task of socialism is to develop the forces of production, create ever more social wealth and meet the people's growing material and cultural needs. Socialism does not mean pauperism, for it aims at the elimination of poverty" (Chinese Communist Party 1984, v).

2. China's Seventh Five-Year Plan placed emphasis on "improving economic results" (Chinese National People's Congress 1986, i; Chinese Communist Party 1985, viii).

3. In 1984–85 the goal of economic reform was restated as development of a "planned commodity economy," which apparently can mean little if any directive planning of the traditional sort (see Chinese Communist Party 1984, vii). This represented a considerable advance over the previous slogan of "taking planning as primary and the market as supplementary."

4. China's Seventh Five-Year Plan called for expanding the role of the market mechanism in the allocation of both consumer and producer goods and for greater decontrol of prices (Chinese National People's Congress 1986, xx).

5. Some interesting evidence on this point, based on experiments, is presented in Plott (1982).

6. Both of these criticisms are intimately related to theories of bounded rationality and the behavioral theory of the firm (see Simon 1982; Cyert and March 1963).

7. See chapter 4 for a discussion of competition in Chinese industry, which suggests that it is more akin to competition in international trade than to domestic competition in a well-integrated national market.

8. See Casson (1982), Kirzner (1973; 1979), Ronen (1982), and Schumpeter (1950), among others.

9. This is basically the "exit option" as described by Hirschman (1970) and applied to the Chinese planning system by Tidrick (1987).

10. This is similar to a conclusion of Simon (1984), who found that enterprises producing differentiated products and hence facing a downward sloping demand function would reduce the "quality" of their products in the face of price controls. Also see Raymon (1983).

11. The benefits to buyers in an economy characterized by buffered equilibrium are elaborated in Scitovsky (1985).

12. Effective competition could be defined to involve strong efforts at cost reduction by firms, in which case it would require a considerable degree of financial discipline. In the analysis of China, however, it is useful to separate the question of financial discipline from that of effective competition, since it is possible to have excess supply and fierce competition without strong cost consciousness on the part of firms (chapter 4).

Chapter 3

1. Indeed, at least in the case of machinery some major trade fairs arose directly out of the old materials ordering conferences.

2. Jiangsu and Zhejiang, which had among the highest industrial growth rates in the late 1970s, had a much higher share of collective enterprises in their total industrial output than other provinces. Collectives, mainly rural commune and brigade enterprises, had little access to material inputs through the state plan, so some kind of extra-plan mechanism was necessary for them to obtain energy and raw materials needed to support rapid growth.

3. *Jingji Guanli* Editorial Board (1980, 28) and Liu Guoguang (1980, 30).

4. Inflation and price decontrol may have meant that growth in the real value of these transactions was considerably less than the nominal growth. Figures are from *China Economic Yearbook* Editorial Committee (1985, IV–31; 1986, V–33; 1988, IV–27) and Zhu Rongji (1985, 294).

5. Percentages of total national output of various industrial producer goods transacted through interregional cooperation can be calculated from State Statistical Bureau (1985, 346, 347, 349), *China Economic Yearbook* Editorial Committee (1985, IV–31), and Zhu Rongji (1985, 294).

6. Interenterprise exchange generally works in the same way as interregional cooper-

ation, involving parallel purchase and sales transactions. The nominal prices used in these exchanges typically are state prices, making them largely immune from price controls.

7. China Materials Economics Association (1983, 78). The figure given is 610 million yuan, but this would appear to have a misplaced decimal point, given that amounts reported for the markets at Shanghai and Dalian alone for 1982 totaled 334 million yuan, and the fact that there were sixty-four markets for the means of production in China at the time (Byrd 1985a, 1, 8). It is possible that both the 1979 and 1982 figures include transactions by the material supply system outside the plan but not at markets for the means of production.

8. In October 1986 complete decontrol of the prices of a number of consumer durables was announced, including bicycles, black and white television sets, cassette players, washing machines, refrigerators, electric fans, watches, and some textile products. Prices of more goods reportedly were to be decontrolled later. See *China Daily*, October 1, 1986, Business Supplement, 1.

9. This discussion of the different procurement categories is based on Yu (1984, 373–74), Ma (1982, 295), and *China Economic Yearbook* Editorial Committee (1982, V–258).

10. Plan-based procurement had to go through official channels, with wholesale commercial units assigned to handle different kinds of goods produced by different firms. Sales to retail units bypassed this route and hence were less subject to control via the plan.

11. This last figure contradicts table 3.9, unless some firms did not use their direct marketing authority.

12. For the most part, prices are given in round numbers, and in some cases price changes appear to lag behind those in other cities where movements occur more quickly and continuously (e.g., Shanghai). This suggests that they are probably posted prices, rather than prices determined by some kind of a bidding mechanism.

Chapter 4

1. This information was gathered as part of a collaborative research project between the World Bank and the Institute of Economics of the Chinese Academy of Social Sciences. The quantitative data cover the period 1975–82. Interviews, conducted in 1983–85, particularly focused on 1979–82. Sample characteristics are discussed in detail in Tidrick and Chen (1987, chap. 2).

2. This is the essence of the "quiet life" sought by bureaucrats in a bureaucratic system, where demand for goods or services provided is never a constraint, yet the entity is not under great internal or external pressure to expand output. Byrd and Tidrick (1987) consider the search for such a "quiet life" to be one of the four main goals pursued by Chinese state-owned industrial firms.

3. Two sample firms did fail to increase output over fairly long periods of time, but for understandable reasons. The Sanchazi Forestry Bureau did not expand cutting of timber because of externally and internally imposed limits to preserve the long-term production potential of forestry reserves. Similarly, falling output at the North China Petroleum Administration masked great efforts to maintain production from declining oil fields.

4. This is closely related to the "engineering motive" (Byrd and Tidrick 1987).

5. The data cannot simultaneously support both. If Kornai's hypotheses are correct, then the sample data at least in part confirm the qualitative judgments on market conditions made in table 4.2. If the latter are independently correct, then the data provide some support for Kornai's hypotheses.

6. The very low figures for the two Shanghai firms probably were due to the system of industrial corporations in that city. Low figures for textile plants also may reflect industry-specific technical or administrative aspects.

7. Again, below-average input inventory/sales ratios for some enterprises like the Shanghai Cotton Textile Mill probably can be explained by factors specific to the enterprises or localities concerned.

8. The Shanghai Oil Pump Plant faced a sellers' market for its own output despite the general buyers' market in the oil pump industry. Jiangmen and Qingdao may have been able to reduce output inventories through efficiency improvements despite the prevailing buyers' market. Qingdao had drastically changed its product mix in 1980–81 to be more in line with demand.

9. Before the smelter instituted such tied sales, the price of cadmium on the open market had dropped by 100 percent without eliminating excess supply. Supply was largely price-inelastic, since nearly all cadmium is produced as a by-product of zinc smelting. Demand for cadmium fell sharply after the discovery that using it as an additive in plastic sheets for agricultural use was contaminating food supplies. See Byrd (1985b, 55–56).

10. This refers to sales arranged by enterprises themselves on a voluntary basis with customers, as opposed to sales through mandatory production or delivery plans or required sales to the "official" commercial agency in charge of procuring the firm's products. Direct marketing includes sales to commercial units outside compulsory production or procurement plans as well as direct sales to end-users or consumers, at wholesale or retail.

11. Sales of cement by Xiangxiang to local authorities on an involuntary basis and to railway departments accounted for 1–4 percent of total output and 11–32 percent of total self-sales in 1981–84. Part of the sale of cement in exchange for needed inputs (54–83 percent of total self-sales in 1981–84) also may have occurred on an involuntary basis.

12. Only three sample firms were allowed to engage in large-scale direct exporting. Two of them are large, centrally run enterprises whose exports account for only a small proportion of total sales. The third, Mindong, was one of the first enterprises given direct export authority as part of China's economic reforms.

13. The Anshan Iron and Steel Company was only 85 percent self-sufficient in iron ore resources, while the Xiangxiang Cement plant relied heavily on coal bought from outside. The North China Petroleum Administration operated declining oil fields; the Sanchazi Forestry Bureau had ample forest reserves, but limits were imposed on timber cutting to preserve long-term exploitation potential. Thus, none of these enterprises completely escaped problems with raw materials.

14. A similar finding emerged with respect to the larger sample of 429 industrial enterprises referred to in chapter 3 (CESRRI 1986a, 62).

15. Government response in China can be contrasted with "planned" adjustment to a weak market, where the planning and distribution systems continue to procure all output but administrative pressure is brought to bear on firms to adjust product mix, improve quality, and so on.

16. Retail commercial units do not keep large inventories; when demand falls, they cut down their orders from wholesale units. Unlike in the Soviet Union, the bulk of commercial inventories in China in the early 1980s (88.5 percent) were at the wholesale level rather than at the retail level (Ma 1982, 291).

17. A policy of "selective purchase" by commercial units, under which they were allowed to refuse poor-quality or unmarketable goods, had been tried in China in 1956–57 and again in 1961–63. The first attempt was interrupted by the Great Leap Forward, while the second appears to have been limited in scope and was wiped out by the political currents that led to the Cultural Revolution (see Solinger 1984, 220–30). Wiles (1962) argues that selective purchase was an important Chinese innovation. But the driving force in the early 1980s was strong buyers' markets in certain industries. Designation of goods for selective purchase (and the variant "purchase by order") often lagged behind actual developments, merely validating rather than deter-

mining changes in commercial procurement practices (see chapter 3).

18. The scope for users to further build up inventories of producer goods may be limited. Capital goods purchased for specific investment projects would not be bought if the project is rejected or canceled. Moreover, users' preexisting inventories of many producer goods were already very large due to hoarding.

19. This compartmentalization and insulation would tend to break down in the face of persistent excess supply, however.

20. Wong (1985, 268–75) argues that local governments increasingly act like "economic agents" maximizing revenues. The orientation toward local industrialization is a legacy of the Cultural Revolution period.

21. Mindong once tried to set up a sales outlet in Chongqing City, as a joint venture with a local collective firm. The director and other leading cadres of that firm were removed from their positions by the local government for their collaboration with Mindong. Eventually they were reinstated when the central government found out about the case, but this is a good example of the barriers and delays in penetrating other regional markets. Mindong also tried vainly for three years to set up a sales outlet in Shanghai before it finally succeeded.

22. The Chongqing Clock and Watch Company's joint ventures with small producers in Guizhou and Yunnan provinces were motivated by the desire to maintain dominance over the watch market in these provinces (Byrd and Tidrick 1984, 20).

23. This supports the assertion of Kornai (1980, 340–41) that firms in centrally planned economies are sensitive to price but not quantity signals on the output side and vice versa on the input side.

24. A possible exception is the sharp increase in the state price of sulphuric acid in 1984, which may have brought the market for this commodity at least temporarily into balance.

25. A good example is the No. 2 Auto Plant, which reduced its truck prices by a cumulative 28 percent in three stages in 1980–82. Approval by the State Price Bureau was required, but reductions occurred at No. 2's initiative. Prices were cut because of sharp declines in unit costs as production grew rapidly and the need to match lower prices charged by the No. 1 Auto Plant.

26. There were a few exceptions in the sample, if the enterprise was under tight administrative control and particularly if its supervisory agency was also in charge of suppliers of the goods concerned. The Chengdu Locomotive and Rolling Stock Plant had to purchase many supplies from distant plants under Ministry of Railways jurisdiction, even though goods were available locally at lower prices. The Northwest No. 1 State Cotton Textile Mill was ordered to buy spindles locally, but it refused to and in the end was able to prevail.

27. These conflicts could be minimized if the allocation system merely replicated past patterns, giving users the same allocations they had received before.

28. The Qingdao Forging Machinery Plant, for example, had to reduce sharply production of large friction presses and shift to small presses, which were in great demand by rural enterprises.

29. This contrasts with American corporations, whose first response to a weak market tends to be cost-cutting measures (Williamson 1964, 94–121).

Chapter 5

1. This section relies heavily on Tidrick (1987) and, in the area of material supply, on Wong (1985) and Byrd (1984).

2. Targets are disaggregated to firms in a "layered" fashion, with ministries and provinces in principle able to reallocate output targets and input allocations among their

subordinate firms. Only a tiny handful of enterprises are given targets directly in the State plan, like the No. 1 and No. 2 Auto Plants, which had line items in the state plan starting in 1984 (interview information, October 1984).

3. Even for watches there was some local variation. This discussion of the price system for different goods is based on Li Peichu (1982).

4. China Materials Economics Association (1983, 92). The fifteen types of rolled steel are not counted separately in reaching the total of 256 Category I materials, which means that the number of commodities actually balanced at the central level may have been somewhat higher than 256.

5. The central government provided funds for the development of the "five small industries," but much larger amounts went into investment to support the development of the "Third Front," an attempt to build an industrial base in remote, inaccessible regions safer from a Soviet attack (see Naughton 1988).

6. See Byrd (1985b, 30–35) for a discussion of the 1970–71 decentralization of enterprise administration and its effect on the Shenyang Smelter.

7. This is evident from the experience of the twenty-firm sample (chapter 4), as well as from available information at a more aggregate level (chapter 3).

8. Command planning refers to directive planning of production and allocation of inputs and outputs by government authorities at all levels, not just by the central government. Thus, the distinction is between directive planning and market allocation, not between central planning and other forms of resource allocation (including local planning and the market).

9. Interview information, March 1983. This behavior contrasts with the preform pattern of firms arguing for lower targets that would be easy to fulfill.

10. Though no preform surveys are available for comparison, plan fulfillment would have been rated much higher by managers then.

11. This argument will be demonstrated formally in chapter 6 using a general equilibrium model.

12. These percentages were calculated by taking the share of firms reported to have no market transactions in table 5.4, dividing this by the share of large and medium-sized enterprises and that of state enterprises in the sample, and then subtracting the result from one.

13. "Economic benefits" (jingji xiaoyi) really means "financial benefits" or profits. The response to the question posed is suggestive but not conclusive, since it was not asking about managerial goals in general.

14. The hypotheses of these authors differ in detail but yield the same general results. Baumol assumes sales maximization subject to a minimum profit constraint. Ames postulates maximization of output subject to a zero profit constraint. Portes assumes maximization of gross output value subject to a minimum profit constraint, which he terms the "resource" constraint.

15. State grants for working capital, an important source of funds in the past, were phased out in the early 1980s.

16. Starting in 1985, credit controls became tighter, and even large firms had trouble obtaining bank credit to finance working capital. Under this pressure, many firms relied more on trade credit, a common response to a tight credit policy in centrally planned economies (see Byrd 1983a, 116–18).

17. This is the essence of the "soft budget constraint" and chronic shortage phenomenon analyzed by Kornai (1980).

18. A number of models show that greater tautness of production targets induces higher production by enterprises. See Hunter (1961) and Keren (1972), among others. Slackness of Chinese production plans is in relation to capacity, not necessarily in relation

to plan-allocated material inputs and energy.

19. As reforms have progressed, state-owned enterprises (and their workers) have come to have some vague, poorly defined "property rights" over their assets and income flows. This is implicit in profit-sharing schemes; retained profits go to workers' benefits and productive investment.

20. But "leakages" may dissipate much of the benefit to the government. Wages have been increasing at a fast pace in recent years despite controlled prices for many goods. Government control over the total nominal wage package of workers may be limited. Furthermore, even if low-priced consumer goods permit lower nominal wages, some of the resulting higher profits may be kept at the enterprise level.

21. This calculation is based on the assumption that all rolled steel produced outside the central plan is sold at the parallel market price, which is clearly unrealistic and results in an underestimate of the share of embodied rents.

22. There is a burgeoning literature on rent-seeking behavior, based on seminal work by Tullock (1967) and Krueger (1974).

23. Since the Chinese system involves enterprise-specific levies, in principle it would be possible to achieve a greater degree of redistribution than with product-specific indirect taxes.

24. There are numerous examples of this, ranging from the Chongqing Clock and Watch Company gaining a 2 percent lower tax rate (Byrd and Tidrick 1984, 23) to the entire construction industry of Liaoning Province getting a very high profit-retention rate in the late 1970s and early 1980s (Byrd 1987b).

25. It greatly reduces the impact of mistakes in the short-run production sphere, though it may transmit the effect to the financial sphere, for example if under-allocation of inputs forces market purchases at higher costs.

26. See, among others, Grossman (1977). Ericson (1984), using a mathematical model, demonstrates that the second economy can generate Pareto-superior allocations.

27. See Bhagwati (1982) for a taxonomy of what he calls directly unproductive profit-seeking (DUP). Sometimes such activities may be second-best welfare improving.

28. The price of a new product is usually set by the enterprise itself for the first several years of production, on a cost-plus basis. Approval by price authorities is required but appears to be pro forma.

Chapter 6

1. These observations and the evidence on which they are based were discussed in chapters 3, 4, and 5.

2. The degree of validity of this assumption in the Chinese context and various alternative choices for the enterprise objective function were discussed in some detail in chapter 5.

3. This assumption is harder to defend. Nevertheless, from the late 1970s until the mid-1980s, wage and bonus ceilings were in place. Fixed nominal wages are not strictly necessary for most of the model's results.

4. Investment goods only enter into the utility functions of "investors" (defined below), consumer goods only enter into the utility functions of consumers, and neither of the two are inputs into production. Intermediate goods do not enter into either but are in enterprises' production sets (as inputs for some, outputs for others).

5. To avoid excessive complexity, it is assumed that the first commodity enters the utility functions of consumers and investors but does not serve as an input or output of any production set. The supply is exogenously fixed (it could be affected by government monetary policy in a more sophisticated version of the model). The reason for having

money as a medium of exchange, carrying a different price from money as the accounting unit, will become apparent in the subsequent general equilibrium analysis. Without "anchoring" plan prices to the market price of some commodity, the normalization of market prices, which is arbitrary, can have an effect on outcomes.

6. Note that this means all q_k move proportionately with changes in p_1.

7. Unless otherwise indicated, summation covers all of the items to which the subscript letter applies (i.e., $\Sigma = \Sigma_{j=1,m}$).

8. For convenience, all assumptions needed in the proof of existence of equilibrium are numbered consecutively, while formulae and equations are numbered separately.

9. This last assumption implies free disposal of commodities. $\{-R^h\}$ is the negative orthant in the space of the h commodities.

10. For notational simplicity, the p_1 in the denominator is assumed to be already incorporated in all the w_{ij}, so it does not need to be explicitly written.

11. The operation * multiplies each coordinate in the first vector by the corresponding coordinate in the second vector, preserving vector dimensions.

12. This stipulation is needed to rule out the situation where $y_{jk} = v_{jk}$, but v_{jk} just happens to be the level of production or purchase that the firm would have freely chosen in the absence of the plan target or allocation.

13. Formally, (1) there must exist a $y_j' \in Y_j$ for which $y_j'^+ = v_j^+$, and (2) there must also exist a $y_j'' \in Y_j$ such that $y_j''^- = v_j''^-$. Under the simpler condition $V_j = \{v_j \in Y_j\}$, firms always could fulfill output targets using only plan input allocations. The model must allow for the possibility that plans force firms to buy some inputs on the market in order to fulfill them.

14. The operation " $\cdot$ " is the inner product of two vectors.

15. The strict preference relation $a >^{C_i} b$ is defined as "not $b \geq^{C_i} a$."

16. As in the case of producers, it is possible that $c_{ik} = x_{ik} \neq 0$, but c_{ik} happens to be the level of consumption of the good that would have been chosen by consumer i even in the absence of the plan allocation. Thus, for a consumer to be plan-constrained, not only must $c_{ik} = x_{ik} \neq 0$ hold, but also a small reduction in c_{ik} must result in an equal decline in x_{ik}.

17. A plausible alternative would be for each investor to receive a fixed share of total profits s, but this would not guarantee $f_g \geq q \cdot d_g$.

18. The strict preference relation $a >^{I_g} b$ is defined as "not $b \geq^{I_g} a$."

19. This is analogous to the well-known fact that profit-maximizing firms in a pure market environment face no income effects from changing input and output prices (see Portes 1968).

20. In general this will also lead to changes in other inputs and outputs for which the producer is not plan-constrained.

21. The reason for assuming resource endowments on the interior of possible consumption and investment sets is not to generate such an attainable state but rather to ensure that the demand correspondences are upper-hemicontinuous.

22. This assumers that $s \geq q \cdot d$. If $s < q \cdot d$, financial balance can still be verified, given that $s + w = f + w$.

23. It can also be verified that this balance holds when $y = 0$ and all plan targets and allocations are set at zero.

24. Nor does the assumption used in the original Arrow-Debreu proof that the intersection between the aggregate production set Y and the positive orthant is only the point 0.

25. The planning system is not considered an agent in the competitive equilibrium "game." It determines the values of certain parameters, subject to the consistency requirements already specified, prior to the determination of market equilibrium by the actions and interactions of the various agents.

26. This is apparent from inspection of the budget constraints of consumers and investors and the profit functions of producers.

27. Note that this will always be true if $s^* > q^* \cdot d^*$. It can be verified from inspection that $\sum a_g^{**} = 1$.

Chapter 7

1. If producers' plan output quotas could be resold (possibly at negative prices, or by "buying out" users with input allocations), then no producer would be plan-constrained on the output side, either.

2. An explicit bonus system for enterprises and/or their managers, related to plan fulfillment, could eliminate this indeterminacy. Enterprises would choose the amount of inputs to use for plan production and associated probability of failure to achieve output plan targets in response to incentives embodied in the bonus scheme. Bonuses related to plan fulfillment are typically used in models of enterprise behavior in Soviet-type economies, but they have not been incorporated in the model in chapter 6, given the assumptions of slack planning and absolute priority accorded to plan fulfillment by firms.

3. The meaning of the profit constraint is unclear if it cannot override the plan constraint. If the profit constraint is related to financial resources needed for production in the short run, to assume that the enterprise could ignore it and produce more to fulfill the output plan would be inappropriate.

4. Lancaster (1979, chap. 2) has developed consumer theory on the basis of products that enter utility functions not in themselves but rather as bundles of different characteristics.

5. This result holds with a fixed set of products that can vary in different characteristics, but it is not necessarily true when the products themselves are endogenously developed and chosen by firms.

6. The Anshan Iron and Steel Company in 1984 was given mandatory plan output targets for 14 kinds of rolled steel, but supply contracts covered some 300 varieties. Even this level of detail is dwarfed by the 60,000 different technical product specifications (interview information, October 1984).

7. Subsidies might be necessary to compensate some producers for negative rents and are implicitly allowed in the model.

8. See Krueger (1974), Buchanan et al. (1980), and Bhagwati (1982) for analyses of rent-seeking behavior and its effect on efficiency.

Chapter 8

1. Also see Heytens (1986) for a distinct theoretical derivation of the same empirical method of analysis.

2. Heytens (1986, 28) suggested an alternative specification, as follows:

$$P_{it} - P_{it-1} = d_0 + d_1(P_{it-1} - R_{t-1}) + d_2(R_t - R_{t-1}) + d_3 R_{t-1} + gV_i + e_{it}.$$

This is equivalent to equation (1), though of course the coefficient values for various hypothesis tests are different.

3. At the Shanghai Market for the Means of Production in 1979–80, "high" and "low" transaction prices were reported for each trade fair, and the gap between the two was frequently very large (see Byrd 1985a). Two different prices for the same commodity and locality at the same time were sometimes reported in the post-1984 period, and there

were often substantial differences in prices for the same product, city, and date in different newspapers.

4. Market prices were reported in *Wuzi shangqing* with a lag of about one month, so the resulting flow of information was relatively slow. (This is another reason why monthly intervals are preferable to ten-day periods as the time unit for analysis.) It is likely that price information was also transmitted among market centers through telecommunications, however.

5. It would be useful to marshall more evidence in favor of or against Shanghai as the reference market. Market price information itself should not be used in selection of the reference market, however. For example, if the market whose price levels and trends are most highly correlated with those in other localities is chosen as the reference market, results of hypothesis tests might well be biased toward acceptance of market integration.

6. The general form of the equation for determination of the reference market price is shown in Ravallion (1986, 104).

7. It is possible, of course, that cities exhibiting market segmentation in relation to Shanghai are actually well integrated with markets in other cities. Thus, using a different city as the reference market might result in a higher degree of observed market integration for some cities.

Chapter 9

1. For many consumer durables there was no multiple pricing during the prereform period. Prices were set high to tax consumption, so even the highest-cost firms could make profits and hence multiple pricing on cost grounds was unnecessary. In the watch industry in 1980, unit production costs ranged from a low of 11 yuan to a high of 41 yuan, but the price of a first-grade watch was 70 yuan and that of a second-grade watch 55 yuan, leaving ample room for profits even for high-cost producers (State Economic Commission 1983, 36).

2. Price reform in Chinese industry is treated in Chai (1987), which cites many useful Chinese sources on this topic.

3. See Xinhua News Agency, December 31, 1979, translated in BBC, 1/23/80, A5–6, and *China Economic Yearbook* Editorial Committee (1982, V–41).

4. In the case of coal the price decline was due primarily to a strong supply response to high prices by small rural coal mines.

5. Diversion of plan-allocated materials for sale at higher prices by government organizations has been cited as a problem of the two-tier system, but its magnitude is not clear (State Council Economic, Technical, and Social Development Research Center 1986, 9).

6. This term has been used as a description of Chinese reform strategy by Naughton (1986a, 605).

7. In addition to evidence from interviews, Tidrick cites some statistical tests. When enterprise profits increase, retained profits also tend to increase (correlation coefficient 0.66), whereas when they decline, there is little correlation with changes in retained profits (0.15). This suggests an asymmetric situation where the ratchet effect is not working in the upward direction but does operate in the downward direction. Some incentive schemes do contain a built-in ratchet effect, however, leading to complaints by enterprises that if they performed well in one year, targets were jacked up in the following year.

8. *Shichang zhoubao*, July 19, 1983, 1. Through the majority of the transactions the goods remained in the same warehouse!

9. Anshan fulfilled only 23 percent of its state-contracted supply of pig iron, only 7.8 percent of its contract with the Ministry of Machine Building, and none of its contract with the China National Auto Corporation. These figures may refer to contracted amounts

for the year as a whole or to the first half of the year only, but in either case there was a substantial shortfall (Xinhua News Agency, August 9, 1985, translated in BBC, 8/14/85, BII–11). Anshan claimed that inability to meet pig iron delivery targets was related to chronic shortfalls in plan allocations of steel scrap it received (interview information, June 1987).

10. The events of April–June 1989 were not a direct or indirect reaction to the two-tier system, except insofar as they represented a powerful expression of distaste for corruption. But at least for a time, the subsequent political-ideological currents posed a threat to the two-tier system from the opposite direction—by attempting, apparently with little success, to reimpose unified central planning.

11. This figure is based on the initial production plan for 1985, which was exceeded by 22 percent, so the share of the central plan in total realized output was most likely less than 42 percent.

12. See, for example, statements cited in Naughton (1986c, 13–14).

13. As early as January 1986 there were reports of further increases in market prices for cement in some localities, attributed in part to the rise in the state price (*Jingji cankao*, January 16, 1986, 4).

14. The following discussion is based on Hebei Provincial and Shijiazhuang Municipal Material Supply Bureaus (1985), Li Wenzhi (1986), and *Jingji cankao*, January 20, 1986, 1.

15. See Kui and Liu (1986) on a similar experiment in Shashi Municipality, modeled on the Shijiazhuang system.

16. If this is true, the political developments of June 1989 and thereafter may lead to at least a temporary revival of the two-tier system, though the decline in plan fulfillment in 1988 in particular should give pause for thought to those interested in promoting it.

References

Ames, Edward. 1965. *Soviet Economic Processes*. Homewood, IL: Richard D. Irwin, Inc.

Arrow, Kenneth J. 1959. "Toward a Theory of Price Adjustment." In *The Allocation of Economic Resources*, 41–51. Stanford: Stanford University Press.

Arrow, Kenneth J., and Gerard Debreu. 1954. "Existence of an Equilibrium for a Competitive Economy." *Econometrica* 22, 3 (July): 265–90.

Baumol, William J. 1959. *Business Behavior, Value and Growth*. New York: Harcourt Brace Jovanovich.

Baumol, William J., J. C. Panzar, and R. D. Willig. 1982. *Contestable Markets and the Theory of Industrial Structure*. New York: Harcourt Brace Jovanovich.

———. 1986. "On the Theory of Perfectly Contestable Markets." In *New Developments in the Analysis of Market Structure*, edited by Joseph E. Stiglitz and G. Frank Mathewson, 339–65. Cambridge: MIT Press.

BBC (British Broadcasting Corporation). *Summary of World Broadcasts: The Far East* [translation series].

Bhagwati, Jagdish N. 1982. "Directly Unproductive, Profit-seeking (DUP) Activities." *Journal of Political Economy* 90, 5 (October): 988–1001.

Blyn, George. 1973. "Price Series Correlation as a Measure of Market Integration." *Indian Journal of Agricultural Economics* 28, 2: 56–59.

Buchanan, James M., Robert D. Tollison, and Gordon Tullock. 1980. *Toward a Theory of the Rent-Seeking Society*. College Station: Texas A&M University Press.

Byrd, William A. 1983a. *China's Financial System: The Changing Role of Banks*. Boulder: Westview Press.

———. 1983b. "Enterprise-Level Reforms in Chinese State-Owned Industry." *The American Economic Review* 73, 2 (May): 329–32.

———. 1984. "Reform of the Material Supply System." Unpublished paper.

———. 1985a. "The Shanghai Market for the Means of Production: A Case Study of Reform in China's Material Supply System." *Comparative Economic Studies* 27, 4 (Winter): 1–29.

———. 1985b. "The Shenyang Smelter: A Case Study of Problems and Reforms in China's Nonferrous Metals Industry." *World Bank Staff Working Papers*, no. 766.

———. 1987a. "The Impact of the Two-Tier Plan/Market System in Chinese Industry." *Journal of Comparative Economics* 11, 3 (September): 295–308.

———. 1987b. "Reforms in China's Construction Industry and Their Significance for Future Development." In *China's Economic Reforms*, edited by Joseph C. H. Chai and Chi-Keung Leung, 214–47. Hong Kong: Centre of Asian Studies, University of Hong Kong.

———. 1987c. "The Role and Impact of Markets." In *China's Industrial Reform*, edited by Gene Tidrick and Chen Jiyuan, 237–75. New York: Oxford University Press.

———. 1989. "Plan and Market in the Chinese Economy: A Simple General Equilibrium Model." *Journal of Comparative Economics* 13, 2 (June): 177–204.

Byrd, William A., and Gene Tidrick. 1984. "Adjustment and Reform in the Chongqing Clock and Watch Company." In "Recent Chinese Economic Reforms: Studies of Two Industrial Enterprises," by William A. Byrd et al., 1–69. *World Bank Staff Working Papers*, no. 652.

———. 1987. "Factor Allocation and Enterprise Incentives." In *China's Industrial Reform*, edited by Gene Tidrick and Chen Jiyuan, 60–102. New York: Oxford University Press.

Carlton, Dennis W. 1986. "The Rigidity of Prices." *The American Economic Review* 76, 4 (September): 637–58.

Casson, Mark. 1982. *The Entrepreneur: An Economic Theory*. Totowa, NJ: Barnes and Noble Books.

Caves, Douglas W., and Laurits W. Christensen. 1980. "The Relative Efficiency of Public and Private Firms in a Competitive Environment: The Case of Canadian Railroads." *Journal of Political Economy* 88, 5 (October): 958–76.

CESRRI—China Economic System Reform Research Institute, Comprehensive Investigation Group, ed. 1986a. *Gaige: Women mianlin de tiaozhan yu xuanze* (Reform: The challenges and choices we face). Beijing: Zhongguo Jingji Chubanshe.

———, ed. 1986b. *Gaige: Women mianlin de wenti yu silu* (Reform: The problems we face and our ideas). Beijing: Jingji Guanli Chubanshe.

Chai, Joseph C. H. 1987. "Reform of China's Industrial Prices 1979–1985." In *China's Economic Reforms*, edited by Joseph C. H. Chai and Chi-Keung Leung, 584–698. Hong Kong: Centre of Asian Studies, University of Hong Kong.

Chai, Joseph C. H, and Chi-Keung Leung, eds. 1987. *China's Economic Reforms*. Hong Kong: Centre of Asian Studies, University of Hong Kong.

Chamberlin, Edward H. 1956. *The Theory of Monopolistic Competition: A Re-orientation of the Theory of Value*. 7th ed. Cambridge: Harvard University Press.

Chen Jiyuan, Xu Lu, Tang Zongkun, and Chen Lantong. 1984. "Management Reforms in the Qingdao Forging Machinery Plant." In "Recent Chinese Economic Reforms: Studies of Two Industrial Enterprises," by William A. Byrd et al., 71–98. *World Bank Staff Working Papers*, no. 652.

Chen Kuan, Wang Hongchang, Zheng Yuxin, Gary H. Jefferson, and Thomas G. Rawski. 1988. "Productivity Change in Chinese Industry: 1953–1985." *Journal of Comparative Economics* 12, 4 (December): 570–91.

China Economic Yearbook Editorial Committee. 1981, 1982, 1983, 1984, 1985, 1986, 1987, 1988. *Zhongguo jingji nianjian* (China economic yearbook). Beijing: Jingji Guanli Chubanshe.

China Encyclopedia Editorial Committee. 1980, 1981, 1982, 1983, 1984, 1985. *Zhongguo baike nianjian* (China encyclopedia yearbook). Beijing and Shanghai: Zhongguo Da Baike Quanshu Chubanshe.

China Materials Economics Association, ed. 1983. *Zhongguo shehui zhuyi wuzi guanli tizhi shilue* (A brief history of China's socialist materials management system). Beijing: Wuzi Chubanshe.

Chinese Communist Party. Central Committee. 1984. "Decision of the Central Committee of the Communist Party of China on Reform of the Economic Structure" (October 20, 1984). *Beijing Review*, October 29, I-XVI.

———. 1985. "Proposal of the Central Committee of the Chinese Communist Party for the Seventh Five-Year Plan for National Economic and Social Development" (September 23, 1985). *Beijing Review*, October 7, VI-XXIV.

Chinese National People's Congress. 1986. "The Seventh Five-Year Plan of China for Economic and Social Development (1986–1990)" (excerpts—approved April 12, 1986). *Beijing Review*, April 28, I-XXIII.

Clark, John Maurice. 1961. *Competition as a Dynamic Process*. Washington, DC: The Brookings Institution.

Conn, David. 1984. "The Evaluation of Centrally Planned Economic Systems: Methodological Precepts." In *Comparative Economic Systems: Present Views*, edited by Andrew Zimbalist, 15–46. Boston: Kluwer-Nyhoff.

Cyert, Richard M., and James G. March. 1963. *A Behavioral Theory of the Firm*. Englewood Cliffs, NJ: Prentice-Hall.

Debreu, Gerard. 1959. *Theory of Value: An Axiomatic Analysis of Economic Equilibrium*. New York: John Wiley and Sons.

———. 1982. "Existence of Competitive Equilibrium." In *Handbook of Mathematical Economics*, edited by Kenneth J. Arrow and Michael D. Intriligator, 2:697–743. Amsterdam: North-Holland.

———. 1983. *Mathematical Economics: Twenty Papers of Gerard Debreu*. Cambridge: Cambridge University Press.

Donnithorne, Audrey. 1972. "China's Cellular Economy: Some Economic Trends since the Cultural Revolution." *The China Quarterly* 52 (October–December): 605–19.

Ericson, Richard E. 1984. "The 'Second Economy' and Resource Allocation under Central Planning." *Journal of Comparative Economics* 8, 1 (March): 1–24.

Grossman, Gregory. 1977. "The Second Economy of the USSR." *Problems of Communism* 26 (September–October): 25–40.

GWYGB—*Zhonghua Renmin Gonghe Guo Guowuyuan gongbao* (Bulletin of the State Council of the People's Republic of China).

Han Yongwen. 1986. "Jiaqiang tongpei wuzi guanli, baozheng guojia zhongdian shengchan jianshe" (Strengthen management of unified-allocation materials, guarantee key state production and construction works). *Wuzi guanli* (Materials management) 1986, 7 (July): 9–10, 17.

Harding, Harry. 1987. *China's Second Revolution: Reform after Mao*. Washington, DC: The Brookings Institution.

Harriss, Barbara. 1979. "There Is Method in My Madness: Or Is It Vice Versa? Measuring Agricultural Market Performance." *Stanford Food Research Institute Studies* 17, 2: 197–218.

Hayek, Friedrich A. 1945. "The Use of Knowledge in Society." *The American Economic Review* 35, 4 (September): 519–30.

———. 1948. *Individualism and Economic Order*. Chicago: University of Chicago Press. Gateway Edition, Chicago: Henry Regnery Company, 1972.

———. 1984. "Competition as a Discovery Procedure." In *The Essence of Hayek*, edited by Chiaki Nishiyama and Kurt R. Leube, 254–64. Stanford: Hoover Institution Press.

He Shengde. 1982. "Cong shedui meikuang yuanmei chengben bianhua tan jiage, shuishou tiaozheng de biyaoxing" (A discussion of the necessity of adjusting coal prices and taxes, based on changes in the production costs of commune and brigade coal mines). *Jingji wenti* (Economic questions) 1982, 5 (May): 41–42.

Hebei Provincial and Shijiazhuang Municipal Material Supply Bureaus. Joint Investigative Group. 1985. "Xiang kaifang de shengchan ziliao shichang maichu de yibu—Guanyu Shijiazhuang Shi dui jihuanei, wai gangcai, mucai shixing tongyi shichang jiage de diaocha baogao" (The first step toward an open market for means of production—Investigative report on unified market pricing of rolled steel and timber within and outside the plan being tried out by Shijiazhuang Municipality). *Wuzi guanli* 1985, 9 (September): 8–11.

Hessian, Charles R. 1971. "The Metal Container Industry." In *The Structure of American Industry*, edited by Walter Adams, 302–34. New York: Macmillan.

Heytens, Paul J. 1986. "Testing Market Integration." *Stanford Food Research Institute Studies* 20, 1 (February): 25–41.

Hirschman, Albert O. 1970. *Exit, Voice, and Loyalty: Responses to Decline in Firms, Organizations, and States.* Cambridge: Harvard University Press.

Hua Sheng, He Jiacheng, Zhang Xuejun, Luo Xiaopeng, and Bian Yongzhuang. 1986. "Weiguan jingji jichu de chongxin gouzao—Zailun Zhongguo jinyibu gaige de wenti he silu" (Reconstruction of the microeconomic foundation—Another discussion of questions and solutions in China's further reform). *Jingji yanjiu* (Economic research) 1986, 3 (March): 21–28.

Hua Sheng, Zhang Xuejun, and Luo Xiaopeng. 1989. "Zhongguo gaige de qianjing yu fanglue" (Prospects and strategy of China's reform). *Zhongguo: Fazhan yu gaige* (China: Development and reform) 1989, 2 (February): 21–26.

Hunter, Holland. 1961. "Optimum Tautness in Developmental Planning." *Economic Development and Cultural Change* 9, 4, 1 (July): 561–72.

Ji Shi. 1988. "Yijiubaqi nian shengchan ziliao shichang jiage jianjie" (A brief introduction to market prices for production materials in 1987). *Jingji yanjiu cankao ziliao* (Economic research information materials), no. 88, 29–57.

Jingji cankao (Economic information). Daily newspaper.

Jingji Guanli Editorial Board. 1980. "Jingji tizhi gaige xuyao jinyibu yanjiu de yixie wenti" (Some questions on economic system reform that need further research). *Jingji guanli* (Economic management) 1980, 8 (August): 28–30.

JPRS EC—Joint Publications Research Service. *China Report: Economic Affairs.* Springfield, VA: National Technical Information Service [translation series].

Keren, Michael. 1972. "On the Tautness of Plans." *The Review of Economic Studies* 39, 4 (October): 469–86.

Kirzner, Israel M. 1973. *Competition and Entrepreneurship.* Chicago: University of Chicago Press.

———. 1979. *Perception, Opportunity, and Profit: Studies in the Theory of Entrepreneurship.* Chicago: University of Chicago Press.

Kornai, Janos. 1971. *Anti-Equilibrium.* Amsterdam: North Holland.

———. 1980. *Economics of Shortage.* 2 vols. Amsterdam: North Holland.

Kornai, Janos, and A. Matits. 1984. "Softness of the Budget Constraint—An Analysis Relying on Data of Firms. *Acta Oeconomica* 32, 3–4: 223–49.

Krueger, Anne O. 1974. "The Political Economy of the Rent-Seeking Society." *The American Economic Review* 64, 3 (June): 291–303.

Kui Xueshi and Liu Weizhi. 1986. "Shashi Dui jihuanei, wai gangcai shixing tongyi gongying jia de zuofa yu chengxiao" (Shashi Municipality's method of instituting unified supply prices for rolled steel within and outside the plan and its results). *Wuzi guanli* 1986, 10 (October): 13.

Lancaster, Kelvin. 1979. *Variety, Equity, and Efficiency.* New York: Columbia University Press.

Li Peichu. 1982. "Zhonggongye chanpin dingjia wenti" (Questions on price-setting for heavy industry products). *Jiage lilun yu shijian* (Price theory and practice) 1982, 5 (September): 7–8.

Li Wenzhi. 1986. "Shijiazhuang Shi dui zhuyao wuzi gongying jiage shixing disanbu gaige qude chengxiao" (Shijiazhuang City's implementation of the third-stage reform of supply pricing of primary materials has achieved results). *Wuzi guanli* 1986, 9 (September): 7–8.

Ling Yuxun. 1986. "Duanzheng dangfeng, jianchi gaige, fazhan you jihua de shengchan ziliao shichang" (Rectify party methods, support reform, develop a planned market for means of production). *Wuzi guanli* 1986, 4 (April): 2–11.

Liu Dingfu, ed. 1982. *Gongye qiye wuzi gongying guanli* (Material supply management in industrial enterprises). Taiyuan: Shanxi Renmin Chubanshe.

Liu Guoguang. 1980. "A Brief Discussion on Problems of Planned Adjustment and Market Adjustment." *Jingji yanjiu* 1980, 10 (October): 3–11. Translated in JPRS EC, no. 104, December 16, 1980, 22–35.

Liu Yi. 1982. "Shangye shichang huoyue fanrong wending" (Commercial markets are brisk, flourishing, and stable). *Caimao jingji* (Finance and trade economics) 1982, 10 (October): 7–9.

Lyons, Thomas P. 1986. "Explaining Economic Fragmentation in China: A Systems Approach." *Journal of Comparative Economics* 10, 3 (September): 209–36.

Ma Hong, chief ed. 1982. *Xiandai Zhongguo jingji shidian* (Modern China economic dictionary). Beijing: Zhongguo Shehui Kexue Chubanshe.

Marris, Robin, and Dennis C. Mueller. 1980. "The Corporation, Competition, and the Invisible Hand." *Journal of Economic Literature* 18, 1 (March): 32–63.

Means, Gardiner C. 1935. "Industrial Prices and Their Relative Inflexibility." U.S. Senate Document 13, 74th Congress, 1st Session. Washington, DC: GPO.

———. 1972. "The Administered-Price Thesis Reconfirmed." *The American Economic Review* 62, 3 (June): 292–306.

Michaely, Michael. 1954. "A Geometrical Analysis of Black-Market Behavior." *The American Economic Review* 44, 4 (September): 627–37.

Ministry of Agriculture. 1981, 1982. *Zhongguo nongye nianjian* (China agricultural yearbook). Beijing: Nongye Chubanshe.

Ministry of Coal Industry. 1982, 1983, 1985, 1986. *Zhongguo meitan gongye nianjian* (China coal industry yearbook). Beijing: Meitan Gongye Chubanshe.

Ministry of Commerce. Commercial Economics Research Institute, ed. 1984. *Xin Zhongguo shangye shigao, 1949–1982* (A history of new China's commerce, 1949–1982). Beijing: Zhongguo Caizheng Jingji Chubanshe.

Ministry of Metallurgy. Planning Department. 1986. *Zhongguo gangtie gongye tongji, 1985* (China iron and steel industry statistics, 1985). Hong Kong: Jingji Daobao She.

Naughton, Barry. 1986a. "Finance and Planning Reforms in Industry." In *China's Economy Looks Toward the Year 2000, Volume 1: The Four Modernizations*, U.S. Congress, Joint Economic Committee, 604–29. Washington, DC: GPO.

———. 1986b. "Saving and Investment in China: A Macroeconomic Analysis." Ph.D. dissertation, Yale University.

———. 1986c. "Summary of Findings." In *Economic Reform in China: Report of the American Economists Study Team to the People's Republic of China*, edited by Janet A. Cady, 6–25. Washington, DC: National Committee on U.S.-China Relations.

———. 1988. "The Third Front: Defence Industrialization in the Chinese Interior." *The China Quarterly* 115 (September): 351–86.

Nelson, Richard R., and Sidney G. Winter. 1982. *An Evolutionary Theory of Economic Change*. Cambridge: Harvard University Press.

Neuberger, Egon, and William Duffy. 1976. *Comparative Economic Systems: A Decision-Making Approach*. Boston: Allyn and Bacon.

Olson, Mancur. 1982. *The Rise and Decline of Nations: Economic Growth, Stagflation, and Social Rigidities*. New Haven: Yale University Press.

Perkins, Dwight H. 1966. *Market Control and Planning in Communist China*. Cambridge: Harvard University Press.

———. 1988. "Reforming China's Economic System." *Journal of Economic Literature* 26, 2 (June): 601–45.

Plott, Charles R. 1982. "Industrial Organization Theory and Experimental Economics." *Journal of Economic Literature* 20, 4 (December): 1485–1527.

Portes, R. D. 1968. "Input Demand Functions for the Profit-Constrained Sales-Maximizer: Income Effects in the Theory of the Firm." *Economica* 35 (August): 233–48.

———. 1969. "The Enterprise under Central Planning." *The Review of Economic Studies* 36, 2 (April): 197–212.

Ravallion, Martin. 1985. "The Performance of Rice Markets in Bangladesh during the 1974 Famine." *Economic Journal* 92 (April): 15–29.

———. 1986. "Testing Market Integration." *American Journal of Agricultural Economics* 68, 1 (February): 102–9.

Raymon, Neil. 1983. "Price Ceilings in Competitive Markets with Variable Quality." *Journal of Public Economics* 22, 2 (November): 257–64.

Ronen, Joshua, ed. 1982. *Entrepreneurship*. Lexington: Lexington Books.

Sah, Raaj Kumar. 1983. "How Much Redistribution Is Possible Through Commodity Taxes." *Journal of Public Economics* 20, 1 (February): 89–101.

Samuelson, Paul Anthony. 1947. *Foundations of Economic Analysis*. Cambridge: Harvard University Press.

Schumpeter, Joseph A. 1934. *The Theory of Economic Development*. Cambridge: Harvard University Press.

———. *Capitalism, Socialism and Democracy*. 1950. 3d ed. New York: Harper and Row.

Scitovsky, Tibor. 1985. "Pricetakers' Plenty: A Neglected Benefit of Capitalism." *Kyklos* 38, 4: 517–36.

Shen Yulao and Han Demin. 1986. "1985 nian zhuyao wuzi shichang jiage biandong fenxi" (An analysis of market price movements for the most important materials in 1985). *Wuzi jingji yanjiu* (Materials economics research) 1986, 3 (March): 18–19.

Simon, A. 1984. "The Role of Prices and Supply in Shortage." *Acta Oeconomica* 33, 3–4: 321–36.

Simon, Herbert A. 1982. *Models of Bounded Rationality*. 2 vols. Cambridge: MIT Press.

Solinger, Dorothy J. 1984. *Chinese Business Under Socialism: The Politics of Domestic Commerce, 1949–1980*. Berkeley: University of California Press.

State Council Economic, Technical, and Social Development Research Center. Price Group. 1986. "Guanyu shengchan ziliao liangzhong jiage wenti he hongguan guanli cuoshi—Fu Shijiazhuang, Wuhan, Changsha, he Guangdong Sheng diaocha baogao" (On the dual price system for production materials and macro management measures—Report on an investigation in Shijiazhuang, Wuhan, Changsha, and Guangdong Province). *Jiage lilun yu shijian* 1986, 1 (January): 9–14.

State Economic Commission, Investigation and Research Office. 1983. "Woguo shoubiao gongye jingji xiaoyi fenxi" (Analysis of the economic efficiency of our country's watch industry). *Jingji diaocha* (Economic investigations) 1: 33–36.

State General Bureau of Industrial and Commercial Administrative Management. 1982. *Nongcun jishi maoyi de kaifang he guanli* (The opening up and management of rural free markets). Beijing: Gongshang Chubanshe.

State Price Bureau, Comprehensive Planning Office, Investigation Group. 1986. "Dui shige qiye de gangcai gongying he kucun qingkuang de diaocha" (An investigation of the supply and stockpiling of rolled steel in ten enterprises). *Wuzi guanli* 1986, 2 (February): 18–19.

State Statistical Bureau. *Statistical Yearbook of China*. 1982, 1983, 1984a, 1985a, 1986b, 1987a. Hong Kong: Economic Information and Agency (1982–86), Orient Longman (1987).

———. 1984b. *Zhongguo maoyi wujia tongji ziliao, 1952–1983* (China commerce and prices statistical materials, 1952–1983). Beijing: Zhongguo Tongji Chubanshe.

———. 1985b. *1949–1984 Zhongguo gongye de fazhan* (Development of China's industry, 1949–1984). Beijing: Zhongguo Tongji Chubanshe.

————. 1985c. *Zhongguo gongye jingji tongji ziliao, 1949–1984* (Statistical materials on China's industrial economy, 1949–1984). Beijing: Zhongguo Tongji Chubanshe.

————. 1986a. *China: A Statistical Survey in 1986*. Beijing: Xin Shijie Chubanshe.

————. 1987b. *Zhongguo gongye jingji tongji ziliao 1986* (Statistical materials on China's industrial economy, 1986). Beijing: Zhongguo Tongji Chubanshe.

————. 1988a. "Statistics for 1987 Socio-Economic Development" (February 23, 1988). In *Beijing Review*, March 7–14, I–VIII.

————. 1988b. *Zhongguo tongji nianjian 1988* (1988 China statistical yearbook). Beijing: Zhongguo Tongji Chubanshe.

————. 1989a. "Statistics for 1988 Socio-Economic Development." *Beijing Review*, March 6–12, I–VIII.

————. 1989b. *Zhongguo gongye jingji tongji ziliao 1988* (Statistical materials on China's industrial economy, 1988). Beijing: Zhongguo Tongji Chubanshe.

Stigler, George J., and James Kindahl. 1970. *The Behavior of Industrial Prices*. New York: Columbia University Press.

Stigler, George J., and Robert A. Sherwin. 1985. "The Extent of the Market." *Journal of Law and Economics* 28, 3 (October): 555–85.

Tian Xin and Pi Gong. 1981. "Cong Dongshan meikuang yuanmei shengchan chengben de bianhua tan meitan jiage tiaozheng de biyaoxing" (A discussion of the necessity of adjusting coal prices, based on changes in coal production costs at the Dongshan coal mine). *Jingji wenti* 1981, 1 (January): 16–17, 4.

Tidrick, Gene. 1986. "Productivity Growth and Technological Change in Chinese Industry." *World Bank Staff Working Papers*, no. 761.

————. 1987. "Planning and Supply in Chinese State-Owned Industry." In *China's Industrial Reform*, edited by Gene Tidrick and Jiyuan Chen, 175–209. New York: Oxford University Press.

Tidrick, Gene, and Chen Jiyuan, eds. 1987. *China's Industrial Reform*. New York: Oxford University Press.

Timmer, C. P. 1974. "A Model of Rice Marketing Margins in Indonesia." *Stanford Food Research Institute Studies* 13: 145–67.

Tullock, Gordon. 1967. "The Welfare Costs of Tariffs, Monopolies and Thefts." *Western Economic Journal* 5 (June): 224–32.

von Mises, Ludwig. 1936. *Socialism: An Economic and Sociological Analysis*, translated by J. Kahane. London: Jonathan Cape. Reprinted Indianapolis: Liberty Press, 1981.

Wagner, Karin. 1980. "Competition and Productivity: A Study of the Metal Can Industry in Britain, Germany and the United States." *Journal of Industrial Economics* 29, 1 (September): 17–35.

Wang Xiaolu, Diao Xinshen, Yan Xiaozhong, Xu Hui, and Xu Gang. 1986. "Jiegouxing duanque yu jiage gaige—Luye jiegou he tizhi maodun shizhe" (Structural shortage and price reform—A preliminary analysis of structural and systemic contradictions in the aluminum industry). In *Gaige: Women mianlin de wenti yu silu*, edited by CESRRI, 189–211. Beijing: Jingji Guanli Chubanshe.

Wiles, P. J. D. 1962. *The Political Economy of Communism*. Cambridge: Harvard University Press.

————. 1977. *Economic Institutions Compared*. New York: John Wiley and Sons.

Williamson, Oliver E. 1964. *The Economics of Discretionary Behavior: Managerial Objectives in a Theory of the Firm*. Englewood Cliffs, NJ: Prentice-Hall.

————. 1975. *Markets and Hierarchies: Analysis and Antitrust Implications*. New York: The Free Press.

————. 1985. *The Economic Institutions of Capitalism*. Cambridge: Harvard University Press.

Wong, Christine. 1985. "Material Allocation and Decentralization: Impact of the Local

Sector on Industrial Reform." In *The Political Economy of Reform in Post-Mao China*, edited by Elizabeth J. Perry and Christine Wong, 253–78. Cambridge: Harvard University Press.

———. 1986. "Ownership and Control in Chinese Industry: The Maoist Legacy and Prospects for the 1980s." In *China's Economy Looks Toward the Year 2000, Volume I: The Four Modernizations*, U.S. Congress, Joint Economic Committee, 571–603. Washington, DC: GPO.

World Bank. 1985. *China: Long-Term Development Issues and Options*. Baltimore: Johns Hopkins University Press, 1985.

Wu Tong. 1986. "Yijiu bawu nian quanguo wuzi xitong jingying qingkuang" (Business situation of the national material supply system in 1985). *Wuzi jingji yanjiu* 1986, 4 (April): 9–10.

Wuzi shangqing (Materials market situation). Weekly newspaper.

Xia Junbo. 1985. "Guanyu banhao qiche maoyi zhongxin de jige wenti" (Several questions concerning handling of vehicle trading centers). *Wuzi guanli* 1985, 4 (April): 4–5, 3.

Xue Muqiao. 1985a. "Rural Industry Advances Amidst Problems." *Beijing Review*, December 16, 18–21.

———. 1985b "Yijiu qijiu nian yilai wending he tiaozheng jiage wenti" (Problems in stabilizing and adjusting prices since 1979). *Jingji yanjiu* 1985, 6 (June): 39–53.

Yu Guangyuan, ed. 1984. *China's Socialist Modernization*. Beijing: Foreign Languages Press.

Zhao Ziyang. 1985. "Explanation of the Proposal for the Seventh Five-Year Plan" (September 18, 1985). *Beijing Review*, October 7, I–V.

Zhongguo wuzi bao (China materials news). Weekly newspaper, retitled version of *Wuzi shangqing* from 1989 on.

Zhou Taihe, chief ed. 1984. *Dangdai Zhongguo de jingji tizhi gaige* (Economic system reform in contemporary China). Beijing: Zhongguo Shehui Kexue Chubanshe.

Zhu Defa and Wen Zaixing. 1983. "Dangqian tigao jinshu cailiao liutong jingji xiaoyi jidai jiejue de yige wenti" (A problem that urgently awaits resolution to improve the economic efficiency of circulation of metallurgical materials). *Wuzi guanli* 1983, 1 (January): 30.

Zhu Rongji, chief ed. 1985. *Dangdai Zhongguo de jingji guanli*. Beijing: Zhongguo Shehui Kexue Chubanshe.

Zou Gang, Gu Zhongzhi, Huang Tieying, and Sun Haiming. 1986. "Duanquexia de jingji zengzhang—Qingdao gongye fazhan de weiguan fenshi" (Economic growth under shortage—A microeconomic analysis of industrial development in Qingdao). In *Gaige: Women mianlin de wenti yu silu*, edited by CESRRI, 147–60. Beijing: Jingji Guanli Chubanshe.

Index

adjustment tax, 12
administered-price thesis, 27–28
advertising, 33
Ames, Edward, 116–17, 231n.14
Anhui Province, 106
Anshan Iron and Steel Corporation, 70, 73, 75, 76, 79, 83, 84, 99, 107, 124, 131, 206, 229n.13, 234n.6, 235n.9
arbitrage, market mechanism and, 28–29, 30
asset management responsibility system, 13, 14
Austrian School, 23–24
autonomy of transactors, 25–27

backward integration, 4–5
banking system, 9, 10, 117
Baoji Nitrogen Fertilizer Plant, 70, 73, 75, 79, 80, 83, 84, 124
barter, 45, 66–67, 114
Baumol, William J., 116–17, 231n.14
Beijing, 190
black markets (underground markets), 48, 65, 127–28
Blyn, George, 171
bonuses, 6, 8, 12, 234n.2
budgets: declining profits passed on to, 102; general equilibrium model and, 158–59; investment financed by, 99–100; price adjustments' effect on, 94. See also soft budget constraint
buyers' markets, 37–41; conditions for emergence and durability of, 98–100; enterprise response to, 71–74, 85–86, 94; governmental response to, 87–90, 96; in socialist economies, 100–102; in two-tier system, 198–99

Canada, 26
capital goods. See industrial producer goods

capital markets, 9, 10, 31
Carlton, Dennis W., 27
Caves, Douglas W., 26
cement, case study of, 210–11
central planning: bargaining process emphasized, 106; Chinese uniqueness in, 103–9, 118–19; command planning, 109, 195–97, 231n.8; conclusions about, 218–19; as constraint on reforms, 19; decentralization of, 107–8, 109; and extra-plan mechanisms, 45; financial discipline discouraged by, 28, 102; in general equilibrium model, 137–39, 148–50, 152, 154–56, 157–58, 161; industrial producer goods in (1980–88), 50–51; investment and, 99–100; in prereform period, 5, 44, 107–8, 126; in reform period, 108–9, 111–12, 113–14; "second economy" and, 127; sellers' and buyers' markets in, 37–38, 100–102; slack and loose nature, 110–11, 119, 195. See also price control; redistribution
Chamberlin, Edward H., 32
Changsha, 190
Chen Jiyuan, 7, 71, 83, 124
Chengdu Locomotive and Rolling Stock Factory, 70, 73, 75, 78, 79, 83, 84, 124, 230n.26
China Economic System Reform Research Institute, 125
China Economic Yearbook Editorial Committee, 49, 51, 54, 155, 200
Chinese Communist Party, 10, 11, 13, 226n.1
Chongqing, 56, 230n.21
Chongqing Clock and Watch Company, 69–70, 72, 73–75, 79, 83, 84, 91, 93, 95, 105, 106, 124, 230n.22, 232n.24
Christensen, Laurits W., 26

Clark, John Maurice, 24, 31, 34–35
coal, case study of, 208
collective enterprises, 4, 89, 227n.2
command planning, 195–97, 109, 231n.8
competition: effective, 34–37, 40–42,
    223–25, 227n.12; financial discipline
    encouraged by, 28; Hayekian, 34;
    interregional, 91–92; market
    mechanism and, 31–32;
    monopolistic, 21, 22, 32, 33;
    nonprice, 32–33, 36, 91; potential,
    36; protection of producers from,
    89–90; by publicly owned firms,
    26–27; Schumpeterian, 34; types of,
    32–34; whether possible in China, 26
consumer goods: buyers' market in,
    87–88, 96–97, 98; commercial
    procurement of, 47, 48; dynamic
    adjustment in, 95–97; Ministry of
    Commerce's supervision of, 50, 55;
    1980s market allocation of, 54–57;
    rationing of, 54, 87; relaxation of
    price controls for, 49; reporting of
    prices for, 63; wholesale markets for,
    49, 55, 56–57, 228n.10
consumers, in general equilibrium model,
    135–36, 140–42
contractual responsibility systems, 13–14
Cultural Revolution, 198: commercial
    organization suppressed in, 29;
    employees' bonuses abolished
    during, 226n.5; lax inventory
    management in, 76; local
    industrialization in, 107, 230n.20;
    price freeze in, 6

Daqing Oilfield, 107
decentralization, 5, 23, 107–8
depreciation, in reform period, 12
directly unproductive profit seeking
    (DUP), 232n.27
disequilibrium, definition of, 37
Dongshan Coal Mine, 108
Donnithorne, Audrey, 103

economic responsibility system, 12
electricity, 114
"enterprise fund" scheme, 9
entrepreneurship, 30, 35
equilibrium, 37, 39, 41
exit option, 35, 37, 227n.9

exports, 81, 86, 229n.12

factor productivity, 7
factory director, 10, 12–14
financial discipline, 28, 40, 41
financial incentives, 6, 8–9, 10, 165
First Ministry of Machine Building, 47, 71
five-year plans: First, 105; Seventh,
    226n.2, 227n.4
free markets, 57, 58
freedom of entry, 37
Freedom of exit. See exit option
Fuzhou, 190

Gang of Four, 7
general equilibrium model (of plan and
    market in Chinese economy),
    132–52, 221–22: assumptions and
    limitations of, 153–59; efficient
    properties of, 145–51; general
    equilibrium in, 140–45;
    microeconomic framework of,
    133–40; possible extensions of,
    159–67; rents and rent-seeking
    behavior in, 168–70; as static model,
    156–57
government supervisory agencies:
    competition and, 26–27; in
    prereform period, 5, 44–45, 46;
    provincial and local, 63–67, 91,
    104, 107–8, 131; in reform period,
    10, 11; response to market forces
    by, 86–90, 96; targets negotiated
    and adjusted by, 12, 110; two-tier
    system supported by, 213
Great Britain, 36
Guangzhou, 65
Guizhou Province, 230n.22

Han Demin, 200
Hangzhou, 190
Harriss, Barbara, 171, 180
Hayek, Friedrich A., 23–24, 34
Hebei Province, 212
Heilongjiang Province, 106
Henan Province, 125
Hessian, Charles R., 36
Heytens, Paul J., 180
hoarding, 38
Hua Sheng, 26
Hungary, 124, 216, 217

industrial producer goods: extra charges and fees on, 205, 214; inventories of, 230n.18; late 1970s decline in plan fulfillment for, 214–16; markets for, 47–54, 65, 88, 97–99, 192; prices for, 62–63, 105, 171–77, 213–14; rationing of, 87; State Material Supply Bureau's supervision of, 50
industrial reforms, 7–14
inflation, 193
innovation, 34
input markets, 85–86
Institute of Economics of the Chinese Academy of Social Sciences, 228n.1
interior provinces, defense industrialization program in, 7, 226n.8, 231n.5
international trade, 91–92
interregional trade, 44–45, 46, 52–53, 91–92, 108
inventories, 38–39, 74–76, 230n.18; 229n.16
investment: budget-financed, 99–100; continuing governmental control over, 11; in firm's response to market conditions, 82–83; in general equilibrium model, 136–37, 140–41, 158–59; governmental controls on, 89, 90; profitability and, 86–87; redistribution's effect on, 130–31
investment goods. See industrial producer goods

Jiangmen Nanfang Foodstuffs Factory, 70, 73, 75, 76, 79, 81, 83–85, 91, 96, 124, 229n.8
Jiangsu Province, 46, 227n.2
Jilin, 65
Jingji cankao, 63, 210
Jinling Petrochemical General Corporation, 70, 73, 75, 79, 81, 83, 84, 124

Kindahl, James, 27
Kirzner, Israel M., 23, 24, 30, 35
Kornai, Janos, 28, 37–38, 40, 74–75, 100, 124, 166–67
Kui Xueshi, 65

labor allocation, 9, 10, 31, 116
Lancaster, Kelvin, 33

leakages, 232n.20; 160–61
Liaoning Province, 131, 226n.6, 232n.24
Lin Yuxun, 105
Liu Dingfu, 53
Liu Weizhi, 65
Lyons, Thomas P., 44, 103

macroeconomic control, 10
Mao Zedong, 7
market integration, 192–94; method of testing, 177–87; results and analysis, 187–92
market mechanism: inventories in, 38–39; "marginal" role of, 112–13; in neoclassical economics, 20–24; in prereform period, 6, 44–46; prerequisites for effective functioning of, 25-31, 223–25; as process rather than state, 23–25, 31; realistic working definition of, 22–23; in reform period, 9, 10, 19–20, 24–25, 46–68, 227n.4
market segmentation. See market integration
markets: conclusions about, 219–24; functioning of, in Chinese industry, 62–68; incomplete, 22; input and output, 85–86; nonfunctioning, in general equilibrium model, 150–51; parallel, 86, 117, 120, 127, 131, 156, 168; specialized, 53
materials allocation conferences, 45
materials cooperation, 46
materials trade centers, 48, 53–54
Matits, A., 28, 124
Means, Gardiner, 27
Metal can industry, competition in, 36
middlemen, market mechanism and, 28–29, 30
Mindong Electrical Machinery Corporation, 70, 73, 75, 79, 81, 83–85, 89, 92, 124, 206, 229n.12
Ministry of Coal Industry, 208
Ministry of Commerce, 50, 55
Ministry of Material Supply, 182
Ministry of Metallurgy, 45
Ministry of Railways, 230n.26
monopolistic competition, 21, 22, 32, 33
monopoly, 21, 32, 34, 36–37
multiheaded leadership, 5, 226n.4
multiplant firms, 4

multiproduct firms: general equilibrium model and, 164–65; product mix of, 71–72, 77–78, 93, 97, 105–6

Nanchang, 190
Nanjing, 190
Nanning Silk and Linen Textile Mill, 70, 73, 75, 79, 81, 83, 84, 93, 124
Naughton, Barry, 7, 111, 200
neoclassical model of the market, 20–22, 23–24, 30
nonstate enterprises, 201. *See also* collective enterprises
North China Petroleum Administration, 70, 73, 75, 79, 83, 84, 124, 228n.3, 229n.13
Northwest No. 1 State Cotton Textile Mill, 70, 73, 75, 83, 84, 90, 230n.26
No. 1 Automotive Plant, 71, 107, 231n.2
No. 2 Automotive Plant, 70, 71, 73, 75, 77, 79, 83, 84, 90, 99, 124, 206, 210, 211, 230n.25, 231n.2

oligopoly, 21, 27, 36
output markets, 85–86
output maximization theory of firms, 116–18, 163–64
ownership: private, 25; public, 26–27; of state-owned enterprises, 10, 11, 14

Pareto optimality, 20, 146–48, 151
pensions, 5
Pi Gong, 108
planned commodity economy, 227n.3
planning. *See* central planning
political developments of 1979, 14, 19, 223, 236nn.10, 16
Portes, R. D., 116–17, 231n.14
poverty, elimination of, 226n.1
prereform period, 4–7
price controls, 27–28, 29, 48; competition and, 33; on consumer goods, 54, 63, 227n.4, 228n.8; extent and speed of governmental response on, 88–89, 94–95; in general equilibrium model, 155–56; lack of influence of, 193; local, 63–65; multiple, 104–5, 108, 235n.1; in 1970s, 49, 53; two-tier system and abolition of, 213, 216

prices: Chinese reporting of, 62–63, 182–84, 235n.4; floating, 200; late 1970s' increases in, 213–14; for local vs. outside sales, 108; "market," 200–201; market mechanism and, 20–22, 27–28, 41, 62–65, 90–95; negotiated, 200; of new products, 232n.28; product, 6, 9; redistributive system and, 127–28; reference market for, 185–86, 190, 235n.5; regional patterns and differentials in, 177–79. *See also specific types of goods*
private ownership of means of production, 25
private wholesalers, 56–57
privatization, 10, 24
producers, in general equilibrium model, 134–35
product mix, 71–72, 77–78, 93, 97, 105–6
product quality: of consumer goods, 54; floating prices and, 200; general equilibrium model and, 164–66; in prereform period, 6–7; price controls and, 227n.10; price differentiation and, 33, 90–91, 214; selective purchase and, 229n.17
profits: buyers' markets and, 101–2; entrepreneurship and, 30; firm's response to market conditions, 82, 84–85, 86–87; market mechanism and, 28; by middlemen and arbitrageurs, 29; as objectives of enterprises, 114–19; retained by state-owned enterprises, 6, 8, 9, 11–12, 235n.7; windfall, 67
protectionism, internal, 90; redistribution and, 131

Qingdao Forging Machinery Plant, 70, 72–75, 79, 81, 83–85, 91, 124, 229n.8
Qingdao Municipality (Shandong Province), 58–60
Qinghe Woolen Textile Mill, 70, 73, 75, 79, 83, 84, 124
Qingyuan County Economic Concession, 70, 73, 75, 79, 83, 84, 124

ratchet effects, 12, 14, 203, 235n.7
Ravallion, Martin, 171, 180, 182
Raymon, Neil, 68

redistribution (in Chinese economic planning), 107, 110, 119–31; advantages of, 126–28; distinctive Chinese features of, 122–25; drawbacks of planning as, 128–30; dynamic pressures due to, 128; general equilibrium model and, 159; mechanism of, 119–20; as process rather than objective, 126; rents in, 120–22

reform: 1989 political developments and, 14, 19, 223, 236n.10, 236n.16; objectives of, 19–20; pragmatic and experimental character of, 19–20. *See also* industrial reforms

rents: definition of, in Chinese context, 120; distinctive Chinese features of, 122–25; embodied in goods allocated by the plan, 121–23, 131–32, 212–13; in general equilibrium model, 168–69; generation and flow of, 120–21; magnitude of, 121–22; "negative," 121

rent-seeking behavior, 33–34, 123, 128, 130–31, 169–70

resource allocation (factor allocation): by central planning, 106, 110–11, 118–19; in general equilibrium model, 151–52; general equilibrium model and, 157; market mechanism and, 31, 112–13; in prereform period, 6, 45; in reform period, 9, 10, 20, 31, 111

rural free markets, 57, 58

Sah, Raaj Kumar, 123

Sanchazi Forestry Bureau, 70, 73, 75, 79, 83, 84, 124, 228n.3

Schumpeter, Joseph A., 23, 24, 30, 34

selective purchase, 229n.17

sellers' markets, 37–38; enterprise response to, 69–71, 72–74, 85–86, 94; governmental response to, 86–87; in two-tier system, 198–99

service charges, 205, 214

Shandong Province, 212

Shanghai, 47, 48, 200; market prices in, correlated with other cities, 177–79; as reference market for prices, 185–86, 190, 235n.5; steel market price data for, 171–73

Shanghai High-Pressure Oil Pump Plant, 70, 73, 75, 79, 83–85, 124, 228n.6, 229n.8

Shanghai Market for the Means of Production, 62, 64, 234n.3

Shanghai No. 17 State Cotton Textile Mill, 70, 73, 75, 79, 83, 84, 124, 228n.6, 229n.7

Shanxi Province, 108

Shashi Municipal Material Supply Bureau, 65

Shenyang Cable Factory, 106

Shenyang Municipality, 131

Shenyang Smelter, 70, 73, 75, 77–78, 79, 83, 84, 89, 93, 98, 99, 106, 107, 110, 164, 214, 226n.4

Shen Yulao, 200

Sherwin, Robert A., 171

Shijiazhuang, 190

Shijiazhuang Municipal Material Supply Bureau, 212–13

Singapore, 81

socialism, 19, 226n.1

soft budget constraint, 28, 40, 231n.17

Soviet Union: bonuses and profit retention in, 6; Chinese planning compared with that of, 104, 105, 108, 218; exchange or barter between enterprises in, 45; free markets in, 25; 1950s aid to China by, 226n.3; "second economy" in, 127

State Material Supply Bureau, 50, 99, 105, 182

state-owned enterprises: attempt to force lower prices for suppliers to, 93; decision-making by, 8, 9, 12–13, 112, 113, 114–19; exchange or barter between, 45, 66–67; financial autonomy for, 11; inefficiency of, 7, 11, 19; local governmental intervention in, 65–67; objectives of, 114–18; output maximization by, 116–18, 163–64; ownership reform for, 10, 11, 14; passivity in ("the quiet life"), 69, 228n.2; percentage of output of, 4; plan shares for, 113–14; in prereform period, 4; pricing decisions by, 94–95; profit retention by, 8, 9, 11–12, 123–25; "property rights" of, 232n.19; in reform period, 11–14;

state-owned enterprises (*continued*)
    response to market conditions by,
    69–86, 88; retail sales by (direct
    marketing), 45, 50, 52, 57–61,
    78–81, 210, 211; social
    responsibilities of (workers'
    benefits), 5, 9, 11, 125; targets of, 12,
    110, 195, 207, 214–16, 230n.2,
    231n.18; weak financial discipline
    of, 102; Workers' Representative
    Assembly in, 13
State Planning Commission, 104, 105
Steel, case history of, 211–12
Stigler, George J., 27, 171
stock-outs, 38, 39
stocks and bonds, 10, 14

Taiyuan, 108, 190
taxation: indirect, 123, 126; of profits, 11,
    12, 94, 120; workers' benefits and, 67
technology, 4, 6–7, 76–78, 226n.8
Third Front defense industrialization
    program, 7, 226n.8, 231n.5
Tianjin Color Textile Corporation, 70, 73,
    75, 79, 83, 84, 124
Tidrick, Gene, 7, 10, 31, 55, 69, 70, 78, 83,
    87, 88, 91, 100, 110, 116, 124, 202, 203
Timmer, C. P., 171, 180
trade fairs, 47, 227n.1
transportation, 106, 184
trucks, case study of, 208–10
two-tier system, 86, 95, 109; basic
    definition of, 197–98; buyers' and
    sellers' markets in, 198–99;
    conclusions about, 221–23; dynamic
    impact of, 201–8, 217; government
    pricing policies and, 199–201;
    1980s' evolution of, 207–16; 1989
    political developments and,

two-tier system (*continued*)
    236nn.10, 16; prereform roots of,
    198; rent-seeking behavior and, 132;
    static impact of, 201–2; as
    transitional system, 216–17

underground markets. *See* black markets
United States, 36
urban free markets, 57, 58

von Mises, Ludwig, 23

Wagner, Karin, 36
Wang Xiaolu, 66, 67
Wen Zaixing, 106
West Germany, 27, 36
Wholesalers. *See* consumer goods;
    wholesale markets for
Williamson, Oliver E., 77
Wong, Christine, 7, 107
World Bank, 26, 27, 228n.1
Wu Tong, 54
Wuzi shangqing, 63

Xia Junbo, 210, 212
Xian, 190
Xiangxiang Cement Plant, 70, 73, 75, 79,
    80, 83, 84, 93, 124, 229n.13
Xue Muqiao, 114

Yugoslavia, 116
Yunnan Province, 106, 230n.22

Zhao Ziyang, 19
Zhejiang Province, 227n.2
Zhengzhou, 190
Zhongguo wuzi bao, 215
Zhu Defa, 106
Zhu Rongji, 105

William A. Byrd is an economist for the World Bank in New Delhi. In 1987, he received his Ph.D. in Economics from Harvard University. Dr. Byrd's many publications on the Chinese economy include *China's Financial System: The Changing Role of Banks*, and, as editor, *Chinese Firms in the New Environment* (forthcoming).